International
Economics

Søren Kjeldsen-Kragh

International Economics

Trade and Investment

Copenhagen Business School Press

International Economics

© *Copenhagen Business School Press*, 2002
Cover design: Kontrapunkt
Set in Plantin and printed by Narayana Press, Gylling

Printed in Denmark
1. edition 2002

ISBN 87-630-0037-7

Distribution:

Scandinavia
Djoef/DBK, Siljangade 2-8, P.O. Box 1731
DK-2300 Copenhagen S, Denmark
phone: +45 3269 7788, fax: +45 3269 7789

North America
Copenhagen Business School Press
Books International Inc.
P.O. Box 605
Hendon, VA 20172-0605, USA
phone: +1 703 661 1500, fax: +1 703 661 1501

Rest of the World
Marston Book Services, P.O. Box 269
Abingdon, Oxfordshire, OX14 4YN, UK
phone: +44 (0) 1235 465500, fax: +44 (0) 1235 465555
E-mail Direct Customers: direct.order@marston.co.uk
E-mail Booksellers: trade.order@marston.co.uk

Contents

Preface

The aim of this book is to give an overview of what can be stated about international trade and international investments based on our economic knowledge today. International economics is traditionally divided into two subtopics. The first topic deals with international trade and international investments that influence the production distribution among the countries. The second topic deals with monetary issues such as balance of payment problems, exchange rates and the impact of macroeconomic policies. This book only deals with the first type of problems.

International trade and investments raise a series of central questions. What determines the size and pattern of international trade? Which economic consequences are connected with international trade and international investments? To which extent are the economic consequences positive or negative? As far as international trade is concerned these questions are not new, as they date back to the beginning of modern economics which is normally related to Adam Smith in the second half of the 18ᵗʰ century. However, the answers are to a large extent new. During the last 20-30 years many new theories have appeared.

The objective of the book is to give an overall presentation in a hopefully understandable language of the knowledge that we possess today. It has by no means been the intention to give a strict formalized presentation. The aim has been to give the reader an intuitive understanding of the prevailing relationships and mechanisms determining causes and effects. Therefore graphic presentations are used to a large extent.

As to subject field the book is divided into three parts. In the first part (chapters 1-4) there is a presentation of the ideas and tools that are used in the analyses in the succeeding parts. The purpose is by way of introduction to give an overall presentation of the conditions and assumptions that are normally included in the analyses, and it has also been the intention to provide a deeper understanding of the circumstances that lie behind the graphic presentations used.

In the second part (chapters 5-11) is given an overall presentation of the theories at our disposal today, when searching for explanations of international trade and its consequences. Two sets of theory types crystallize. You have the traditional theories, where the factor portion theory, based on all the premises of the neo-classical theory, has been crucial. Since the 1960s a large number of theories that depart from the traditional assumptions have been developed. The two sets of theory types should not be considered as competitive but as theories supplementing each other.

The theories in part II are static analyses. These analyses are supplemented in part III (chapters 12-15) by introducing economic growth. In this part the effects of capital movements and direct foreign investments are also analysed. What is the background of factor movements across frontiers and which are the consequences? Finally it is shown that when trade and factor movements occur simultaneously cumulative processes may arise, which may result in greater inequality among countries.

The theories are divided into two categories, viz. descriptive theories and normative theories. Descriptive theories describe the actual circumstances, if the chosen conditions of the theories are in accordance with reality. Normative theories indicate how one should act to achieve a given aim.

This book concentrates on the descriptive theories. The normative question as to whether interventions related to commercial policy under certain circumstances are preferable to free trade is not dealt with in this book. However, it is treated in my book "International Trade Policy", Copenhagen, 2001. It is obvious that this book and the book "International Trade Policy" supplement each other. On the other hand the two books are planned in such a way that they can be read and used separately.

This book is a slightly revised version of a Danish edition. The Danish text has been translated by Steven Harris, Lindfield, UK, with whom I have had an excellent cooperation.

Søren Kjeldsen-Kragh
Copenhagen, 2002

Part I
The methods and concepts
of international trade

1. Different methods of analysis

This first chapter a short introduction to the analysis of international trade and its consequences.

There are three sets of factors which determine international trade. These factors are linked to the conditions of:

The supply
The demand
The market.

These conditions can be analysed by various methods. It is possible to construct a general equilibrium model to explain international trade, or to construct partial models. It is also possible to divide the models between static models and dynamic models. This second division can cut across the first; general equilibrium models can thus either be static or dynamic, and the same applies to partial models.

If an analysis is made of the conditions at a given period, it is a static analysis. It can become a comparative statics analysis when the conditions in two different periods are compared with each other. In contrast to static analysis there is dynamic analysis which shows developments as a sequence through time. What happens in the first period affects conditions in the second period, which in turn affects what happens in the third period, and so on.

In Section 1.1 there is a brief description of a general equilibrium model. There is a more detailed look at this model and its assumptions in Chapter 2. Section 1.2 looks at the particular characteristics of a partial equilibrium model and Section 1.3 shows how the choice of the type of model should depend on the nature of the problem to be analysed. Finally, Section 1.4 illustrates how a dynamic equilibrium works.

1.1 A general equilibrium model

In a general equilibrium model there must be at least two countries and
at least two goods. For the sake of simplicity it is assumed that there
are two countries called country A and country B. They each produce
the two final products, good a and good b, and each has a demand for
these two goods. The goods are produced using production factors.
There are assumed two be two factors, being capital K and labour L.
To describe the conditions of production there is a production function
for each of the two goods in each of the two countries.

How much the individual country can produce of the two goods
depends on the quantity of capital and of labour which is available to
the country in the period concerned. For an individual country the
production functions for goods a and b can be written, in non-specific
form, thus:

$$X_a = X_a (K_a, L_a)$$
$$X_b = X_b (K_b, L_b)$$

Where X_a and X_b is the production of the two goods, K_a and K_b the
amount of capital used, and L_a and L_b the amount of labour used.
The same model can be made for the second country, but the form of
the functions of production can differ from the first country because
the production technology differs in the two countries.

In each of the two countries there are limits to the capacity of
production of each of the two goods. Thus, for one country the following applies:

$$\overline{K} = K_a + K_b$$
$$\overline{L} = L_a + L_b$$

where $\overline{K}$ and $\overline{L}$ are the amount of capital and the amount of labour
available in the country. This means that if the country expands its
production of good a it must use more capital and labour for this, so
that production of good b must be reduced. The same applies to the
second country, where the factor endowment can of course be different from the first country. On the basis of the production functions it
is possible to find the transformation curve for each country. A transformation curve is a curve which shows the maximum combinations
of the two finished goods a country can produce. How a transformation curve is derived will be shown in the next chapter in Section 2.5.

There is demand for the two goods in each of the two countries. This demand is conditioned by the fact that use of these goods gives consumers some utility. In each of the two countries there is a social utility function.

$$U = U (C_a, C_b)$$

where C_a and C_b are the consumption of good a and good b in the country in question.

Against the background of this utility function it is possible to derive a set of indifference curves for each country. An indifference curve is an expression of which combinations of the two final goods give the same utility or the same satisfaction of needs in the country in question. Typically, if the consumption of one good is reduced there must be an increased consumption of the other good in order to achieve the same satisfaction of need as in the initial situation. Chapter 3 contains a more detailed discussion of indifference curves.

These conditions of supply and demand can be shown as in Figure 1.1.a for country A and Figure 1.1.b for country B.

In the two countries there is a transformation curve TT. At the same time there is an set of indifference curves in each of the two countries. Two indifference curves, I_1 and I_2 are drawn, but there is a whole set of indifference curves in the co-ordinate system. Each point along the co-ordinates lies on an indifference curve. What characterises an indifference curve is that the further out it is along the co-ordinates, the greater the utility associated with it.

Figure 1.1: Transformation curves and indifference curves for two countries

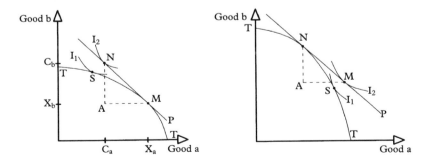

Figure 1.1.a: Country A   Figure 1.1.b: Country B

If there is no trade, which means that the economy is self-sufficient, it will be optimal for the two countries to produce and consume at the point S. There is no other point on the transformation curve which can be higher on an indifference curve.

On the contrary, at all other points on the transformation curves there are associated indifference curves which lie below I_1.

Assuming that there is perfect competition, it is possible to show (see the next chapter, Section 2.4) that the numerical value of the slope of the tangent at S gives the relative prices P_a/P_b. These tangents are not drawn in the Figures above. The slope of the tangents differ in the two countries, so the relative prices also differ.

S is the point of equilibrium in the two countries when there is no international trade. If international free trade is now introduced, there will be a set of world market prices which apply in both countries. For the sake of simplicity it is assumed that there are no transport costs.

The relative prices of the finished goods P_a/P_b are now equal to the numerical value of the slope at P. This means that the optimal production points in countries A and B are now M and N respectively. Meanwhile the optimal consumption point in countries A and B shift to N and M respectively. In country A production takes place at point M where the production of the two goods a and b is X_a, X_b. Consumption is at N where the consumption of the two goods is C_a, C_b.

Country A will export a quantity $X_a - C_a$ of good a while importing a quantity $C_b - X_b$ of good b. The figures indicate that AM for country A is equal to AM for country B, which is the same as country B's import of good a. AN is country A's import of good b. The length of this section of the line corresponds to the length of AN which is country B's export of good b.

As stated above, the numerical value of the slope of the tangent through NM is equal to the relative prices P_a/P_b. The slope can also be written as follows:

$$\frac{AN}{AM} = \frac{C_b - X_b}{X_a - C_a}$$

which means that:

$$\frac{P_a}{P_b} = \frac{C_b - X_b}{X_a - C_a}$$

Based on this fraction one gets:

$$P_a(X_a - C_a) = P_b(Cb - X_b)$$

which is the same as saying that there is equilibrium in the balance of trade or equilibrium in the current items of the balance of payments, if there are no 'invisible' items, such as trade in services.

If the model is looked at in more detail it will be seen that the trade equilibrium shown in Figure 1.1 is dependent on there being equilibrium in the balance of payments. The central point in the general equilibrium model is that it is not possible to change production of one good without changing production of the other. The same applies to consumption.

The consequences of international trade can be seen in that for country A there is movement from the consumption at point S under conditions of self-sufficiency to consumption at point N under free trade. In the model, welfare is linked to the utility level attainable. The utility level can be said to be relative in the sense that an indifference curve that is positioned further out in the co-ordinate system than another indifference curve has higher utility. In Figure 1.1.a indifference curve I_2 which passes through point N is higher than indifference curve I_1 which passes through point S. This means that country A's utility or welfare increases when moving from self-sufficiency to free trade. In country B there is movement from the consumption point S under self-sufficiency to consumption point M under free trade. As M is on indifference curve I_2 which is positioned further out in the co-ordinate system than indifference curve I_1, where S is positioned, welfare also increases in country B.

1.2 A partial equilibrium model

In a partial equilibrium model it is possible to look at the conditions for a single good or group of goods without taking into consideration all the other goods. For example, increased demand for a good will lead to increased expenditure on consumption of the good but it is not assumed to have any influence on the demand for other goods. On the supply side an increased supply will require the use of an increased amount of production factors, which can lead to a change in factor prices. This is not taken account of in the partial model because it is assumed that the scope for production of other goods is unaffected by the increased supply of the first good.

It is again assumed that there are two countries A and B, and that there are two final goods a and b and two production factors L and K. It is possible to write the demand curve D_a and the supply curve S_a for good a in country A as follows:

$$D_a = D_a(P_a, \overline{P}_b, \overline{Y})$$
$$S_a = S_a(P_a, \overline{P}_b, \overline{P}_L, \overline{P}_K)$$

where P is price and Y is income. P_a and P_b are the prices of final goods and P_L and P_K are the prices of the means of production. The lines above the variables express the assumption that they will be constant.

The demand curve for good D_a is the relationship between the price and the volume of demand, when the price of the other good and income are assumed to be constant. Similarly, the supply curve is only dependent on the price of the good, since the price of the other good and the factor prices are constant.

The functions of supply and demand in country A, as shown above, can be shown graphically as supply and demand curves as in Figure 1.2.a. In country B there are also supply and demand functions for good a, corresponding to the functions described above for country A. These functions can also be drawn in a figure which shows suppy and demand curves, as in Figure 1.2.b.

If the two countries do not trade with each other, then in each of the national markets a price will be established, P_A in country A and P_B in country B. This will be the case as long as there is perfect competition in the markets of the two countries.

The possibility of cross-border trade is now introduced. This means that a world market is established for good a. The conditions of this world market are drawn in Figure 1.2.c where E_A is country A's export supply and M_B is country B's import demand. These two curves can be derived from the conditions in countries A and B which are shown in Figures 1.2.a and b.

At price P_A country A will be self-sufficient, since the demand at this price is equal to the quantity supplied at the same price. At price P_A country A will not have an export surplus. If the price goes up to, for example P, the demand will be PF and the domestic supply will be PG. In this situation the country will have an export supply of FG, as drawn in Figure 1.2.c, which shows the conditions on the world market. If a horizontal subtraction is made between the domestic supply and the domestic demand with alternative prices which are higher than P_A, the result will be country A's export curve E_A.

Figure 1.2: Supply and demand curves for a single product

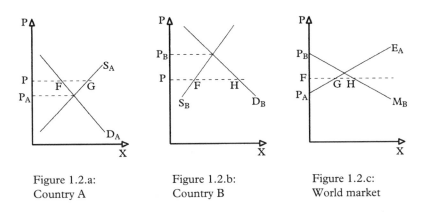

Figure 1.2.a:
Country A

Figure 1.2.b:
Country B

Figure 1.2.c:
World market

With a price of P_B country B will be self-sufficient in the good, but this will not be the case if the price falls below P_B. If the price is P, country B's domestic demand will be PH and the domestic production will equal PF. At price P there will be an import demand in country B equal to FH. This is shown in Figure 1.2.c. It is now possible to calculate the differences between domestic demand and domestic supply at other prices in country B. Thus it is possible to derive country B's import demand curve M_B.

It should also be noted that country A's export supply curve at a given price has a greater price elasticity than country A's domestic supply curve. This is not so surprising. If, for example, the price goes up 10%, supply in country A will also go up by 10%, if the price elasticity of supply is equal to 1. However, this 10% increase in the supply quantity is a greater proportion of exports which are less than production. The price elasticity will be greater for this reason alone. Furthermore, exports increase by more than the increase in supply, because the higher price leads to a fall in consumption. Similarly, it can be shown that import elasticity in country B is greater than demand elasticity.

On the world market a new price is now created where E_{Aa} (country A's export supply) intersects M_B (country B's import demand) in Figure 1.2.c.

What is the effect of trade on welfare? In partial models it is usual to measure welfare by looking at consumer surplus and producer surplus. Figure 1.3 shows what is meant by these terms. D is the demand curve, S is the supply curve, and P is the market price. The market price, which a purchaser is willing to pay, is an expression of the value which the purchaser ascribes to the good. In Figure 1.3.a it will be seen that if the price is P_1, there is one household that is willing to buy one unit of the good, but the household has only to pay the market price P.

Figure 1.3: Consumer surplus and producer surplus

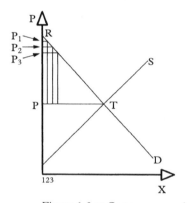

Figure 1.3.a: Consumer surplus

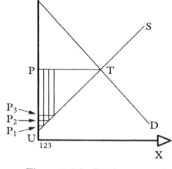

Figure 1.3.b: Producer surplus

The difference P_1 – P is therefore an expression of the difference between the utility which the household obtains and the cost paid in order to obtain that utility. If the price is P_2 there is a second household which is now willing to buy one unit of the good. In this case the utility minus the cost is P_2 – P. At the price P_3 a third household is willing to buy one unit and this household's consumer surplus (utility less cost) is equal to P_3 – P. The total consumer surplus is calculated by adding together the consumer surplus of the individual households. The total consumer surplus in Figure 1.3.a is equivalent to the size of the area PRT.

It is possible to make similar arguments on the supply side. It is assumed that there is one producer who has a marginal cost curve which is equal to the supply curve of the market. The producer is willing to sell the good at the marginal cost. In Figure 1.3.b the producer is willing to sell the first unit at the price P_1, the second unit at the price P_2 and the third unit at price P_3, etc. The producer obtains the market price of P for all the units produced. The total producer surplus is therefore the sum of $P - P_1$, $P - P_2$, $P - P_3$ etc. This means that the producer's surplus, i.e. its earnings minus the production costs (not including the fixed costs) will be equal to the area PUT.

These concepts can be used to describe the welfare effect of international trade in a partial model. The curves from Figure 1.2 are drawn in Figure 1.4. In Figure 1.4 in the situation without trade the prices in countries A and B are P_A and P_B respectively. When there is trade there is a world market price of P_V. The changes to welfare when there is international trade, compared with the position with self-sufficiency, can be measured by the sum of changes to consumer surplus and producer surplus. From Figure 1.4 it appears that the following changes take place when international trade is introduced:

Country A:	Increase in producer surplus	$= P_A P_V GO$
	Diminished consumer surplus	$= P_A P_V FO$
	Net gain	$= OFG$
Country B:	Diminished producer surplus	$= P_B P_V FO$
	Increase in consumer surplus	$= P_B P_V GO$
	Net gain	$= OFG$

In each of the two countries welfare will be increased by the two triangles OFG for country A and OFG for country B. These two areas are equal to the areas $P_V P_A O$ and $P_V P_B O$ in Figure 1.4.c.

Figure 1.4: Changes to welfare through trade

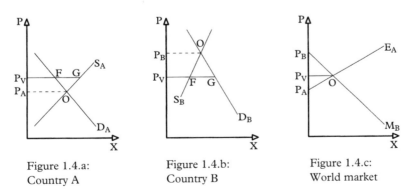

Figure 1.4.a:	Figure 1.4.b:	Figure 1.4.c:
Country A	Country B	World market

What is the core of the partial model? In the initial situation it is assumed that there were two goods a and b, for which there were both supply and demand in the two countries. In the general equilibrium model consumption and production are linked. The same applies to price formation.

The partial model deals with a situation where the supply curves and the demand curves show a link between price and volume when other conditions remain the same. Changes to the production volume and price of good a has no influence on the supply and price of good b. Changes to the production of good a does not affect factor prices nor the quantity of production factors available for good b. Nor do the changes to the conditions of product a have any influence on the incomes of the households.

As seen from the functions of supply and demand for good a on page 18, all the elements that can influence supply and demand are fixed since they are externally determined (exogenously fixed elements). Only the price of the good has influence. The mutual dependence in the general equilibrium model is not assumed to exist in the partial equilibrium model.

1.3 Which type of model is best?

International trade is analysed above by using a general equilibrium model and a partial equilibrium model. The differences between the two types of model have been shown. It is reasonable to ask if one model is better than the other. The answer is that it is not possible to generalise; it depends on the problem to be analysed. What are important are the kind of goods put into the model, and the type of country on which the model is used. A number of examples will illustrate this.

If there is a small country like Denmark, and if the market for carrots is to be analysed, then a partial model showing only Denmark will be satisfactory. Danish carrots play only a marginal role on the world market, so the world market prices for carrots will be externally determined. Similarly, the derived effect of a change in the supply or demand for Danish carrots will be of entirely marginal significance for the supply and demand of other goods in Denmark.

If, on the other hand, it is the EU which is considered and the market for cereals is to be analysed, it is reasonable to analyse the cereals market by itself. It can be assumed that the effect on markets for other goods in the EU will be marginal. However, it is reasonable to take into account the cereals market in the rest of the world because the EU plays such a dominant role in the world market for cereals, so that a change to the situation in the EU will influence prices in the world market.

If there is a requirement to analyse the relations between two large regions, for example between industrial countries and developing countries, and if the relations between industrial goods as one good and primary products as another good are to be considered, it is best to use a general model with two countries and two goods. The inter-relationship between countries and goods is so important that a partial model will not be adequate.

If there is a requirement to analyse the relationship between industrial and primary goods in Uruguay, it is best to use a general model for Uruguay since the two types of products are of such significance to Uruguay. On the other hand Uruguay plays such a small role in the world market that it is unnecessary to include the rest of the world in such a model.

1.4 Dynamic models

The general and the partial equilibrium models illustrated above are static models, or more correctly, comparative static models. They show a comparison between two static situations, namely the conditions under self-sufficiency and the conditions under free trade. A static model can be defined as one in which all the variables refer to the same period.

A dynamic model is one which shows the economic path over time. The model shows how the economic variables of an earlier period contribute to the determination of current economic variables which in turn influence the economic outcome in the succeeding period. A dynamic analysis can be defined as one in which there is at least one equation which links variables which relate to different periods.

The difference can be shown in an example. In Figure 1.5 and Figure 1.6 there is a comparative static model and a dynamic model each describing price formation. In Figure 1.5 there is a supply curve S, in which supply is immediately adjusted when there are price changes. In the initial situation there is demand D_1 and the price in equilibrium is P_1. This is a static analysis, which can become a comparative static analysis when it is assumed that in the following period the demand will be D_2. Because the supply adjusts immediately to the price change, there will immediately be a new equilibrium price of P_2 and a production volume of X_2.

In Figure 1.6 it is assumed that the supply is adjusted after a certain delay. This means that during the period t the supply is determined by the price in the foregoing period t - 1. In the initial situation (period 1) there is demand D_1 which means that the price is P_1, and the volume produced is X_1. In the following period (period 2) the demand curve moves to D_2. The adjustment of supply occurs after a period of delay which means that in period 2 the supply X_2 continues to be the same as the supply in period 1 since the supply in period 2 is determined by the price P_1 which applied in period 1. In period 2 the market price is P_2, which is at the intersection between the vertical supply curve X_1 and D_2. In the next period demand D_2 is fixed while prices will fluctuate. In period 3 the supply will be X_3 as determined by the price in period 2. However, the increased supply X_3 can only be sold at price P_3 which becomes the market price in period 3.

This model is called the cobweb theory which explains price fluctuations by the fact that the adjustment of supply takes time. This phenomenon is known in the production of primary products such as coffee, cocoa and pig meat.

Figure 1.5: A comparative statics price formation model

Figure 1.6: A dynamic price formation model

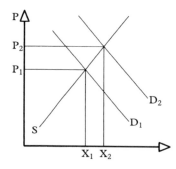

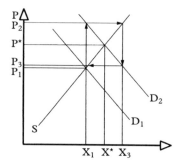

The difference between the two models can best be illustrated by describing the models arithmetically.

Static model:
$D(t) = D(P_t)$
$S(t) = S(P_t)$
$D(t) = S(t)$

Dynamic model:
$D(t) = D(P_t)$
$S(t) = S(P_{t-1})$
$D(t) = S(t)$

In the static model both supply and demand in period t are determined by the price in the same period. In the dynamic model, as shown here, demand in period t is determined by the price in period t, while supply in period t is determined by the price in the preceding period $t - 1$.

A dynamic model must be linked to a static model if there is a need to show whether the equilibrium reached is a stable equilibrium. A stable equilibrium is defined as an equilibrium which is returned if there is a disequilibrium, i.e. if the state of equilibrium is departed from because of a 'turbulence', for example a bad harvest.

The dynamic model in Figure 1.6 shows whether a new equilibrium is reached with price $P^\star$ and volume $X^\star$ after an increase in demand. If a new equilibrium is reached, the model can show how long the adjustment will take.

Another type of dynamic model is described below. It is a model which traces the development of points of equilibrium through time and shows how a number of macro-economic factors develop through time. It is a dynamic general equilibrium model which illustrates the central links between the savings in a society which are used for investments increasing the capital stock which creates the potential for increased production in future.

It is a model for a closed society, in other words a society without external trade and where there are two product sectors. The two sectors produce X_a and X_b respectively of the two goods a and b, using capital K and labour L. The following production functions apply to the two sectors:

$X_a = X_a (K_a, L_a)$
$X_b = X_b (K_b, L_b)$

The volume of capital and labour used in the two sectors amount to the total capital stock and labour force. It therefore applies that:

$$K = K_a + K_b$$
$$L = L_a + L_b$$

The demand of good a is for consumption, while the demand of good b is both for consumption and investment. The idea that a good can be used both for consumption and investment may be thought a little fanciful, but this can be overcome by using a three-sector model, in which the first two sectors produce consumer goods and the third produces investment goods.

If the two sector model is still used, it applies that:

$$C_a = X_a$$
$$C_b + I = X_b$$

where C_a and C_b are the consumption of the two goods and I is investments.

In addition to this there is a utility function which defines utility as the function of the volume of the two goods which are available. Thus:

$$U = U(X_a, X_b)$$

This utility function helps determine the demand for the two goods.

On the basis of the production it is possible to calculate the national product Y, which is:

$$Y = (P_a/P_b)X_a + X_b$$

where P_a/P_b are the relative prices of the goods a and b. Y is measured by using a numeraire equal to the price of good b.

There are savings in the society. The savings are that part of the national product which is not used for consumption. Savings are assumed to be directly proportional to the national product. The following applies:

$$S = sY$$

where s is the savings ratio.

In a closed economy the investments required are equal to the savings. Therefore:

$$S = I$$

In contrast to the static equilibrium model in Section 1.1, K and L are no longer constant. They change over time. It is precisely these dynamic relationships that are described by the model.

If the capital stock is permanent it will grow year on year by the size of the investments. This means that:

$dK/dt = I$

At the same time it is assumed that the population grows by n per cent per year. This can be expressed as follows:

$L = L_o e^{nt}$

where L_o is the labour force in the initial situation, e is the base number of the logarithm, n the annual growth in the population and t the time unit.

Such a model gives a description of the variables through time. The core of the model is shown in Figure 1.7. In the initial situation, i.e. in period 1, there is a transformation curve $T_1 T_1$ and an indifference curve I_1. This means that in period 1 there is a point of equilibrium at A_1. In period 1 there are investments and the labour force increases so that in period 2 $T_2 T_2$ is the new transformation curve with a point of equilibrium at A_2. In period 2 there are further investments and a further increase in the labour force, which lead to the transformation curve in period 3 being $T_3 T_3$ which gives a level of welfare corresponding to the indifference curve I_3.

Figure 1.7: A dynamic model of growth

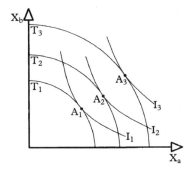

The model used here is for a closed economy. A corresponding model for a second country can be made. It is assumed that the two countries do not initially trade with each other. This gives the development through time for each of the two countries. Next it is assumed that trade is introduced, which gives different developments for the two countries.

The benefit of trade is the difference between the national product with trade and the national product without trade in each of the two countries. A comparison can be made of development through time.

1.5 Summary

In this introductory chapter a distinction is made between different methods of analysis or different types of models. There are two sets of model types. A distinction is made between partial and general models and between static and dynamic models. These distinctions cut across one another, and there are thus four possible combinations.

The characteristic of the general model is that it takes account of capacity limitations. It is only possible to increase production volume of one good by diminishing the production volume of the second good because there is only a given quantity of production factors. The same applies to consumption since the consumption of one good can only be increased if the consumption of the other good is diminished. The income earned sets limits to consumption. If the partial equilibrium model is used, these capacity limits are disregarded. In many cases it is reasonable to use a partial model.

In Chapters 2 to 4 there will be a more detailed review of the general equilibrium model, which is often used in international trade theory. But in many cases the use of the partial model will cause no problems.

The comparative static analysis method compares states of equilibrium, for example the situation before and after the introduction of international trade. The dynamic model, which links variables related to different periods, shows the development through time. General and partial models can supplement one another. The same applies to static and dynamic models. The interaction between growth and trade can be analysed by using both types of models. In analysing economic growth a dynamic model is the primary method, but when looking at growth and trade the comparative static model will often be satisfactory, as will be seen in Chapter 12.

Literature

The theories of international trade and factor movements are based on a comprehensive literature in books and articles. It is not intended to give an exhaustive reference to this literature. The references given here are to books which give an overview of international economic conditions and which also contain comprehensive references to the literature. Reference can be made to the following publications which give an overview:

Bhagwati, J.N. (ed), *International Trade: Selected Readings,* Cambridge, MIT Press, 1987.

Caves, R.E. and H.G. Johnson (eds), *Readings in International Economics,* Homewood, 1968.

Greenway, D., (ed), *Current Issues in International Trade,* Macmillan, 1996.

Greenaway, David and Alan Winters (eds), *Surveys in international Trade*, Blackwell, 1997.

Jones, Ronald and Peter Kenen (eds), *Handbook of International Economics,* Volume 1 and 2, Elsevier Science Publishing Company, 1984.

After each chapter references will be given to certain recommended publications which deal with the issues covered in the chapter.

2. Production conditions

In Chapter 1 there was a discussion of the use of the general equilibrium model to explain international trade. The model showed that trade depends on the shapes of the transformation curves in the two countries and the shapes of the indifference curves which mirror the preferences in the two societies. It is not sufficient to 'explain' international trade by drawing transformation curves and indifference curves while assuming that there is perfect competition. It is necessary to look closer at the assumptions about the conditions of production that determine the form of transformation curves. It is also necessary to look closer at the assumptions which lie behind the social indifference curves and which determine demand. Finally, it is natural to look at the benefits which may be associated with trade, including the question of how international terms of trade are determined.

These questions concerning production, demand and trade will be analysed in Chapters 2 to 4. The analysis is based on neo-classical microeconomics governing supply and demand. Chapter 2 deals with the conditions of supply, including the assumptions which must be made to be able to work with transformation curves. Chapter 3 deals with the necessary conditions for working with social indifference curves, and also links the conditions of supply and demand in a general equilibrium model for a closed society. The concepts of the Walras equilibrium and Pareto optimality are explained. Chapter 4 analyses the effects of trade, and the establishment of international terms of trade is studied in a model which links two equilibrium models for two countries which trade with each other.

2.1 Cost minimisation in firms

There is production in a single country in a large number of firms. It is assumed that these firms minimise their costs. In the society two final goods are produced, a and b. In the production of the two final goods each firm has its own production function which shows the relationship between the production of the final good and the inputs of capital and labour. The production functions for good a, in an non-specified form, can be described as:

$$X_a = X_a(L_a K_a)$$

It is possible to make the production functions specific by assuming that they are of the Cobb-Douglas type:

$$X_a = A_a L_a{}^\alpha K^{1-\alpha}$$

where A_a and α are parameters.

The production functions can be described by a set of isoquants. An isoquant is a curve which shows the different possible combinations of the two production factors which make it possible to produce a given volume of the final good. There are three isoquants drawn in Figure 2.1. One shows the combination of L and K which enable the production of the volume X_1. A higher isoquant shows the combination of factors which enable the production of the volume X_2, which is greater than X_1. X_3 is an isoquant with which even greater production is related.

The isoquants are convex, i.e. they are inwardly curved in relation to the system of co-ordinates staring at O.

Figure 2.1: An isoquant diagram

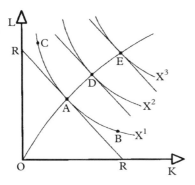

The marginal rate of substitution indicates how much more of the one factor is needed if the input of the other factor is diminished, in order to maintain constant production of the final good. The marginal rate of substitution is dL/dK. This is the slope of the tangent at a given point on the isoquant. At point B, where there is a relatively high use of K, dL/dK is relatively small. At point C, where there is relatively low use of K, dL/dK is big. The marginal rate of substitution in the use of factors is determined by the marginal productivity of the production factors. In general it is the case that:

$$dX = \partial X/\partial L \cdot dL + \partial X/\partial K \cdot dK$$

where $\partial X/\partial L$ and $\partial X/\partial K$ are the marginal productivity of the labour force and the capital stock respectively. When on a given isoquant dX = 0. Therefore:

$$-\frac{dL}{dK} = \frac{\partial X/\partial K}{\partial X/\partial L} \tag{2.1}$$

It is now assumed that a firm is confronted with a given set of factor prices P_L = w and P_K = r, where w is the wage rate and r is the price for using a capital unit. The concept of the isocost curve is now introduced; it is a curve which shows the combinations between two production factors L and K which give a uniform cost of Z. The equation for such an isocost curve is:

$$Z = w \cdot L + r \cdot K$$

which can be expressed as:

$$L = -\frac{r}{w} \cdot K + \frac{Z}{w}$$

The line RR in Figure 2.1 is such an isocost line, where the slope of the line r/w is the ratio between the factor prices, and where Z/w is equal to the segment of the line OR which is cut off at the L axis.

When a firm wants to produce a volume of X^1 this takes place at point A, where the isocost curve touches the isoquant for X^1. At this point the relative factor prices r/w are equal to the marginal rate of substitution for factor use dL/dK, which in turn is equal to the ratio between the marginal productivity of the production factors.

If production levels X^2 and X^3 are chosen, the production is most economically done at points D and E, as long as the relative factor prices are equal to r/w corresponding to the slope of RR. The slope of the tangents at points D and E are equal to the slope of the tangent RR. It is possible to link the points OADE as shown in Figure 2.1. This curve describes the points at which the isocost lines with the relative factor prices r/w corresponding to the slope RR, touches the

set of isoquants which express the production function. The curve
OADE shows the combinations of production factors which, at a
given set of factor prices, gives the lowest costs. A curve such as
OADE is called the expansion line. The curve shows how it is possible
to combine the production factors used in order to increase production of final goods while minimising costs.

2.2 Homogeneity and returns to scale

As referred to in the previous section, production functions can have
different characteristics. It is important to define concepts such as
homogeneity and returns to scale precisely. A production function is
said to be homogeneous to the degree of k if the following applies:

$$\lambda^k X(K,L) = f(\lambda K, \lambda L) \tag{2.2}$$

If inputs of K and L increase by 20 per cent, then $\lambda = 1.2$, which
means that the production of final goods is increased by λ^k, where k
is a constant, compared with the initial situation.

When production functions are homogeneous to the degree of k, it
is possible to distinguish between constant returns to scale, economies
of scale and diseconomies of scale. If $k = 1$, then a 20 per cent increase
in the inputs of both L and K gives a production increase of 20 per
cent. If $k > 1$ there are economies of scale, because the production
increase will be more than 20 per cent. If $k < 1$, there will be diseconomies of scale because 20 per cent increase of L and K gives less
than 20 per cent increase in production.

The Cobb-Douglas production function is a homogeneous production function. If the sum of the exponents of L and K together is 1,
there will be constant returns to scale. If the sum of the exponents is
greater than 1 there is a rising return to scale, and if the sum is less
than 1 there is a falling return to scale.

Figure 2.2 shows a production function which is homogeneous.
Three isoquants X^1, X^2 and X^3, and a straight line OABC have been
drawn. The isoquants are drawn so that OB is one and a half times
OA and OC is twice OA. If production is homogeneous in the first
degree, the ratios of X^3 and X^2 to X^1 1 are 2 and 1.5 respectively.

The slope of the tangents at points A, B and C indicate the marginal rates of substitution in the use of factors, which are equal to the

relationship between the marginal productivity of capital and labour, cf. Equation 2.1. It is possible to compare the marginal productivity at points A, B and C. When the production function is homogeneous the Equation 2.2 applies. If Equation 2.2 is differentiated first with regard to K and then with regard to L, there are the following equations:

$$\lambda^k \frac{\partial X(K,L)}{\partial K} = \frac{\partial f(\lambda K, \lambda L)}{\partial(\lambda K)} \cdot \lambda$$

$$\lambda^k \frac{\partial X(K,L)}{\partial L} = \frac{\partial f(\lambda K, \lambda L)}{\partial(\lambda L)} \cdot \lambda$$

(2.3)

where $\partial X/\partial K$ and $\partial X/\partial L$ are the marginal productivity of capital and labour respectively, for example, at point A in Figure 2.2. $\partial f/\partial(\lambda K)$ and $\partial f/\partial(\lambda L)$ are the corresponding marginal productivities, for example at point C.

If the production functions are homogeneous in the first degree, which means that there is constant return to scale, then $k = 1$. In this situation the marginal productivity of capital and labour is the same at points A and C, which also applies to other points along the line OABC. If there are economies of scale then $k > 1$, which means cf. Equation 2.3 that the marginal productivity of capital and labour increases as one moves from A to B and then on to C. If there are diseconomies of scale then $k < 1$, which means that the marginal productivity of both capital and labour fall as one moves from A to B and on to C.

Absolute marginal productivities develop differently, depending on whether there are neutral returns to scale, economies of scale or diseconomies of scale, when moving along a curve such as OABC. However, if the relative marginal productivities that are obtained by dividing the second equation in 2.3 into the first equation are considered, it will be seen that the relative marginal productivity is constant when the production functions are homogeneous, regardless of the degree of homogeneity. This means that the slopes of the tangents at A, B and C are always the same when the production functions are homogeneous.

Along every factor trajectory, such as OABD, the slopes of the tangents are the same when the production functions are homogeneous. This can also be expressed so that, if the production functions are homogeneous, the expansion line, for example OABD, will always be a straight line. The optimal combination of L and K given by the slope of the line OABC is constant with given relative factor prices, regardless of the volume of production.

Figure 2.2: A homogeneous produc- Figure 2.3: A production function tion function   which is not homogeneous

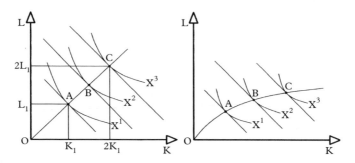

Figure 2.3 shows a production function which is not homogeneous. The expansion line OABC is curved so the optimal combination between L and K will vary according to the volume of production.

In the following it is assumed that the production function is homogeneous in the first degree, so constant returns to scale are assumed.

2.3 Cost minimisation in firms which produce different goods

Figure 2.1 illustrates cost minimisation with given relative factor prices for a firm which produces the good a. In another firm, which produces good b there is another production function. Also, for this firm there is cost minimisation when the relative factor prices are equal to the marginal rate of substitution in the use of factors, which in turn is equal to the ratio between the marginal productivity of the factors.

When the two firms, each producing their own good, have the same factor prices, the relationship between the marginal productivity of the factors must be the same for the two productions, as long as both minimise costs. This relationship can be illustrated in the box diagram in Figure 2.4.

The length of the box indicates the total quantity of capital which is available to the society. The height indicates the total labour force.

Figure 2.4: Cost minimisation for two firms each producing its own good

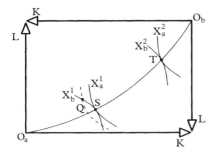

Taking the starting point of the co-ordinate system LO_aK, the isoquants for the production of good a are shown. With the staring point in the system of co-ordinates LO_bK, which is turned on its head, the isoquants for the production of good b are shown.

These isoquants touch at points S and T. If further isoquants are drawn, which are all characterised by the fact that the marginal rate of substitution in the use of factors is the same for both productions, the curve O_aO_b will be found. The slope of the tangent at S, which is not drawn, shows the relationship of dL/dK which is the same for both productions. The situation is similar at point T where dL/dK is also the same for both productions, but greater than at point S.

The curve O_aO_b is called a contract curve. On this curve it is impossible to increase production of good a by changing the mix of the factors used, without causing a fall in the production of good b. However this is not the case when one is outside the contract curve.

If the production takes place at point Q, it is possible, by changing the mix of the factors used to move production to point S, for example, where the production of good b will be the same as at point Q but where the production of good a will be greater than at point Q. All the points on the contract curve show a distribution of production factors between the two manufactures of final goods where the use of factors is optimal.

At each point in the box diagram there is an isoquant for good a for good b. For example this applies to point Q in Figure 2.4. The ratios for the marginal rates of substitution are:

$$\frac{dL_a}{dK_a} = \frac{\partial X_a/\partial K_a}{\partial X_a/\partial L_a} \quad \text{and} \quad \frac{dL_b}{dK_b} = \frac{\partial X_b/\partial K_b}{\partial X_b/\partial L_b} \tag{2.4}$$

It is assumed that the production factors are remunerated according to the value of their marginal product. For example, the following applies at point Q:

$$\begin{aligned}
\partial X_a/\partial Ka &= r_a/P_a \\
\partial X_a/\partial L_a &= w_a/P_a \\
\partial X_b/\partial K_b &= r_b/P_b \\
\partial X_b/\partial L_b &= w_b/P_b
\end{aligned} \tag{2.5}$$

If Equation 2.5 is combined with Equation 2.4 the result is:

$$\frac{dL_a}{dK_a} = \frac{r_a}{w_a} \quad \text{and} \quad \frac{dL_b}{dK_b} = \frac{r_b}{w_b} \tag{2.6}$$

If there are perfect markets the production factors will move instantaneously from the sector with low factor return to the sector with higher return, which implies that wages and the cost of capital will be the same in the two sectors. On the basis of Equation 2.6 there is the following outcome:

$$\frac{dL_a}{dK_a} = \frac{dL_b}{dK_b} = \frac{r}{w} \tag{2.7}$$

Equation 2.7 is true for all points along the contract curve.

At every point on the contract curve the marginal rate of substitution in the use of factors corresponds to dL/dK, which is identical for the two productions. At point S it is equal to the slope of the tangent at point S. If the relative factor prices r/w are equal to the slope of the tangent at point S, then S is the point of optimal production. If the price of capital rises in relation to wages, the slope of the tangent will be steeper. If the new relative prices are equal to the slope of the tangent at point T, then T will be the optimal point of production.

While the changing use of production factors moves production from point S to point T, it also changes the mix of final products. Production of good a is increased, while production of good b is reduced.

2.4 The optimisation of the amount of production

In Section 2.3 the task was to minimise the costs of the firms. The firms must also decide what volumes X_a and X_b to produce of the final goods a and b.

Each firm not only has given prices for factors, it also has given prices for final goods. For both firms the additional costs for expanding production of goods a and b can be written as:

$$dZ_a = w \cdot dL_a + r \cdot dK_a$$
$$dZ_b = w \cdot dL_b + r \cdot dK_b$$

which gives an increase in production of dX_a and dX_b respectively. This means that the marginal costs for the two productions MC_a and MC_b can be written as:

$$\frac{dZ_a}{dX_a} = \frac{w \cdot dL_a + r \cdot dK_a}{dX_a} = MC_a$$

$$\frac{dZ_b}{dX_b} = \frac{w \cdot dL_b + r \cdot dK_b}{dX_b} = MC_b$$

$$(2.8)$$

When each of the two firms has minimised its production costs, i.e. when they are on the contract curve, then one firm can only expand its production if the other firm reduces its production. This is illustrated above in Section 2.3. This is because the society only has a limited amount of labour L and a limited amount of capital K. All the production factors are fully used so that:

$$L = L_a + L_b$$
$$K = K_a + K_b$$

All the production factors are being used as effectively as possible. This means that in Equation 2.8 any increase in the production of good a by using dL_a and dK_a must mean a reduction in the production of good b, since $dL_a = -dL_b$ and $dK_a = -dK_b$. If this is included in the equation the result is:

$$\frac{dZ}{dX_a} = MC_a \quad \text{and} \quad -\frac{dZ}{dX_b} = MC_b$$

If – dZ/dXb is divided by dZ/dXa, the result is:

$$- \frac{dX_b}{dX_a} = \frac{MC_a}{MC_b} \qquad (2.9)$$

The left hand side refers to the marginal rate of transformation of production. It shows how much of the production of good b must be given up, dX_b, to obtain extra production of good a, dX_a. When firms minimise costs, this rate will be equal to the relation between the marginal costs.

The firms will also expand their production until their respective marginal costs are equal to the respective final good prices, since it is assumed that there is perfect competition in the market for final goods. There is therefore an optimisation of the production of final goods when the following conditions are met:

$$- \frac{dX_b}{dX_a} = \frac{P_a}{P_b} \qquad (2.10)$$

With a given set of relative factor prices the firms minimise their costs. This determines the relative marginal costs which are equal to the marginal rate of transformation. There will only be an optimal combination of final goods production if the relative prices for final goods fulfil the terms of Equation 2.10.

2.5 A graphical derivation
of the transformation curve

On the basis of a box diagram, corresponding to Figure 2.4 where the two sets of isoquants are shown, it is possible to derive the society's transformation curve.

In Figure 2.5 a box diagram is drawn in a slightly different form. The two starting points for the co-ordinate systems, O_a and O_b are moved to the bottom right hand and the top left hand corners.

Starting at the bottom left hand corner, at the point S, two new axes are drawn which show the volumes produced of goods a and b respectively. It is assumed that there are constant returns to scale in both productions, cf. Section 2.2.

This means that if the isoquant X_a^1 is twice as far out in the co-ordinate system as isoquant X_a^2 then production of good a will be twice as much. If isoquant X_a^1 is twice as far out as X_a^2 this means that if a straight line is drawn from O_a, for example the diagonal O_aO_b, it will intersect X_a^1 and X_a^2 at M and P, where the length of O_aM is twice that of O_aP.

Figure 2.5: Derivation of the transformation curve

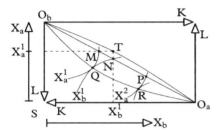

In the initial situation production is at point Q. Point M is at the point where X_a^1 intersects the diagonal. The horizontal dotted line leads the ordinate of M to the X_a axis, where the final good production, X_a^1, which takes place at point Q is positioned on the axis. If production is at point R, then X_a^2, the production of good a, will only be half the production at X_a^1. If again a horizontal dotted line is drawn to the X_a axis from point P, it is possible to show the production volume X_a^2 which is half X_a^1.

Similarly it is possible to show the production volume of good b from the X_b axis. The X_b^1 isoquant intersects the diagonal at point N. A dotted vertical line is drawn through N which hits the X_b^1 axis. The production volume X_b^1 is put on the X_b axis.

If the two dotted lines are extended horizontally and vertically, the point where they intersect is point T. With the co-ordinate system X_sSX_b the volumes of the two final goods that are linked to production at point Q have been determined at point T.

When this exercise is carried out for the other points on the contract curve, it is possible to derive other points in the co-ordinate system X_sSX_b which show the combinations of production of the two goods. A curve thus derived is O_bTO_a with its starting point in the co-ordinate system X_aSX_b.

The curve which has now been derived is a transformation curve which shows the alternative combinations of final goods which it is possible to produce when all the production factors are used optimally.

In Figure 2.5 the transformation curve is concave, i.e. outwardly curved in relation to point S. The slope of the tangent at a given point, for example point T is $- dX_a/dX_b$. This describes the marginal rate of transformation.

There is a relationship between the appearances of the production functions, the contract curve and the transformation curve. If the two production functions are very different the contract curve will be strongly curved. When the contract curve is strongly curved then the transformation curve will also be strongly curved. The more alike the production functions the weaker will be the curvature of the contract curve and the transformation curve. In the extreme case, where the two production functions are identical, the contract curve will be the diagonal, and the transformation curve will also be a straight line.

It has now been shown that there is a link between the production functions and the transformation curve. Figure 2.5 also illustrates that there is a linked variation between the points on the contract curve and the points on the transformation curve.

This also means that there is a linked relation between the prices in equilibrium in the market for factors and the prices in equilibrium in the market for goods. If there is a factor price ratio r/w which is equal to the curve of the isoquants at point Q in Figure 2.5, then Q is the optimal production point. Point T corresponds to it on the transformation curve, where the marginal rate of transformation is $- dX_a/dX_b$. In the market for goods there is only equilibrium if this rate is equal to the relative prices of final goods, cf. Equation 2.10 in Section 2.4. This condition will be met if there is perfect competition in the market for goods, where the prices for goods are equal to the marginal costs when there is equilibrium.

2.6 Summary of the conditions for production

At each point on the contract curve the marginal rate of substitution in the use of factors is identical for goods a and b:

$$\frac{dL_a}{dK_a} = \frac{dL_b}{dK_b}$$

As long as the production factors are remunerated according to the value of their marginal product, the marginal rate of substitution for the two goods will be equal to r/w. Therefore the following applies:

$$\frac{dL_a}{dK_a} = \frac{dL_b}{dK_b} = \frac{r}{w} \qquad (2.7)$$

In a situation of equilibrium, the marginal rate of substitution of factor usage (abbreviated to MRS^F) will be the same for the different manufactures.

At each point on the contract curve there is a corresponding point on the transformation curve where:

$$-\frac{dX_b}{dX_a} = \frac{MC_a}{MC_b} \qquad (2.9)$$

When there is perfect competition in the production of goods, production of the individual good will be expanded until the marginal costs are equal to the price. This means that, in a state of equilibrium there is

$$-\frac{dX_b}{dX_a} = \frac{P_a}{P_b} \qquad (2.10)$$

dX_a/dX_b, called the marginal rate of transformation (abbreviated to MRT), shall be equal to the relative prices of final goods.

Because of the definitions, the total factor remuneration in each of the two productions of good a and b shall be equal to the production value in the two sectors. This will be the case when it is assumed that there are constant returns to scale in the two productions.

When the production functions are homogeneous in the first degree the following applies to each of the two sectors, according to Euler's theorem:

$$X = \frac{\partial X}{\partial K} \cdot K + \frac{\partial X}{\partial L} \cdot L \qquad (2.11)$$

In Equation 2.7 it is assumed that the production factors are remunerated according to the value of their marginal product, which gives the following when the factor remuneration r and w is the same everywhere:

$$\frac{\partial X}{\partial K} = \frac{r}{P} \quad \text{and} \quad \frac{\partial X}{\partial L} = \frac{w}{P} \qquad (2.12)$$

where P is the price of final goods.

If Equations 2.12 and 2.11 are combined the result is:

$$P \cdot X = r \cdot K + w \cdot L$$

which shows that the value of production of the goods corresponds to the total factor remuneration of the production in question. An equilibrium model is thus created for the production sector.

Literature

The chapter is based on general microeconomic theory. Apart from the references to the general works referred to in connection with Chapter 1, reference can also be made to the first publication showing the derivation of the transformation curve on the basis of production functions:

Savosnick, K.M., 'The Box Diagram and the Production – Possibility Curve', *Ekonomisk Tidsskrift*, 60, 1958.

3. Demand conditions

3.1 The individual household has a preference structure

In the economy under consideration there are two goods which are available to the individual household. It is assumed that it is possible to describe the preference structure of the individual household by using a utility function:

$$U = U (C_a, C_b)$$

where the utility depends on the consumption of the two goods. Such a utility function can be shown graphically by using a set of indifference curves, as in Figure 3.1. An indifference curve, for example I_1 is a curve which describes the combination of the goods a and b which give the same utility.

At point Q, the slope of the tangent which is not shown, is equal to dC_b/dC_a. This ratio is called the marginal rate of substitution in consumption. The rate is determined by the relationship between the marginal utilities of the two final goods. It thus applies that:

$$dU = \partial U/\partial C_a \cdot dC_a + \partial U/\partial C_b \cdot dC_b$$

On an indifference curve dU will be zero. Therefore:

$$-\frac{dC_b}{dC_a} = \frac{\partial U/\partial C_a}{\partial U/\partial C_b}$$

The curves I_1 and I_2 are convex, i.e. they are inwardly curved from their point of origin. This means that a good's marginal utility is relatively small if, in the initial situation, there is a large quantity of this good and a small quantity of the other good. There is a level of utility linked to every indifference curve. The utility of consuming the combinations of goods that lie on the curve I_1 is less than the utility level on curve I_2. It follows from the utility function that it is possible to rank all indifference curves in relation to each other according to how far they lie from the point of origin. This only a relative, not an absolute measure of utility, as there is no objective standards against which to measure the utility. It is usual to refer to ordinal utility, measured is by relative ranking, rather than cardinal utility, which is measured in absolute units.

Figure 3.1: Indifference curves for a household

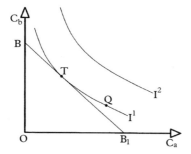

The household has a given income Y_1, and there are given prices on final goods, P_a and P_b. The household wishes to maximise its utility, but this can only be achieved within the household's budget restrictions, which can be described as an isocost curve:

$$Y_1 = P_a C_a + P_b C_b$$

$$C_b = - \frac{P_a}{P_b} C_a + \frac{Y_1}{P_b}$$

The line BB_1 in Figure 3.1 is such an isocost curve, with its position is determined by Y_1, P_a and P_b.

The slope of the isocost curve is $-P_a/P_b$, i.e. the slope is determined by the relative prices of the final goods. The section of the line OB is equal to Y_1/P_b, i.e. the household income measured in the maximum number of units which it can buy of good b. An isocost curve describes the combination of goods which a household can buy at given final goods prices when the household has a given income.

With the given income and given prices which fix BB_1 the household will achieve maximum utility by using at point T. At this point the relative prices are equal to the marginal rate of substitution, which is equal to the ratio between the marginal utilities.

In order to work with a utility function for a household on the basis of which indifference curves can be calculated, two conditions must be met.

First, the household must always be able to rank each set of combinations of goods in relation to another set (the consistency criteria). There are two sets of combinations of goods $R = (C_a, C_b)^R$ and $S = (C_a, C_b)^S$. The household must be able to decide whether the two sets give the same satisfaction of need, or whether set R gives a greater or lesser satisfaction than set S. If set R leads to there being more of both goods than set S, there the satisfaction level of R is greater than S.

In Figures 3.2 and 3.3 there are two sets of indifference curves. In one case the indifference curves do not intersect each other, while in the other they do. In both cases it is possible to compare the combinations of goods. Thus $R > S$, $S = S_1$, and $S_1 > T$, where $>$ means greater satisfaction and $=$ means equal satisfaction.

Figure 3.2: Indifference curves which do not intersect   *Figure 3.3: Indifference curves which intersect*

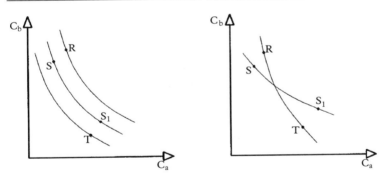

The other condition which must be met for indifference curves is that if $R > S$ and $S > T$, then it must be that $R > T$. This is called the transitivity criteria which is met in Figure 3.2 where the indifference curves do not intersect. However this condition is not met in Figure 3.3, where the following applies:

$R > S$ since at R there is more of both goods
$S = S_1$ since the two points are on the same indifference curve
$S_1 > T$ since there is more of both goods at S_1

From this it should be possible to deduce that R > T, but this conflicts with the fact that R and T are on the same indifference curve,
which should give the same level of satisfaction. The transitivity criteria require that the indifference curves should not intersect.

3.2 Social utility

The preceding discussion concerns the conditions for an individual
household. It is possible to work with a utility function for an individual household and the indifference curves derived from them. The
question now is whether it is possible to work with a utility function
for society as a whole, from which it may be possible to derive a set of
indifference curves which can rank the various combinations of goods
according to their social utility.

If there is one household in the society, there is no problem. This
household's indifference curves, which are assumed to fulfil the two
criteria referred to in the preceding section, will constitute society's
indifference curves.

However, if there are two or more households a problem arises with
regard to the distribution of income. The first thing to be noted is that
the condition for obtaining an optimal situation for consumption is
that the households' overall marginal rate of substitution of consumption (abbreviated to MRS^C) is the same.

To simplify things it is assumed that there are two households,
referred to as 1 and 2. It makes no difference to the argument whether
there are two or more households. If there are more than two it merely
makes the presentation of the argument more complicated. The two
households each have their own utility functions which are:

$$U_1 = U_1 (C_{a1}, C_{b1})$$
$$U_2 = U_2 (C_{a2}, C_{b2})$$

from which it is possible to derive two sets of indifference curves,
which are different. It is assumed that in the society there is a given
quantity of consumer goods to be shared between the households.

Figure 3.4 is a box diagram in which the lengths of the axes indicate
how much of the two goods are available to two households. Household 1's indifference curves are drawn with their starting point in the
co-ordinate system $C_b O_1 C_a$ and household 2's indifference curves are
drawn with their starting point on the co-ordinate system $C_a O_2 C_b$.

The two households each have budget limitations which are respectively:

$$C_{b1} = - \frac{P_a}{P_b} C_{a1} + \frac{Y_1}{P_b}$$

$$C_{b2} = \frac{P_a}{P_b} C_{a2} + \frac{Y_2}{P_b}$$

as shown, for example, by the line BB in Figure 3.4. If the two households have a volume of goods corresponding to Q on the budget line BB, each of the households will have improved welfare if household 1 sells the quantity $Q_b - T_b$ of good b in return for the quantity $T_a - Q_a$ of good a. By moving from Q to T each of the households moves out along the indifference curves to a point associated with greater utility.

With the distribution of income corresponding to the budget line BB, the optimal consumption point T is where the indifference curves for the two households I_1^0 and I_2^0 touch each other at point T. At this point the marginal rate of substitution of the two households is the same, and is equal to the relative prices of the goods which correspond to the slope of the budget lime BB.

If the two households' budget line is equal to DD, there is a different income distribution, since household 1 is wealthier than in the initial situation, where the budget line was BB. Correspondingly, household 2 is poorer. With the new income distribution and with the relative prices for final goods which corresponds to the slope of DD, the optimal point of consumption will be at S.

The curve $O_1 TSO_2$ is the contract curve on which the two households' marginal rates of substitution are always the same. When the two households each try to maximise utility, they will consume a combination of the goods a and b which lies on the contract curve. This is referred to as a Pareto-optimality, which is a situation where it is not possible to improve the welfare of one household without worsening the welfare of the other. Points which do not lie on the contract curve are not Pareto-optimal. For example, it is possible to increase the welfare of both households by moving from Q to T. However, all points along the contract curve are Pareto-optimal. In moving from T to S, household 1 will increase its welfare since the household will be able to obtain more units of each good, but this is

at the expense of the other household, which has reduced availability
of both goods.

*Figure 3.4: Two households' consumption of two goods whose quantity is
given*

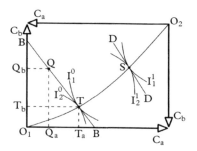

*Figure 3.5: Utility combinations with the distribution of given quantities of
goods*

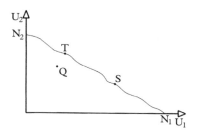

In Figure 3.5 both households' utilities are shown with alternative
distributions of given quantities of the consumer goods a and b. In
Figure 3.4, when moving along the contract curve from O_1 to O_2 one
moves from N_2 to N_1 in Figure 3.5. In Figure 3.5 the points T, S and
Q correspond to the equivalent points in Figure 3.4.

It will be seen that the social utility at T is greater than at Q because both households are better off. However it is not possible to
deduce anything about the social utility in moving along N_2N_1 in
Figure 3.5. This is because it is impossible to measure utility for an
individual household in absolute terms. It is only possible to rank the
utility associated with different combinations of goods.

3.3 Social indifference curves

Is it possible to make an aggregation of the indifference curves of individual households so as to be able to talk of a social indifference curve?

Social indifference curves correspond to the indifference curves of individual households. They must show a ranking of different combinations of goods from the point of view of society. For a social indifference curve to have any meaning it must have consistency and transitivity. If social indifference curves intersect one another, the requirement for transitivity will not be met, and there will be no purpose in working with social indifference curves.

There is a further requirement for social indifference curves. The utility of both households must be constant in moving along a given social indifference curve. If the utility of one increases and the other decreases it is not possible to say that the social utility is unchanged. If one household is on a higher social indifference curve, the social utility is only greater if the individual utility of both households is greater than on the lower social indifference curve.

The utility functions are different

It is possible to derive a social indifference curve by putting the indifference curves of the two households together in a box diagram, as shown in Figure 3.6, where the indifference curves of the two households differ. The initial situation is at point T. The welfare of the two households is equal to the utility associated with I^1_1 and I^1_2 respectively. These two levels of utility are maintained. It is possible to shift the co-ordinate system, which is turned on its head, so that household No. 2's indifference curve I^1_2 always touches I^1_1. Such a point is T', to which there is a corresponding point O_2'. If the point of contact is T" then this corresponds to $O_2"$.

The curve $O_2'O_2O_2"$ is a curve describing how the starting point of the co-ordinate system, which is turned on its head, moves. This is a social indifference curve. The social utility is the same with alternative combinations of goods because the two households obtain the same utility regardless of which combination is chosen. The social indifference curve is characterised by the marginal rate of substitution for the two households being the same at every point along the curve.

Figure 3.6: Derivation of social indifference curves

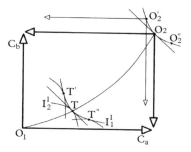

Figure 3.7: Social indifference curves with different income distribution

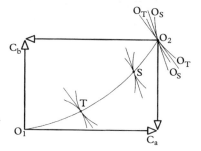

However, there is a problem because the social indifference curve $O_2'O_2O_2''$ is linked to the income distribution at point T. If social indifference is calculated on the basis of some other income distribution, the result will be another social indifference curve. In Figure 3.7 O_TO_T is the same social indifference curve as is shown in Figure 3.6. However, if the calculation is based on the income distribution at point S, this will result in a different social indifference curve which has the same slope at point O_2 as the indifference curve at point S. The result now is a social indifference curve O_SO_S. For each point along the contract curve O_1TSO_2 it is possible to derive social indifference curves which will intersect each other.

The conclusion is that as long as the two households have different needs which result in each having its different sets of indifference curves, it is not possible to derive social indifference curves which do not intersect each other, which is necessary if the transitivity criteria are to be met.

The utility functions are the same

The question now is whether it is possible to derive social indifference curves if the needs, and thus the indifference curves, of the two households are the same. The answer is that it is possible in some cases, but not in all cases.

Figure 3.8: Non-homothetic utility function which is identical for the two households

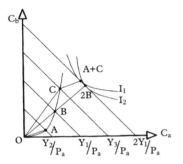

In Figure 3.8 there is a set of indifference curves which are the same for the two households. These are not shown. A set of parallel isocost lines are drawn in the figure because there is a given set of relative prices, P_a/P_b. The isocost lines indicate differences in income.

The income level at the isocost line furthest out is four times as high as the level at the isocost line furthest in, twice as much as the next line out, and 1 1/3rd times the income at the next isocost line out after that. OABC is the expansion line which shows the tangent points between the indifference curves, which are not shown, and the isocost lines.

In the initial situation there are two households, each with the income Y_1. In this case the total consumption for the whole of society will be 2B, on the isocost line furthest out, which is the isocost line for society since the national income is $2Y_1$. In the next situation, the national income is still $2Y_1$ but one of the household's income is reduced to Y_2, halving it in relation to Y_1. The household is taxed, and this income is given to the other household which thus obtains an income of Y_3. This means that society has a consumption of A + C, which is different from 2B.

The total national income is the same, but the distribution between the households is different. Even if the utility function for the two households is the same, there will be two different consumption points for society in the two situations. If a corresponding calculation is now made for alternative relative prices in relation to the indifference curves, which touch at the points A, B and C, it will be possible to derive social indifference curves for the two situations with identical national incomes but different income distribution. The two social indifference curves are I_1 and I_2 respectively. The two social indifference curves for each of the income distributions intersect one another. The transitivity criteria are not fulfilled so that it is impossible to derive any meaningful social indifference curves.

Figure 3.9: Identical homothetic utility functions in the two households

Figure 3.10: Identical quasi-homothetic utility functions in the two households

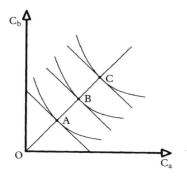

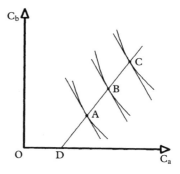

The reason for this is that the utility function is not homothetical. In Figure 3.9 a set of indifference curves is drawn which result from a homothetical utility function. A function is called homothetical when the expansion line OABC, which gives the optimal combination of consumption of the goods a and b, is a straight line. If a utility function is homothetical this means that doubling a households' income will lead to a doubling of the consumption of each of the goods a and b, if their relative prices remain unchanged. If the utility function is homothetical this means that the income elasticity for both the goods is equal to one.

Figure 3.8 shows an expansion line is that is not straight. The income elasticity for good a is less than 1, and the income elasticity for good b is greater than 1.

In the case where the utility function is not merely the same for the two households but also homothetical, it is possible to construct social indifference curves that do not intersect one another. This can be illustrated in Figure 3.9.

In the first situation there are two households which each have the same income, for example corresponding to the budget line which is the tangent to point B. The total consumption for society is 2B. In the second situation the first household's income is halved, which means that the first household consumes at point A. The second household gets the income which the first loses, and the richer household will therefore consume at point C. The total consumption is equal to A + C. Since A + C is equal to 2B the total consumption in society will be the same regardless of income distribution.

With different relative prices the consumption of the two goods in the society will also be the same, regardless of income distribution. Where the utility function is the same and is homothetic it is thus possible to derive a social indifference curve which is the same regardless of income distribution.

If there are indifference curves, as shown in Figure 3.10, it is also possible to derive social indifference curves which do not intersect each other, even if the income distribution changes. This can be illustrated in the same way as above. If, from the staring point of B, one income is increased to C and the other is reduced to A, the consumption in the society will be unchanged. In Figure 3.10 the utility function is homothetic because a straight expansion line does not pass through O. If one disregards the initial consumption, OD, of one good in Figure 3.10, there is a homothetical function. Therefore this function is often referred to as being quasi-homothetical.

When the utility functions are the same for the two households, and when the utility function is homothetic or quasi-homothetic, it is possible to derive social indifference curves which meet the transitivity criteria, i.e. the curves do not intersect each other. There is a core problem remaining, and this is that it is impossible to be certain that the welfare of society is greater on a social indifference curve which is positioned further out in the co-ordinate system.

In Figure 3.11 there are two social indifference curves, S_1 and S_2. The national product corresponding to S_2 is N_2, which is greater than the national product N_1, which corresponds to S_1. It is therefore reasonable to expect that the welfare of society is greater at D than at C. However, it is impossible to state this with certainty since a higher welfare level associated with S_2 requires that both households shall be better off than they were on the social indifference curve S_1. If the incomes of each the two households are equal to Y_1^1 in the first situation, then each of the households has a satisfaction of needs corresponding to the indifference curve I_1^1. The national income is equal to twice Y_1^1. There is now a change, since household 1's income falls to falls to Y_2^1, while household 2's income rises to $N_2 - Y_2^1$. This involves moving up to the higher social indifference curve S_2. It is not possible to say that welfare has increased since household 1 has a lower income ($Y_2^1 < Y_1^1$), and is therefore on a lower indifference curve I_2^1. Only if, in the new situation, both households are on an indifference curve which is not lower than I_1^1 is it possible to say that the social welfare at S_2 is higher than at S_1. This condition will be met if the relative income distribution linked to S_2 is constant compared with the income distribution at S_1.

Figure 3.11: Comparison of welfare with two different social indifference curves

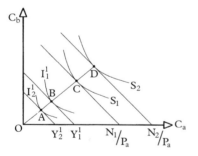

If one of the households finds itself on indifference curve I_1^1 initially and thereafter on I_2^1 there must be a redistribution of income to the advantage of the household which has become worse off, for example by means of taxation policy, before S_2 can be said to give a higher social welfare than S_1.

It is possible to say that welfare at S_2 is potentially higher than welfare at S_1, and it is always possible to redistribute income to ensure that both households have a higher welfare at S_2 than with the social indifference curve at S_1.

If there is always a redistribution of income so that the relative income distribution is constant, it is also possible to rank social indifference curves according to their position in the co-ordinates system. The higher the social indifference curve, the higher the welfare.

3.4 Combining production and domestic demand

In Chapter 2 there was a model for the production sector, in which there was production of two goods using two production factors. In this chapter there is a model for domestic demand, in which there are two households that each consume two products, with due account taken of the income of each. It is now natural to combine the two models into one model for the whole of society, covering both sectors.

In the domestic sector the two households, 1 and 2, will each consume a combination of the goods a and b. For these consumption combinations (C_{a1}, C_{b1}) and (C_{a2}, C_{b2}) the following applies:

$$P_a C_{a1} + P_b C_{b1} = Y_1$$
$$P_a C_{a2} + P_b C_{b2} = Y_2$$

where (P_a, P_b) are the prices of the goods and (Y_1, Y_2) are the household incomes.

The total amount of the two production factors, capital and labour, that is shared between the two households is thus $K = K_1 + K_2$ and $L = L_1 = L_2$ and where household 1 has (K_1, L_1) available to it and household 2 has (K_2, L_2) available to it.

Household incomes are determined by the factor remuneration for capital r and labour w multiplied the amount of production factors which each household has available to it. There is therefore the following:

$$Y_1 = rK_1 + wL_1$$
$$Y_2 = rK_2 + wL_2$$

In the production sector there are productions of X_a and X_b, for which the value of the production of goods is equal to the sum of the factor remuneration of the two factors:

$$P_a X_a + P_b X_b = r(K_a + K_b) + w(L_a + L_b)$$

where (K_a, L_a) and (K_b, L_b) are the factor combinations which are used in the manufacture of the two goods.

Every Walras equilibrium is Pareto-optimal

There is considered to be a general equilibrium, or a Walras equilibrium, in a model when there is:

- a combination of consumption for the two households
- a composition of production of the two goods
- a set of prices for the goods and factor prices

for which it applies that:

- each household maximises its utility at the given prices and incomes
- the firms maximise their profits at the given prices
- the supply and demand in each market is the same

If there is perfect competition in the markets, then this form of market, together with the consumers' maximisation of utility and producers' maximisation of profit, will result in a Walras equilibrium.

The Walras equilibrium is dependent on a set of exogenous factors. These are the distribution of income and assets, the needs structure, technology and the quantity of production factors available. It is particularly to focus on the distribution of income and assets. If these are changed there will be a new set of quantities and prices which fulfil the criteria for a Walras equilibrium.

In a general equilibrium situation the marginal rate of substitution in consumption is equal to the relative prices, and the marginal rate of transformation in production is equal to the relative prices of final goods.

If the assumptions behind this general equilibrium model apply in practice, including the assumption of perfect competition in all markets, this model will describe reality. The question is whether the general equilibrium model is also a normative model which can indicate what course of action should be adopted.

There is a given quantity of the goods a and b. The given quantities are shared between the two households. If the given share means that it is not possible to improve one household's welfare without damaging the other household's welfare, the distribution is an expression of Pareto-optimality. In the box diagram, Figure 3.4, all the points along the contract curve are Pareto-optimal. The points not on the contract curve are not Pareto-optimal. By exchanging goods between households it is possible to improve welfare in both households.

It is possible to look at the effectiveness of production in a similar way. In Figure 2.4 there is only one effective production, as long as one is on the contract curve. If one is not on the contract curve, it is possible to increase production of one good while maintaining production of the other good, if there is a redistribution of the use of production factors.

In a Walras equilibrium the position is always on the contract curve in relation to factor use (see Figure 2.4), on the transformation curve (see Figure 2.5) and on the contract curve for consumption (see Figure 3.4).

It can thus be concluded that when there is a Walras equilibrium there will also be a Pareto-optimality, which means that one household's situation cannot be improved without harming the position of the other household.

There are many points of Walras equilibrium, depending on how income and assets are distributed. It is not possible to suggest which of these points of Walras equilibrium is the most desirable. This is because it is impossible to make an absolute measure of the welfare or utility of individual households. Welfare can only be measured relatively for each household. It is not possible to make any interpersonal comparisons, in other words to compare the utility in one household with the utility in another.

Every Pareto-optimality is a Walras equilibrium after a redistribution of income

Every Walras equilibrium implies Pareto-optimality. The converse also applies, in that for every Pareto-optimal situation there is a set of consumer and factor prices which can ensure a distribution of consumption and production which is at a point of Walras equilibrium, following a redistribution of income. If the necessary redistribution of incomes is made, the markets will establish a Walras equilibrium corresponding to Pareto-optimality.

At a given income distribution there is a corresponding Walras equilibrium, which is also a Pareto-optimality. With different income distribution there is another Walras equilibrium, which gives another Pareto-optimality.

If there is Pareto-optimality initially, there will be prices which will give a Walras equilibrium if there are transfers which alter the income distribution. It will be exceptional if the distribution of production factors between households initially is precisely so that there will be a Walras equilibrium at the given prices. However, there will always be an income distribution that can ensure this equilibrium.

Figure 3.12: Pareto-optimality means Walras equilibrium after income redistribution

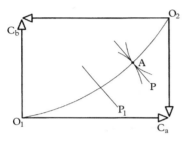

In Figure 3.12 there is a Pareto equilibrium at A. There is a set of consumer goods prices corresponding to this which ensure a Walras equilibrium, as long as the household incomes are such that P is the budget line for the two households. If, as a result of the distribution of production factors between the households, the income distribution means that P_1 is the budget line, then household 2 should be taxed and the money should be transferred to household 1 so that the budget line moves from P_1 to P so that the Pareto equilibrium at point A will also be a Walras equilibrium.

Descriptive and normative models

A distinction is made between descriptive and normative models. A descriptive model shows how things are in fact. A normative model indicates what should be done in order to achieve a desired result.

In many cases models are used both to describe how things are and as a starting point for indicating what should be done. The general equilibrium model is such a model. If all the assumptions behind the general equilibrium model are fulfilled, the model can be used descriptively. The model shows the results of factor use, consumer goods production, consumer goods consumption, relative factor prices, and relative consumer goods prices. Whether or not a model is good at describing reality depends on whether the assumptions behind the model also correspond to reality.

The general equilibrium model can also be used as a normative model, giving some indication of what should be done in order to attain some particular objective. If the assumptions of the model are realistic, the model can show what income transfers shall be made in order to obtain the income distribution required in a society. The desired Pareto-optimality can theoretically be obtained both in a society based on a market economy with perfect competition and in a planned economy in which consumer prices and factor prices are administratively determined. However, in practice it has been shown that in a planned economy it is impossible for the planners to be in possession of all the information necessary to set the 'right' prices. Nor will an unregulated market economy create a Pareto-optimal situation, even after income redistribution, as long as there are monopolies or externalities in production and consumption, for example, in the form of pollution.

3.5 Summary

It is possible to derive an indifference curve for an individual household on the basis of a utility function, as long as certain criteria are met. Even if there is a set of indifference curves for each household, it is only possible to derive social indifference curves in certain circumstances. This is linked to income distribution, which can be changed, and to the requirements of Pareto-optimality which state that a given level of consumption for a plurality of households can only be considered as being better than another level of consumption as long as every household is better off in the new situation or at least not worse off than in the previous situation.

It is only possible to work with social indifference curves as long as the indifference curves are the same and are either homothetic or quasi-homothetic. In addition to this, it is only possible to rank social indifference curves in relation to each other, subject to certain conditions of income distribution.

Even though social indifference curves can only be derived under certain specific conditions, they will nevertheless be used in what follows because they are useful for illustrating a number of conditions. In the next chapter it will be shown that the gains associated with trade are not conditional on whether it is possible to construct social indifference curves. The advantages continue to apply, even if it is not possible to draw social indifference curves, as long as the necessary compensatory payments are made (or changes made to income distribution).

At the conclusion of the chapter a general equilibrium model is shown combining the production sector and domestic demand in a closed economy. In a Walras equilibrium the marginal rate of substitution between the production factors MRS^F is the same overall. For each MRS^F there is a corresponding marginal rate of transformation, MRT, which shall be equal to the prices of final goods. Finally, in consumption, the marginal rate of substitution, MRS^C for the two goods shall be the same for all households as well as being equal to the relative prices of the goods.

There are many points of Walras equilibrium which are also Pareto-optimal, but where the income distribution is different. If there is a given Pareto-optimal position initially, there will always be a corresponding Walras equilibrium, once a necessary redistribution of income has taken place.

Literature

Caves, R.E. and H.G. Johnson (eds), *Readings in International Economics*, Homewood, 1968.

Chipman, J.S., 'A Survey of the Theory of International Trade', *Econonomica* 33, 1965.

Melvin, J.R.,'On the Equivalence of Community Indifference and the Aggregate Consumption Function', *Economica*, 42, 1975.

Samuelson, P.A.,'Social Indifference curves', *Quarterly Journal of Economics*, 64, 1956.

4. Trade and the terms of trade

In the two previous chapters the production conditions and demand conditions in a single country have been analysed. If the two models for production and demand are put together, they form a general equilibrium model for an individual country. This is a model for a closed economy.

It is now assumed that there are at least two countries which can trade with each other. On the world market there is an established set of international prices. This chapter deals with two sets of questions. The first question concerns the benefits of international trade with given international terms of trade. The second question concerns the factors which determine the international terms of trade as well as how the terms of trade can be derived from the offer curves.

4.1 The gains from trade

In the two countries it is assumed that the production conditions can be described by using two concave transformation curves. It is also assumed that the demand conditions can be described by using a set of social indifference curves for both countries. Finally, it is assumed that there is perfect competition, which means that the marginal rate of transformation MRT is equal to the marginal rate of substitution in consumption MRS, which is equal to the prices of final goods. On the basis of these assumptions it is possible to illustrate the conditions in one of the countries before and after trade, as shown in Figure 4.1.

The production in the initial situation the country is described by Point A, where the indifference curve I_1 touches the transformation curve. The country is self-sufficient. The relative prices P_a/P_b are given by the slope of the tangent. International trade is now introduced. It is assumed that good b will be relatively cheaper. The new terms of trade are equal to the slope of the straight line BD, which touches the indifference curve I_2. Since I_2 is further out in the co-ordinate system than I_1, it can be shown that international free trade in the situation described in Figure 4.1, gives higher welfare than self-sufficiency.

Figure 4.1: The gains from trade

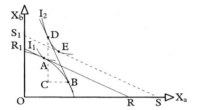

It is also possible to reach the higher positioned indifference curve I_2 differently. The dotted line gives the same relative prices as in the initial situation. It is now assumed that a new transformation curve is reached through economic growth, i.e. through capital accumulation or technological progress, and this touches the indifference curve I_2 at point E.

The equation for the line RR_1 is:

$$Y = P_a X_a + P_b X_b$$

which is equal to:

$$X_b = - \frac{P_a}{P_b} X_a + \frac{Y}{P_b}$$

where Y is the national income, since Y is the value of the total production. If $X_a = 0$, then $Y/P_b = X_b$, which is equal to the line segment OR_1, cut off by RR_1 on the X_b axis. If $X_b = 0$, $Y/P_a = X_a$, which is equal to OR, cut off by RR_1 on the X_a axis. The line segments OR_1 and OR thus give the national income Y, measured in units of good b and good a respectively. For the dotted line SS_1 P_a and P_b are unchanged. This means that the line segments OS_1 and OS now show that the national income has increased in relation to the line RR_1. The growth is equal to R_1S_1/OR_1 calculated in units of good b, and RS/OR calculated in units of good a. As the prices are unchanged, the growth is the same regardless of whether the calculation is made in units of good a or good b.

It is possible to achieve a higher indifference curve either through trade or through growth. The utility level is the same whether this is achieved by trade or by growth. Here, no account is taken of the 'costs' of growth, for example for the expenses of capital accumulation and research, which can differ from the costs associated with the re-allocation of factors that is necessary in moving from A to B through trade.

The effect of trade on consumption can be said to correspond to an increase in income with unchanged relative prices, combined with a substitution effect on consumption, due to changed relative prices. The income effect causes a move from A to E, and the substitution effect causes a move from E to D. With these assumptions, trade gives a growth in real income and a change in the prices of final goods. Consumption of the cheaper good b increases, partly because trade gives increased income (the income effect), and partly because good b is relatively cheaper (the substitution effect). For good a, the income effect will pull in the direction of increased consumption, while the substitution effect will reduce the use of good a, which becomes more expensive. The cumulative effect will depend on whether the income effect is stronger or weaker than the substitution effect. At the same time, domestic production will be changed. Production of good a will be increased and production of good b will be reduced.

The country exports the quantity BC of good a and imports the quantity CD of good b. Since CD/BC is equal to P_a/P_b:

$$BC \cdot P_a = CD \cdot P_b$$

which means there is equilibrium in the balance of payments.

In Figure 4.1, point A is a point of equilibrium without trade and points D and B are points of equilibrium with trade. The analysis does not take account of the fact that such an adjustment takes time, or that the adjustment itself is not without costs.

The gain obtained through trade can be divided between the gain associated with being able to trade, in other words being able to exchange goods, and the gain associated with the changes to the pattern of production. This is illustrated in Figure 4.2, which corresponds to Figure 4.1 as the points A, B and D are identical.

When trade is introduced, the country will find itself at point A, but there will now be trade at international terms of trade which will be equal to the slope of the dotted line which is parallel to the slope of BD. If the production point continues to be A, consumption will be D_1, after trade. This is the advantage from the trade in goods at the new international prices. In time, the production point will move from A to B, because it becomes worthwhile for firms to change product mix with the new pricing conditions. This advantage becomes apparent as the point of consumption moves from D_1 to D.

Figure 4.2: Gains from exchanging goods and gains from specialisation

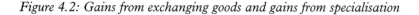

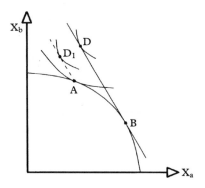

Therefore, the advantage of introducing trade consists of two components, the advantage to consumption from the exchange of goods and the advantage to production from specialisation. / *INSERIRA COME ULTIMA FRASE NELLA SPIEGAZIONE DELLA TEORIA)*

4.2 Trade affects households differently

In the above it is assumed that it is possible to derive social indifference curves where the position within the co-ordinates ranks welfare in situations with and without trade. As shown in Chapter 3, a number of pre-conditions have to be met before it makes any sense to work with social indifference curves.

In moving from a situation without trade to a situation with trade, the conditions for the different households in society will be changed. Firstly, the relative prices will be changed, which will be a disadvantage for households which have a preference for the good which becomes more expensive. Secondly, the changed relative final good prices mean that the rewards for the different production factors which the households can offer, will be changed. There will thus be a change in the incomes of the households. These changed conditions are shown in Figures 4.3 and 4.4, which illustrate the conditions in a society with two households.

In Figure 4.3, I_1^1 and I_2^1 are indifference curves for household 1, and I_1^2 and I_2^2 are indifference curves for household 2. In household 1 there is a relative preference for good b, and in household 2 there is a preference for good a. Before there was trade there were relative prices corresponding to the slope of P_1. Household 1's consumption was A_1 and household 2's consumption was B_1, as long as the incomes of the two households were the same. If, after trade, the incomes of the two households are unchanged, there will be a new budget line P_2, whose slope illustrates the new relative prices. In Figure 4.3 the slope of P_2 is steeper than P_1, which means that good a has become relatively more expensive. After trade the result is that households 1 and 2 consume at points A_2 and B_2 respectively. Household 1, which has a preference for good b, which has become cheaper, experiences an increase in welfare. Household 2, which has a preference for good a, which has become more expensive, has reduced welfare.

Figure 4.3: Changed price relations *Figure 4.4: Changed incomes*

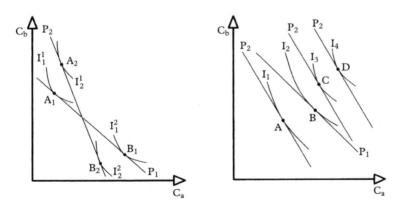

Figure 4.4 illustrates the effect of the change in the incomes of the households. The demand structure in the two households is assumed to be the same. This is illustrated by a common set of indifference curves I_1, I_2, I_3 and I_4. In the initial situation, before trade, the relative prices are equal to the slope of the budget line P_1, which is the same for both households, whose income is assumed to be the same. Consumption is therefore B. After the introduction of trade, the relative

prices are equal to the slope of P_2. If both households get the same increase in income as the result of trade, there will be a new consumption point at C. C gives higher welfare to both households than B. After the introduction of trade there will be different factor prices, as will be discussed in Chapter 6. It is possible that household 1's income will fall, so that household 1 consumes at point A. On the other hand, household 2 gets a considerable increase in income and will, for example, consume at point D. In this situation, in contrast to the other situation in which both households get increased incomes, it is not possible to say whether the welfare of society has increased after the introduction of trade, compared with the situation of self-sufficiency. We are thus back with the problem that was discussed in Chapter 3. Here it was shown that it can only be said that the welfare of society has increased in a situation where it is possible to construct social indifference curves and where each household gets an increased income.

The analysis in section 4.1 concluded that there is a benefit with trade, because a higher social indifference curve is achieved. But this conclusion is based on the assumption that it is possible to construct social indifference curves where all households obtain an increase in their real income.

However, the fact is that it is only in exceptional cases that it is possible to construct social indifference curves which meet the transitivity criteria. Even in these cases it is not possible to say anything about society's welfare if at least one of the households suffers a fall in its real income.

On the basis of this it must be concluded that it cannot be shown that free trade gives society greater welfare than self-sufficiency.

4.3 Utility curves

The conclusion, that it is not possible to say anything about the extent to which free trade is better or worse than self-sufficiency, is naturally unsatisfactory. However, fortunately it is nowadays possible to say something about welfare under conditions of free trade and self-sufficiency even if it is not possible to construct social indifference curves.

It is in fact possible to show that, as long as there is a redistribution of income after the introduction of free trade, the result will always be better with free trade, because each household will be able to obtain greater utility or greater welfare. This is shown by P.A. Samuelson (1939, 1962), and his argument will appear from the following.

Figure 4.5: Consumption possibility curves

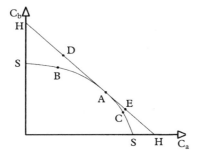

In Figure 4.5 the curve SS shows the country's transformation curve or production possibility curve. Under conditions of self-sufficiency this curve also shows the country's consumption possibilities. In this society the maximum disposable quantity of the good a and good b is shown by the curve SS. If, on the other hand, there is free trade, and if the international prices (the world market prices) P_a/P_b are equal to the slope of HH, then HH will be the consumption possibility curve under conditions of free trade. Apart from at point A, HH lies further out in the co-ordinates than SS. If B is the production and consumption point under conditions of self-sufficiency, and if D is the consumption point after the introduction of free trade, society as a whole will have more goods available to it. This ought to indicate that, on the face of it, free trade is better than self-sufficiency when income distribution is disregarded.

Each point along curve SS shows a given combination of goods a and b which are available to society. The combination of goods which corresponds to B can be shared differently between the two households 1 and 2. This is shown in Figure 4.6a, where the axes represent the utility of the two households. The dotted line BB shows the maximum utility combinations which households 1 and 2 can achieve when the quantity of goods given by point B in Figure 4.5 is shared variously between the two households. Correspondingly it is possible to take the combination of goods shown by point C in Figure 4.5 and share them differently between the two households. In this way one gets the utility combinations shown by curve CC in Figure 4.6a. It is possible to derive similar utility combinations for the two households for all the other points along curve SS in Figure 4.5. These utility combinations could be drawn in Figure 4.6a, but they are not. On the basis of all these utility combinations, which are each associated with a given combination of goods, it is possible to derive all the points which are outer limits attainable, which form the curve SS in Figure 4.6.a. This is an envelope curve which shows the maximum possible utility combinations which can be obtained by moving along the consumption possibility curve SS in Figure 4.5.

Figure 4.6: Utility possibility curves

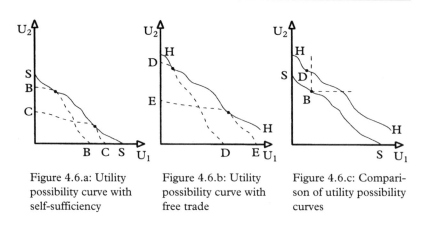

Figure 4.6.a: Utility possibility curve with self-sufficiency

Figure 4.6.b: Utility possibility curve with free trade

Figure 4.6.c: Comparison of utility possibility curves

In Figure 4.6.b the utility possibility curve which corresponds to the consumption possibility curve HH in Figure 4.5 can be derived in a similar way. If there is an assortment of goods D in Figure 4.5, it can be shared between the two households so that the curve DD in Figure 4.6.b describes the utilities. Each point along the curve lies beyond the curve BB in Figure 4.6.a, which corresponds to point B in Figure 4.5. The reason for this is that there is more of both goods to be shared. Curve EE in Figure 4.6.b shows the utility combinations which the two households can achieve when the quantity of goods E in Figure 4.5 is variously shared. By again linking the outer limits available for these curves in Figure 4.6.b, it is possible to derive the utility possibility curve under conditions of free trade.

It is interesting that the utility possibility curve for free trade is further out than the utility possibility curve for self-sufficiency, as shown in Figure 4.6.c. (However, there is a possibility that there could be a common point, corresponding to point A in Figure 4.5.)

It is assumed that, under conditions of self-sufficiency, the country is at point B in Figure 4.5, and that under conditions of free trade, the consumption point is D. The utility combination that corresponds to this in Figure 4.6.c is point B and point D respectively. It is not possible to say that point D under free trade is better than point B under self-sufficiency, since household 1 has reduced welfare under free trade.

Meanwhile, Figure 4.6.c shows that, with a redistribution of income, it is always possible to reach a point on the utility possibility curve HH which means that the welfare of both households will increase under free trade. This situation is reached when redistribution of income in favour of household 1 means that it is on that part of the HH curve which lies between the dotted lines in Figure 4.6.c.

With the assumptions which apply to the general equilibrium model, which are shown here, it can be concluded that free trade is always potentially better than self-sufficiency. The households can always achieve a better utility with free trade, through a redistribution of income, than is possible with self-sufficiency.

In this section, the conclusion that free trade is potentially better than self-sufficiency, is derived without using social indifference curves. Even if it is not possible to derive the social indifference curves, it is nevertheless possible to derive that free trade gives the possibility of achieving greater social utility.

In the following, social indifference curves will be used as they are a suitable instrument for illustrating the argument. The conclusions that can be made using social indifference curves can also be made even if they are not constructed. This requires the use of the technique shown in this section.

4.4 The assumptions for the model

In Chapters 2 and 3 there is a description of a neo-classical general equilibrium model. This model is also the basis for this chapter. For the sake of clarity, it should be emphasised that this model is based on a number of assumptions, which are not necessarily fulfilled. If they are not fulfilled, free trade will have other consequences than those illustrated above. These problems will be dealt with in some of the following chapters. Here, these assumptions are noted.

Firstly, it is assumed that there is perfect competition in the markets for production factors and final goods. The production factors can be substituted by one another in the production of the final goods. This means that the production factors of labour and capital have alternative uses. Because of differences in the education of the labour force, this assumption will not always be fulfilled. Frequently, labour can only be used for new production after re-training. The higher the general level of education, the easier it is to assume that re-training will take place. Capital that is invested in given physical equipment can only be transferred to another sector with the elapse of time. This is done by depreciation in the first sector and making new investments in the second sector. Also, new production is only possible if there is a class of entrepreneurs who are ready to take initiatives. The existence of an industrial environment is important for obtaining the necessary inputs, as for example semi-manufactured goods, for production.

It is also important that price formation in the factor markets is flexible so that the production of goods is competitive. The more limited the alternative employment prospects are for a labour force in a given industry, the more willing the labour force should be to accept lower wages if the industry in question is exposed to competition and if the labour force wants to protect its jobs. There can be a number of such market imperfections which mean that free trade may not necessarily be the best solution.

Secondly, it is assumed that all prices not only reflect private economic utility and private economic costs, but also social economic utility and social economic costs. However, there are also external economies and external diseconomies, in other words, positive and negative externalities which mean that the prices do not always reflect social advantages and disadvantages.

The prices which should be used are those that reflect the social advantages and disadvantages. The effect of economic activities on the environment means that, in practice, there are a number of negative externalities which ought to be calculated in the prices.

Thirdly, the analytical method used is comparative statics. In other words, two situations of equilibrium are compared, without taking account of the adjustment period. Adjustments will always involve costs.

Fourthly, the analysis disregards all the dynamic aspects. The assumptions are based on certain given goods, which have fixed characteristics. This means that there is no room for new products. The quantity of productions factors is given. The quality of production factors is given. The technology used is given.

On the basis of these assumptions, the neo-classical model shows how it is possible to obtain the optimal allocation of resources available at a given point in time.

The quantity and quality of production factors changes over time. The same is true of technology. These changes are not dependent on whether or not there is trade. It is also important to analyse the effects of trade in a dynamic perspective.

4.5 Imperfections in the markets for factors of production

To illustrate what can happen if the assumptions of the model are not fulfilled, it is possible to analyse the results of imperfections in the factor markets.

In the country in question two goods a and b are produced, being textiles and agricultural products, respectively. A given quantity of the production factors of capital and labour are associated with each of the two manufactures. It is assumed that the production factors are immobile since the production factors in one industry cannot be used in the other industry. This could be the case in a less developed country where factor mobility is often limited. In Figure 4.7, ABC gives the transformation curve. An import duty is imposed on good a, which is a textile product. The duty is so high that the country finds itself in a position of self-sufficiency at point B, where all production factors are exploited in both sectors. In conditions of self-sufficiency the relative prices P_a/P_b are equal to the slope of the line DD. The line segment OD on the vertical axis is equal to Y/P_b, where Y is the national income. If P_b is used as a numeraire, P_b is equal to 1. Y is therefore equal to the total of production units of b, which corresponds to OD. Of this national income OD, OA relates to the agricultural sector, and AD relates to the textile sector.

It is now assumed that there are certain rigidities in factor return in the two productions. In neither of the two sectors will the given production factors accept a real return which is less than OA in sector b and AD in sector a, calculated in units of b.

Figure 4.7: Immobile production factors together with rigidities in factor returns

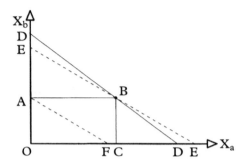

International trade is now introduced, as the tariff protection of good a is removed. This means that P_a falls, while P_b is unchanged and equal to 1. The new price conditions are represented by the slope of the line EE. Good a becomes relatively cheaper. Under 'normal conditions' it could be said that the welfare of society is increased. Instead of the consumption possibility curve ABC under conditions of self-sufficiency, there is now the consumption possibility curve EBE with international trade, when production takes place at point B.

However there is a problem, because the real factor return of the production factors used in the production of good a are no longer AD, but only AE. Therefore production of good a will be abandoned. The production factors for good b will continue to have a real return corresponding to OA.

The result will be that the production point will move from B to A, which means that the total production of good a will be lost. At point A the country has the international terms of trade given by the slope of the dotted line AF.

The line AF indicates the consumption possibility curve under conditions of free trade. The curve ABC indicates the consumption possibility curve under conditions of self-sufficiency. Since AF lies within ABC it is obvious that free trade will be worse in all situations. The conclusion is, therefore, that in this case tariff protection is appropriate until the circumstances which cause a tariff protection to be reasonable are changed. The lack of substitutability of factors, combined with minimum requirements for returns are the reasons why, in this situation, free trade is worse than the situation without trade.

4.6 Supply and demand curves when there is a general equilibrium

In Figure 4.1 the benefits of trade are analysed assuming that the international terms of trade are externally determined. However, the international terms of trade can change. It is therefore natural to asks two questions. The first question concerns the significance which changes to the international terms of trade can have for an individual country. The second question concerns what determines the international terms of trade and what conditions influence changes to the terms of trade.

The first question, on the significance of changes to the terms of trade, can be analysed by using Figure 4.8, in which there is a transformation curve TT and a set of social indifference curves.

Figure 4.8: Equilibrium with various different terms of trade

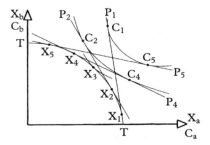

In the figure various different terms of trade P_a/P_b are shown by the slope of the tangents P_1 - P_5. For the sake of simplicity, P_3 is not drawn. In moving from P_1 to P_5, P_a/P_b falls. The production points X_1 - X_5 and the consumption points C_1 - C_5 correspond to the tangents. On the basis of the related production and consumption points it is possible to derive the exports and imports. On the basis of Figure 4.8 it is possible to calculate the relationship between supply, demand, exports, imports and the relative prices of the two goods.

In Figure 4.9 the relative prices P_a/P_b are drawn on the y axis. To the right on the x axis the supply and demand respectively are shown for good a by SS_a and DD_a. To the left on the x axis the supply and demand of good b are shown.

The curves in Figure 4.9 can be derived from Figure 4.8. First the supply curves SS_a and SS_b in Figure 4.9 will be analysed. With a high P_a/P_b only good a is produced, and none of good b. With a falling P_a/P_b there is less and less production of good a and more and more of good b. In the end, only good b is produced. The development of production shown here, with falling P_a/P_b corresponds to moving along the transformation curve in Figure 4.8. Starting on the X_a axis and moving gradually, with a falling P_a/P_b, towards the X_b axis. The quantities produced of good a and good b which correspond to the differing price relations P_a/P_b are drawn as the curves SS_a and SS_b in Figure 4.9.

Figure 4.9: Supply and demand when there is a general equilibrium

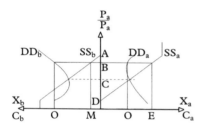

With falling P_a/P_b in Figure 4.8 the consumption points will be $C_1 - C_5$. The demand for good a will first fall from C_1 to C_2. Next, the demand will rise from C_2 to C_5. The demand for good a which follows from these consumption points is drawn as DD_a in Figure 4.9. The demand for good b will fall in moving from C_1 to C_4. A further increase in the price for good b in relation to good a will give an increase in demand from C_4 to C_5. The demand for good b which follows from these consumption points in Figure 4.8 is drawn as DD_b in Figure 4.9.

In moving from right to left on the transformation curve in Figure 4.8, there is movement from A to D in Figure 4.9. Point C in Figure 4.9 corresponds to point X_3 in Figure 4.8, in other words, a situation of self-sufficiency. With relative prices for final goods P_a/P_b greater than C, the country exports good a and imports good b. The traded quantity is the vertical distance between the DD and SS curves at the relevant relative prices. With relative prices lower than point C, good b is exported and good a is imported.

It is important to note that the 'supply' and 'demand' curves which are drawn in Figure 4.9 are quite different from the traditional supply and demand curves which are drawn in connection with a partial analysis, cf. Chapter 1, Section 1.2. The curves in Figure 4.9 are curves which show the supply and demand under conditions of general equilibrium.

4.7 Derivation of the offer curve

By using Figure 4.9 it is possible to derive how much a country with different values for the relative prices P_a/P_b is willing to export of one good in return for an imported quantity of the other good.

In Figure 4.10 there is a co-ordinate system in which trade in good a is situated on the x axis for country A. To the right of the starting point country A exports good a, and to the left of the starting point the country imports good a. The upper part of the y axis indicates country A's imports of good b and the lower part of it shows the country's exports of this good.

At point B in Figure 4.9 there are given terms of trade of P_a/P_b shown on the vertical axis, and it is possible to see the quantity of good a which the country is willing to export in order to obtain a corresponding quantity of the imported good b. These quantities depend on the relative prices of final goods, in other words the terms of trade. These quantities are drawn in Figure 4.10. For exports the quantity is OE and for imports it is OM. The slope of OR is equal to OM/OE.

The model is based on there being neither surplus nor deficit on the balance of trade. Therefore:

$$OE \cdot P_a = OM \cdot P_b$$

which gives:

$$OM/OE = P_a/P_b$$

This means that the slope of the line OR also indicates the relative prices of final goods.

If a corresponding exercise is undertaken for other relative prices of final goods, there will be a curve OR, which shows how much of the export good the country is prepared to 'offer' for a given quantity of the import good. This is why it is called an 'offer curve'. Point O on the offer curve is the position of self-sufficiency. In the first quadrant country A exports good a and imports good b. In the third quadrant country A exports good b and imports good a.

Figure 4.10: Offer curve for country A

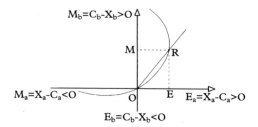

The offer curve is derived on the basis of a general equilibrium model. Therefore, the export and import quantities which the country is willing to trade at various relative prices of final goods are arrived at after there has been a total adjustment of the country's economy. For each set of quantities of exports and imports there is an associated combination of the two goods in domestic demand and domestic production. With different quantities of exports and imports, resulting from the changed relative prices, there will also be changes to the combination of goods in domestic demand and production.

Figure 4.11: Offer curve as an import demand curve

Figure 4.12: The marginal rate of substitution in trade

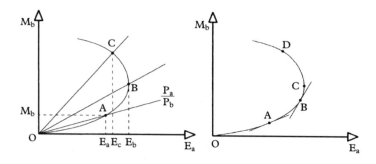

Overall on the offer curve the optimality conditions for the general equilibrium model are met. The marginal rate of substitution in the use of production factors MRS^F is the same in the production of the two goods. The marginal rate of transformation MRT is equal to the relative final good prices. The marginal rate of substitution in consumption MRS^C is the same for the households and equal to the relative final good prices.

The offer curve can be interpreted as an import demand curve. The offer curve shows the demand for an import good at a 'price' which is given in the quantity of the export good which the country is willing to supply in order to obtain the given import quantity. The offer curve from the first quadrant in Figure 4.10 is drawn in Figure 4.11. At point A the terms of trade are P_a/P_b, and at these terms of trade country A is willing to pay Ea of the export good in order to import the quantity M_b of good b. It is now assumed that P_a is constant and the price of the import good b falls. With the lower import price corresponding to the slope OB, country A is willing to export the quantity E_b to obtain a greater import quantity.

At point A the import costs are equal to the export earnings, which are equal to P_aE_a. When the export price P_a is constant, at point B the import costs will be P_aE_b, which are greater than the import costs at point A because E_b is greater than E_a. For the part of the offer curve OAB, which is rising from the left to the right, a fall in price of the import good b will lead to an increase in import costs, since P_aE is increasing while P_a is constant. It can therefore be said that OAB is that part of the 'import demand curve' where elasticity is greater than 1. The percentage increase in imports is greater than the percentage fall in the price of the imported good, which means that the import costs increase. At point B the import demand elasticity is equal to 1. On that part of the offer curve, BC, which turns from the right towards the left, the elasticity of import demand is less than 1. With a fall of the price of the import good from point B to C the import costs will fall from E_b to E_c. Here, the percentage increase in import demand is less than the percentage fall in the import price.

In Figure 4.12 the tangents to the offer curve are drawn at points A and B. The slope of the tangents is dM_b/dX_a, which is the country's marginal rate of substitution in trade with the outside world. In moving along the offer curve from O to A and onwards to C, there will be a rising dM_b/dE_a. This means that if one has only a little M_b, there is a willingness to pay more in the form of dE_a in order to obtain an extra unit of the import good b. At point C, dE_a is zero. If there is a movement from C to D, there is already so large an imported quantity of good b that there is only a willingness to increase imports if the cost in the form the quantity of exported goods falls.

4.8 The terms of trade are determined by the offer curves for the two countries

A general equilibrium for country A is drawn in Figure 4.8 on the basis of a transformation curve and a set of social indifference curves. It is not possible to say anything about the pattern of trade before the international terms of trade are known. Various different terms of trade are drawn in Figure 4.8, and using Figure 4.8 the supply and demand curves for good a and good b are derived. These curves are drawn in Figure 4.9. Figure 4.9 shows how much a country is willing to export at different terms of trade, and how much imports can be demanded for the export quantity.

By using Figure 4.9 it is possible to derive the offer curve for country A in Figure 4.10. In the first quadrant of the figure it can be seen that, with terms of trade corresponding to the slope of OR, country A wishes to offer OE for export in order to obtain OM of the imported good. All the other points along the offer curve show how much the country is willing to export in order to get the import quantity at different terms of trade, as shown on the vertical axis.

Figure 4.13: Offer curves for two countries

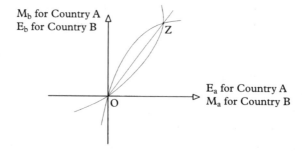

On the basis of similar figures to those in Figures 4.8 and 4.9 it is possible to derive a corresponding offer curve for country B, in the same way as for country A. This offer curve is drawn in Figure 4.13. Country B's offer curve shows how much it is willing to export of good b in order to import a given quantity of good a. Where the two offer curves intersect, there is equilibrium for both countries. Country A's export and import requirements exactly match country B's import and export requirements. The slope of the line OZ represents the international terms of trade which will be established on the international market.

In Figure 4.13, offer curves are drawn for country A and country B, which are two countries of equal economic size. For example, the figure illustrates the trade between the USA and the EU, disregarding the existence of other countries.

If country A is Denmark and country B is the rest of the world, the offer curve which confronts Denmark, i.e. country B's offer curve, will be a straight line. In Figure 4.14 country B has an offer curve of traditional appearance. Since country A is a small country, that part of country B's offer curve which is relevant for country A will be virtually a straight line.

Figure 4.14: Offer curves where country A is a small country and country B is big

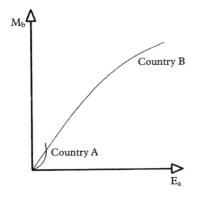

The analysis in Figures 4.13 and 4.14 is a static analysis, which shows what international terms of trade will apply when there is a general equilibrium in both countries. When these conditions are changed in one country, then the offer curve for the country in question will also change its appearance. If there is growth in country A which, with the given relative prices, increases the country's production of the export good a more than the country's demand for it, the offer curve will move from curve I to curve II in Figure 4.15. If this greater increase in production than in demand at the given relative prices takes place in the import competing sector, the import curve will move from I to III. This is discussed further in Chapter 12.

The offer curve for a country will also be influenced by a change in trade policy, see Figure 4.16. In the initial situation, where there is free trade, there is an offer curve I. If the terms of trade are $P_a/P_b = \frac{1}{2}$, A is the point at which the country will export E_A to obtain M_A from abroad. Overall on the offer curve there is neither surplus nor deficit on the balance of trade. i.e. $P_a E_a = P_b M_b$. At point A, $2M_A = 1E_A$.

Now, country A imposes a 25 per cent import duty on the imported good b. If the domestic price, including the duty, is still 2, as is the case at A, the import price without duty must be 1.6. If country A still wants to export the quantity E_A at the price $P_a = 1$, it will now have the possibility of importing M_B for which $E_A = 1.6 M_B$. As a result of the fact that the import price, exclusive of import duty, falls by 20 per cent (from 2 to 1.6), the country can import the quantity M_B, which is equal to $5/4 M_A$, and there will still be equilibrium in the balance of payments.

Figure 4.15: The offer curve changes its shape when there is growth

Figure 4.16: The offer curve depends on trade policy

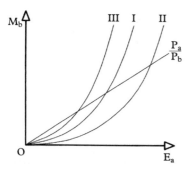

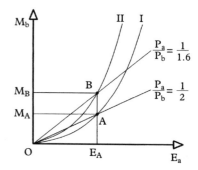

The new import quantity M_B, which corresponds to export costs of E_A, will now be equal to 5/4 M_A. Point B, which is the point on the offer curve after the introduction of a 25 per cent import duty, is therefore 25 per cent above point A, and the price line OB has a slope of 1/1.6.

If the same calculations are made for other points along offer curve I, there will be new points, which are all 25 per cent above the points on offer curve I. These points constitute offer curve II, which is the offer curve after the introduction of an import duty of 25 per cent.

4.9 Summary

By using a transformation curve and social indifference curves it is possible to show the benefit of free trade compared with a situation of self-sufficiency. The international terms of trade are externally (exogenously) determined. The problem with such an analysis is that, simultaneously with the introduction of free trade, the real income of households will change. This is related to the fact that the relative prices of final goods will change and factor prices will change. If the criteria for Pareto-optimality are applied, it cannot be said that welfare is increased if there is at least one household which finds itself on a lower indifference curve after the introduction of free trade.

Instead of using social indifference curves it is possible to use utility possibility curves which show the optimal obtainable utility for two households under conditions either of free trade or self-sufficiency. Such an analysis means that, as long as the assumptions of the general equilibrium model apply, then free trade will always potentially give higher welfare for both households, compared with situations where there is self-sufficiency. It is always possible to combine free trade with a redistribution of income between the households to ensure that welfare is increased for both households.

If the assumptions of the general equilibrium model do not apply, if for example there are imperfections in the market for production factors, then free trade can mean that welfare is decreased.

Taking a general equilibrium model to two countries which are assumed to represent the world, it is possible to determine the international terms of trade. It is possible to derive the supply and demand curves for the individual goods in the two countries. By using these curves it is possible to derive offer curves for the two countries. An offer curve shows a country's import demand measured in relation to the 'price' which is the quantity of another good which the country is willing to export as payment for the import. On the offer curve, the optimality conditions for a general equilibrium model are met. Offer curves for the two countries determine the international terms of trade, which means that there is equilibrium in both countries.

Literature

Chipman, J.S., 'A Survey of the Theory of International Trade', *Econometrica 33*, 1965.

Johnson, H.G. 'International Trade, Income Distribution and the Offer Curve', *Manchester School of Economics and Social Studies*, 27, 1959.

Meade, J.E., *A Geometry of International Trade*, London, 1952.

Samuelson, P.A., 'The Gains from International Trade', *Canadian Journal of Economics and Political Science*, 5, 1939.

Samuelson, P.A., 'The Gains from International Trade Once Again', *Economic Journal*, 1962.

Part II
Theories of international trade

5. The classical theory

The classical school of economics can be related to the period from 1776 to 1870. The beginning of modern economic science is associated with the publication of 'The Wealth of Nations' by Adam Smith in 1776. This was the start of a period up to around 1870 in which the classical economic theory was developed. The great names of this period were Adam Smith, David Ricardo, Thomas Malthius, John Stuart Mill and Karl Marx.

The classical theorists were especially interested in economic growth. As part of this interest they questioned the extent to which growth was dependent on international trade, and what influence trade has on growth.

5.1 The theory of absolute advantage

The theory of the absolute advantage was formulated by Adam Smith. It can be considered as the forerunner to Ricardo's theory of comparative advantage, which is a theory which contains a much more powerful proposition than the theory of absolute advantage. Because of this, the theory of absolute advantage will only be described here briefly.

Just as Ricardo did, Adam Smith based his theory on the assumption that there was only one kind of production factor, labour, and that the production function was linear, i.e.:

$$X_i = k_i L_i$$

where X_i, k_i and L_i are production, labour productivity and the labour involved in production, respectively.

If there is production of two goods, a and b, in two countries, A and B, there will be labour productivity of k_a^A, k_b^A, k_a^B and k_b^B. When the production functions for the two goods are different, and when the production function for each good is different in the two countries, then the four labour productivities will be different. If country A has an absolute production advantage in the production of good b then

$k_a^A > k_a^B$. If country B has an absolute production advantage in the production of good b then $k_b^A < k_b^B$.

Before there is trade, each country will produce both goods. After the introduction of trade, each of the two countries will produce that good in which the country has an absolute production advantage, which in the case of country A will be good a and in the case of country B will be good b. Country A will export good a and import good b.

According to Adam Smith there is only a basis for trade when each of the countries has an absolute advantage in the production of a particular good. There will be a more detailed look at the influence of productivity on trade in connection with Ricardo's theory of comparative advantage in Section 5.3.

5.2 Trade and growth

Specialisation in a dynamic context

The analysis above is a comparative static analysis in which a situation of self-sufficiency is compared with a situation of free trade. However, a central part of Adam Smith's theory is that the replacement of a domestic market with an international market will create the basis for the division of labour which will increase the productivity for both products through specialisation between countries.

The central point in Adam Smith's theory is that labour is the source of welfare. It is through the division of labour that increased productivity is obtained, which creates economic growth and thereby a higher standard of living. These relations should be seen as a process that creates economic development. There is thus a dynamic interrelationship. This idea can be presented in a simple flow chart.

Capital ↘   ↗ Capital
          Division of labour → Productivity → Growth
Market ↗   ↘ Market

An economic surplus (economic rent), which makes the accumulation of capital possible, is necessary for achieving a division of labour. For example there can be a food surplus which can feed an industrial population. It is also necessary for there to be a large market where the specialised production can be sold.

An increased capital accumulation and a larger market create the basis for a division of labour. This division of labour leads to increased productivity which in turn gives economic growth. This increases the possibility for greater capital accumulation, and the market becomes even greater. All trade restrictions internally in the country, as for example under mercantilism, hinder growth. The same applies to trade restrictions between countries.

The developments in agriculture in the nineteenth century and up to the present time illustrate this idea very well. In an agrarian society, such as was quite common in the nineteenth century, the individual farming units were largely self-sufficient. They produced not only food, but also clothing, footwear, candles, furniture and tools. Since then there has been a horizontal specialisation, in other words the product range of the individual producer has been reduced. Everything except the production of food has been delegated to craft workers and industry, where individual businesses have specialised in the production of specific goods.

At the same time there has been a vertical specialisation. For example, the production of bread requires the cultivation of wheat, which must then be milled, before it is baked into bread. The production of textiles requires wool from a flock of sheep. The wool has to be carded, spun and woven, before the textile can be used for making clothes. In an agrarian society all these processes took place on a single farm unit. Today the farmer concentrates on growing cereals or the production of wool. The further processing to the end product takes place in various industrial enterprises.

Such processes requires capital. If, in agriculture, there is no 'capital' in the form of a surplus production of cereals which can be used to feed the urban population which will develop the industrial sector, then specialisation will not be possible. The concentration of production which takes place is only possible as long as there is a large enough market to absorb the production. If the size of the market is reduced through trade restrictions, then the specialised production of goods will be restricted. The same applies to the specialisation of labour and capital.

In the theory of the absolute advantage there is a given production technology which is different in the different countries. The exploitation of these differences gives a one-time gain. In the dynamic specialisation theory, the specialisation will contribute to achieving improved production methods through better training of the work force and through new technology.

Vent for surplus

In the above it is shown that trade gives rise to improved productivity. Trade means that it is possible to exploit absolute productivity advantages and that there will be technological progress. Adam Smith's trade theory says that trade is dependant on absolute productivity advantages, and that trade is associated with increased productivity obtained through specialisation.

Adam Smith also had another trade theory. It is the 'vent for surplus' theory, concerning the outlet for surplus production. With international trade a country will be able to exploit its resources.

A country is able to produce agricultural and industrial products. The given quantity of labour determines the shape of the production possibility curve QR in Figure 5.1.

Without trade the country will produce at point A. Even if there is a capacity for producing further agricultural products corresponding to AB, this will not happen because an increased supply of agricultural products will not be matched by demand.

When international trade is introduced, production will move to B. The country will export agricultural products corresponding to AB, enabling it to obtain industrial products corresponding to AC. International trade gives an outlet for production which would not otherwise take place.

Figure 5.1: Vent for surplus model

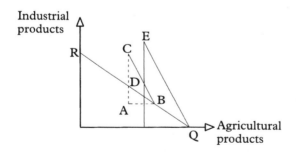

In this theory there is a central question which must be answered. If, under conditions of self-sufficiency, one is at A, it is understandable that the surplus labour will not be used to produce further agricultural products, because there is no demand for agricultural products beyond what corresponds to A. But, how can it be explained that there is not an increase in the production of industrial products, i.e. why is there not a move from A to D?

The explanation for this can be that people prefer more free time rather than an extra quantity of industrial products. By moving some of the labour to industry working time will be longer. The real income growth which the increased labour input will generate will be very small. The transformation between industrial and agricultural products, i.e. the slope of the line QR, gives the relative prices for the two product categories. Industrial products are thus much more expensive in relation to agricultural products. The disadvantage of the greater labour input is judged to be greater than the advantage of the increase in real income, which is small.

When international trade is introduced industrial goods become relatively much cheaper. The supply of labour depends on the quantity of goods which can be obtained through extra effort. This means that there is now a willingness to increase the labour supply, so the production point moves from A to B.

Point B is the new point of equilibrium. When, after the introduction of international trade, the industrial goods are relatively cheaper, the domestic manufactures cannot compete. Production will therefore move from B to Q where there is a total specialisation. The consumption point will be E.

Another explanation why in the initial situation production is at A and not at D, can be the existence of hidden unemployment. Part of the work force has either a very small marginal productivity or even zero marginal productivity in agricultural production. Since the marginal productivity of labour in industry is higher, this should mean that the 'hidden' work force would move to industry. However, it does not happen as long as labour in agriculture is not rewarded according to the value of the marginal product, but according to the value of the average product. In a household in the country the income is shared between the members of the household even though an individual person may have a very small marginal product or even a marginal product of zero.

The vent for surplus model has been used to explain the economic development in the USA and Canada in the nineteenth century. As soon as the export of agricultural products became possible, because the transport costs fell following the building of the railways, the land

began to be used as it had not been used before. However, it was not
the introduction of international trade alone that prompted the farming
of virgin land in these countries. The incorporation of virgin territories
was combined with the inflow of labour and capital from Europe.

5.3 The theory of comparative advantage

Adam Smith's theory of absolute advantage is intuitively easy to understand. By contrast, Ricardo's theory of comparative advantage sets
up less demanding conditions before international trade becomes
advantageous.

An illustration of Ricardo's theory and its assumptions can start
with the following identity:

$$P_i = \frac{L_i}{X_i} \cdot \frac{W_i}{L_i} \cdot \frac{X_i P_i}{W_i} \tag{5.1}$$

where P_i is the price per unit of good i, L_i is the quantity of labour
used in the production of i, X_i is the quantity of final goods produced,
and W_i is the wage costs. If each of the three terms is considered, it
will be seen that L_i/X_i is the technical production co-efficient or the
reciprocal of the labour productivity. W_i/L_i is the hourly wage. Where
$X_i P_i$ is an expression for the total production value or the total costs,
$X_i P_i/W_i$, expresses the division of the production result between labour
and the other production factors.

The equation (5.1), as dealt with above, is an identity. The various
terms are defined in such a way that equation (5.1) always applies. A
theory first arises when one makes some assumptions about the conditions that exist. Ricardo's theory is based on several assumptions.
Firstly, it is assumed that there is only one production factor involved
in the production, and that is labour. This means that the last link in
the equation (5.1) is equal to 1, since the whole of the production
value is allocated to labour as it is the only production factor. Secondly, it is assumed that the wage rate is the same for all manufactures, which means that W/L is constant for all goods. Thirdly it is
assumed that the production function is linear, which means that:

$$X_i = k_i L_i$$

where k_i is the labour productivity for good i, which is constant.

With these assumptions, and by using (5.1), it is possible to see that there are the following connections:

$$\frac{P_a}{P_b} = \frac{k_b}{k_a} \qquad (5.2)$$

This means that under Ricardo's theory, the domestic price relations are determined by the relations between labour productivity.

On the basis of the production functions in the two countries A and B for the two goods, it is possible to derive transformation curves for the two countries. In country A and country B there are the following functions for goods a and b, where the upper character denotes the country and the lower character denotes the good:

$$X_a^A = k_a^A L_a^A \qquad X_a^B = k_a^B L_a^B$$
$$X_b^A = k_b^A L_b^A \qquad X_b^B = k_b^B L_b^B \qquad (5.3)$$

In each of the two countries there is a given quantity of labour L, which is assumed to be the same in both countries.

There is therefore:

$$L = L_a^A + L_b^A = L_a^B + L_b^B \qquad (5.4)$$

If (5.3) is inserted in (5.4) there are the following connections for the two countries:

$$L = \frac{X_a^A}{k_a^A} + \frac{X_b^A}{k_b^A} \quad \text{and} \quad L = \frac{X_a^B}{k_a^B} + \frac{X_b^B}{k_b^B}$$

which can be reformulated as:

$$X_b^A = -\frac{k_b^A}{k_a^A} X_a^A + k_b^A L \quad \text{and} \quad X_b^B = -\frac{k_b^B}{k_a^B} X_a^B + k_b^B L \qquad (5.5)$$

If country A has an absolute advantage in the production of good a, then $k_a^A > k_a^B$, and if country B has an absolute advantage in the production of good b, then $k_b^A < k_b^B$. In this case, the result of drawing the expression of (5.5) as a diagram gives the situation which is shown in Figure 5.2 a.

If, however, there are relative advantages, then country A, for example, will be better able to produce both good a and b than country B. This means that $k_a^A > k_a^B$ and $k_b^A > k_b^B$, but the relative advantages in the two manufactures in country A are different. For example, the relative advantage in the production of good b can be greater than for good a in country A compared with country B. The following therefore applies:

$$\frac{k_b^A}{k_a^A} > \frac{k_b^B}{k_a^B} \tag{5.6}$$

Figure 5.2: Transformation curves with absolute and relative advantages

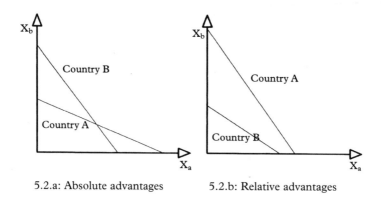

5.2.a: Absolute advantages   5.2.b: Relative advantages

In this case one will get transformation curves as shown in Figure 5.2.b. Overall, country A's transformation curve is further out than country B's transformation curve. However, the slopes of the two curves differ, since the slope which is $-k_b/k_a$ is numerically greater for country A than for country B. This means that country A has a relative advantage in the production of good b and country B has a relative advantage in the production of good a. If (5.2) is inserted in (5.6) it results in:

$$\frac{P_a^A}{P_b^A} > \frac{P_a^B}{P_b^B} \tag{5.7}$$

which means that, under conditions of self-sufficiency, the price of good b, which country A is relatively better in producing, will be relatively low in country A. Similarly, the price of good a, which country B is relatively better at producing, will be relatively low in country B. It is these relative price differences in equation (5.7) being determined by the relative differences in labour productivity, which determine the pattern of trade. Country A exports good b, which is relatively cheap in country A, and country B exports good a, which is relatively cheap in that country.

Even if, in absolute terms, country A is better at producing both goods, there is a basis for trade when the relative productivities in the countries are different. This is the essence of Ricardo's theory of comparative advantage.

What happens when international trade is introduced? A set of world market prices, P_a/P_b, is established which lies between the relative prices existing in the two countries prior to international trade. The result is:

$$\frac{P_a^A}{P_b^A} > \frac{P_a}{P_b} > \frac{P_a^B}{P_b^B}$$

In country A good b will be relatively more expensive, and in country B good a will be relatively more expensive.

The transformation curves from Figure 5.2.b are drawn in Figure 5.3. In the initial situation, without trade, the two countries produce and consume at point S_a and S_b respectively. After the introduction of international trade the two countries specialise in the manufactures in which they have relative production advantages, which is good b in the case of country A and good a in the case of country B. There is trade at international prices which are equal to the numerical slopes of the dotted lines. The consumption points becomes C_A and C_B.

Welfare is increased because each of the two countries has more units of the two goods available after the introduction of trade than before.

The advantage of trade can also be illustrated in another way, as shown in Figure 5.4, where both countries' production possibilities are drawn together as a kind of global transformation curve. The transformation curves of the two countries, as shown in Figure 5.3, are put together. The maximum possible production of good a is

K + L. The curve from K + L to T is country A's transformation curve. The curve from T to M + N is country B's transformation curve. The maximum possible production of good b is M + N.

After the introduction of trade, T is the production point when the relative prices on the world market are between the relative prices in the two countries before trade. The domestic prices before trade are equal to the slopes of the two national transformation curves.

Figure 5.3: The effects of trade

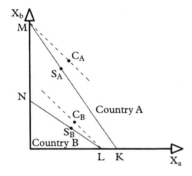

Figure 5.4: Global transformation curve

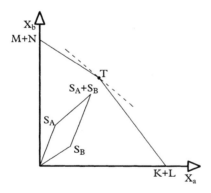

If the consumption possibilities before trade are looked at, it will be seen that these are determined by points S_A and S_B. By adding them together there is the consumption possibility before trade, which is

$S_A + S_B$. This point lies within the global transformation curve, where after the introduction of trade there will be an available quantity of goods corresponding to T.

The concept of the comparative advantage has remained valid since Ricardo first put forward his theory. Ricardo associated comparative advantages with labour productivity. Since then the comparative advantage has been linked to other elements, such as a country's relative factor endowment, as will be seen in the next chapter on factor proportion theory.

It is possible to give many examples from economic history of comparative advantages. The economic conditions of England and Denmark around 1850 show that the effectiveness of production in both the industrial and the agricultural sectors was greater in England. England had an absolute production advantage in both sectors. The repeal of the Corn Laws in England in 1846, which did away with import duties on cereals, can be seen as an acknowledgement that England's comparative advantage lay in industrial production. What happened was that, especially from the 1880s onwards, Danish agricultural production took over a large part of the English market for agricultural products which had previously been supplied by English agriculture. At that point Denmark had a comparative advantage in the production of agricultural products.

When the rate of exchange is in equilibrium, there is the basis for trade between the two countries. In England the industrial sector was developed while, relatively speaking, agriculture stagnated. In Denmark agriculture in particular was developed. The reason for the stagnation of agricultural production in England was not that it was not competitive with Danish agriculture. The reason was that English agriculture could not compete with English industry for the production factors present in the English economy.

5.4 A generalisation of the Ricardian theory

n goods in two countries

Above there has been an analysis of the Ricardian theory of comparative advantage in cases where there are two goods in two countries. It is now assumed that there are still two countries A and B. The number of goods is expanded from two to n. Each of the n goods is identical in the two countries. The other assumptions in Section 5.3 also apply to this analysis.

When there is a multiplicity of goods it is possible to rank the goods so that the good which has the greatest labour productivity in country A compared to country B is ranked first. It is good a. The good which has the next greatest labour productivity in country A compared to country B is ranked second. The last ranked good n will be the one for which the labour productivity in country B compared with country A is the greatest.

$$\frac{k_a^A}{k_a^B} > \frac{k_b^A}{k_b^B} \ ---- \ \frac{k_i^A}{k_i^B} > \ ---- \ \frac{k_n^A}{k_n^B} \tag{5.8}$$

If Ricardo's assumptions about production conditions apply, it will be seen that country A has the greatest comparative advantage in the production of good a, and after that good b. However, country B has the greatest comparative advantage in the production of n, and thereafter in the production of good m, etc.

Since only one production factor is used by Ricardo, then, cf. equation (5.1) in Section 5.3, the result will be that:

$$P_i^A = \frac{1}{k_i^A} \cdot w_i^A \tag{5.9}$$

If the wage rate is the same for all products in each of countries A and B, respectively w_i^A and w_i^B, it can be derived from the expression (5.9) that the ranking of the relative prices is the reverse of the ranking of the relative labour productivity as shown in (5.8).

The result is therefore:

$$\frac{P_a^A}{P_a^B} < \frac{P_b^A}{P_b^B} \ ------ < \ ----- \ \frac{P_i^A}{P_i^B} < \ ------- < \ \frac{P_n^A}{P_n^B}$$

In contrast to the case with two goods, it is no longer possible to distinguish between export products and import products, without taking account of demand conditions. Country A will export goods with the first letters in the alphabet; country B will export goods with the last letters in the alphabet. It is not possible to say where country A's export goods stop and country A's import goods begin purely on the basis of the supply conditions; it is also necessary to take account of the demand conditions.

R is the rate of exchange, and is defined as the quantity of A's currency being required for the purchase of B's currency. It is assumed that for good i, $P_i^A/R = P_i^B$. In this case A will export goods with the letters a, b, ..., h and import goods with the letters j, k, ..., n. Good i will not be traded.

If the rate of exchange R is in equilibrium, there is equality in the balance of payments, in other words, the value of country A's exports is equal to the value of its imports. If there is equality in the balance of payments the following applies:

$$P_a \cdot E_a^A + P_b \cdot E_b^B - - \; + \; P_h \cdot E_h^A = P_j \cdot E_j^B + P_h \cdot E_h^B - - - - - - - P_n \cdot E_n^B$$

The prices P_a, P_b $- - - P_n$ are the world market prices calculated in country B's currency. The values E_a^A $- - - E_h^A$ are the quantities which country A exports, in other words the difference between what country A produces and consumes itself. For example, for good a, $E_a^A = X_a^A - C_a^A$. The values E_j^B $- - - E_n^B$ are the quantities which country A imports. When there is total production specialisation for commodity j then $E_j^B = C_j^A$. In other words country A's imports are equal to its total consumption of the good.

Thus, where there is a multiplicity of goods, it will still be the relative labour productivities which will have a decisive influence on which goods country A exports and which goods it imports.

The dividing line between imported goods and exported goods is no longer exclusively determined by production conditions. The dividing line can be determined by the rate of exchange, the world market prices and the volumes of exports and imports. Each of these factors in turn is determined by the conditions of supply and demand.

In this model there is an interesting connection between productivity, wage levels and the rate of exchange. This can be illustrated by good i, which is assumed to be the good which is not traded because the price in the two countries, calculated in the same currency, is the same, in other words $1/R \cdot P_i^A = P_i^B$. Into this term the equation (5.9), $P_i = w_i/k_i$, is inserted and the following result is obtained, when it is assumed that the wage rate is the same in all productions in each country:

$$\frac{w^A}{k_i^A} \cdot \frac{1}{R} = \frac{w^B}{k_i^B}$$

which can also be written:

$$R = \frac{k_i^B}{k_i^A} \cdot \frac{w^A}{w^B}$$

With the given productivity conditions in the two countries, with k being constant, a more rapid growth of the wage level in country A than in country B will mean that country A's currency must be devalued, so that R must increase in order to avoid a deficit on the balance of payments. If R is not devalued, fewer products will be exported by A and more products will be imported from B.

If there is a desire for a constant exchange rate, the wages in the two countries must develop in parallel, unless the technical progress differs between the two countries. Improved technology will be evidenced by an increase in k. If there is stronger technological development in country A than in country B, there is greater scope for wage increases in country A than in country B, while leaving the exchange rate unchanged.

Two goods in N countries

The Ricardian model of two goods in two countries is now adapted so that instead of two countries there are N countries. Country A is the country where k_a/k_b is greatest. Country B is the country where the relative productivity differences are next greatest. Country N is the country where k_a/k_b is least.

Therefore:

$$\left(\frac{k_a}{k_b}\right)^A > \left(\frac{k_a}{k_b}\right)^B \; ------------ > \left(\frac{k_a}{k_b}\right)^N$$

With the usual assumptions that there is only one production factor, and that the return on it is the same in the individual countries for the production of both goods, this means that:

$$\left(\frac{P_a}{P_b}\right)^A < \left(\frac{P_a}{P_b}\right)^B \; ---- < \left(\frac{P_a}{P_b}\right)^I < \left(\frac{P_a}{P_b}\right)^J < --- < \left(\frac{P_a}{P_b}\right)^N$$

The country with the first letter in the alphabet will export good a. The country with the last letter in the alphabet will export good b.

Where the dividing line between the countries will be depends on the international terms of trade, which in turn are determined by the total demand and production of the two goods.

It is assumed that the international terms of trade P_a/P_b fulfil the following conditions:

$$\left(\frac{P_a}{P_b}\right)^I < \frac{P_a}{P_b} < \left(\frac{P_a}{P_b}\right)^J$$

which means that in this case countries A, B and down to I will export good a, and that countries J to N will export good b.

This situation can be illustrated diagrammatically by drawing the global transformation curve, as shown in Figure 5.5. There will be a curve consisting of a number of straight lines. The dotted line gives the international terms of trade. Point T gives the total world production of the goods a and b. In Figure 5.5 country I will export good a and country J will export good b.

Figure 5.5: The global transformation curve with N countries

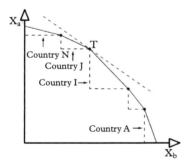

If the global demand for good b increases, the price for good b will increase. The dotted line will be steeper and country I can now be the country that exports good b. It is clear that the countries which lie closest to the two axes, X_a and X_b, will be the countries which get the greatest gains from international trade, as long as the demand conditions are the same in the countries.

5.5 A Ricardian theory
with two production factors

It is now assumed that the production of the two final goods uses two production factors L and K. There is no possibility of substitution between the two factors. This is a case of a production function with fixed technical production coefficients, which means that the production of one unit of the final good requires a fixed quantity of labour and capital.

For example, the following relations apply:

good a
$$K_a = m_a X_a$$
$$L_a = n_a X_a$$

good b
$$K_b = m_b X_b$$
$$L_b = n_b X_b$$

Figure 5.6 shows the production functions in which, for example points A_1, A_2 and A_3 are linked to an increasing production of good a. A doubling of the factor inputs K and L in the fixed ratio m_a/n_a, which gives the slope of the line OA_3 gives a doubling of production.

Figure 5.6: Production function with fixed technical coefficients

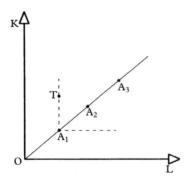

If there is a factor endowment corresponding to T, then the capital quantity $T - A_1$ cannot be used in the production. There is a lack of labour. It is the scarce factor, in this case the labour, which sets the limit to production.

A production function as in Figure 5.6 and a corresponding production function for good b can be put in a box diagram, in which the length of the sides of the box give the quantity of K and L in the society. This is done in Figure 5.7.

Figure 5.7: The transformation curve with fixed technical coefficients

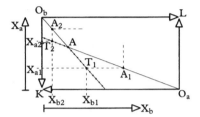

For good a the co-ordinate system KO_aL apply, and the straight line O_aA, shows the factor combination used in the production of good a. For good b the co-ordinate system KO_bL applies, and the straight line O_bA indicates the factor combination used in the production of good b.

At point A_1, the quantity which can be produced is X_{a1}, which is shown on the X_a axis. If there is production at point A, which is assumed to be twice as far from O_a as A_1, it is possible to produce twice as much of good a, which is shown on the X_a axis.

If again production at point A_1 is considered, it will be seen that there will be production of good b at point T_1. The quantity X_{b1} which corresponds to point T_1 is shown on the X_b axis. If there is X_{a1} production of good a, which means that good a is at point A_1, it will be possible to produce X_{b1} of good b. Therefore T_1 is a point on the transformation curve. It is possible to carry out a corresponding exercise for other points, for example point A_2. In this way it is possible to derive the dotted line as the transformation curve. This is the same technique as is used for deriving the transformation curve in Chapter 2.

In cases where there are fixed technical coefficients, there will be a kinked transformation curve. Only at point A will all production factors be used. At point T_1 it is not possible to use the quantity of capital A_1T_1. At point T_2 on the transformation curve it is not possible to use A_2T_2 of the labour.

5.6 *Summary*

When the classical theory of international trade is referred to, this means Ricardo's theory of comparative advantage. Adam Smith's theory of absolute advantage is mostly of interest as the forerunner to Ricardo's theory, which sets up much less strict conditions for countries to be able to trade with each other.

However, it must not be forgotten that it was Adam Smith's ideas about the roles of capital and the market in the process of economic growth that meant that people turned away from mercantilist ideas which promoted the belief that protection was an advantage. The removal of trade barriers promotes welfare. Trade can be an important condition for growth, which gives a greater division of labour. Increased division of labour means, in turn, increased trade.

The vent for surplus model is of more limited significance. It is possible that it can help to explain economic developments in the nineteenth century in the USA, Canada and Australia. Here the growth was strongly marked by the export of agricultural products which was made possible by the development of infrastructure. The question is whether it can help to explain the development in some less developed countries today, for example countries which export primary goods. There should be under-exploited resources which cannot be used in the manufacture of goods for domestic consumption. These can first be exploited when export is made possible by the elimination of the barrier of distance. This can be through the improvement of infrastructure or the removal of protective measures abroad.

Ricardo's theory of comparative advantage is based on relative differences in production technology. It is based on restrictive assumptions, among other things that there is only one production factor, i.e. labour.

Labour productivity plays a central role through technological differences. In the world in which we live today there are many different factors which influence labour productivity. Therefore the question is how much can be explained by using labour productivity as the decisive factor in explaining international trade. In spite of this, it should be recognised that the core idea of the comparative advantage has survived the test of time. The question is rather, what is it that determines the comparative advantage.

Literature

Chipman, J.S., 'A Survey of the Theory of International Trade: Part 1, The Classical Theory', *Econometrica 33*, 1965.

Jones, R.W., *International Trade: Essays in Theory*, Amsterdam, 1979.

Ricardo, D., *On the principles of Political Economy and Taxation*, Penguin, 1991. First published in 1817.

Smith, A., *An Enquiry into the Nature and Causes of the Wealth of Nations*, Penguin 1982. First published in 1776.

6. Factor proportion theory

One of the main propositions of factor proportion theory is that the pattern of international trade is determined by the factor endowment of different countries. Factor proportion theory is a neo-classical theory. The neo-classical theory emerged around 1870 and it was the dominant economic theory up until J.M. Keynes published his most influential book on macroeconomic policies in 1936. The emergence of the neo-classical theory occurred in various places around Europe. Its pioneers were S. Jevons in England, Leon Walras in France and Karl Menger in Austria.

With the emergence of the neo-classical theory, attention switched from economic growth to the allocation of goods and production factors. There is a given quantity of production factors, for example a given quantity of capital and labour. The question is how to get the most efficient production. Which goods and in what quantities should be produced so that households get the greatest possible utility?

6.1 The assumptions behind factor proportion theory

Factor proportion theory is based on the neo-classical general equilibrium model which is considered in Chapters 2-4.

On the production side it is assumed that the production factors are fully divisible. Substitution in the use of production factors is possible. On the demand side, each household has a utility function which indicates the level of utility connected with the consumption of variable amounts of two final goods. Both on the supply side and on the demand side the neo-classical theory uses the concept of marginal changes. It is assumed that producers want to maximise their profits and that households want to maximise their utility. As for the form of the market, the neo-classical theory assumes that there is perfect competition and that the markets are perfect. This applies both to the markets for final goods and for production factors.

The assumption of perfect competition means that there is absolute transparency in the market. No one in the market is able to influence prices, which means that there will be no market distortions as a result of market dominance. The assumption that there is a perfect market means that there is complete mobility of production factors between product sectors. Adjustment takes place without delays and without costs.

Apart from these general assumptions that are usually associated with neo-classical theory in its common form, factor proportion theory is also based on a number of additional assumptions. These assumption are described below.

General assumption:
1. There is a two country, two product and two factor model. A comparison is made between a situation with conditions of self-sufficiency and a situation with free trade, without any political trade barriers in the form of import duties, quotas etc.

Assumptions about production conditions:
2. For each product, the production functions in all countries are identical.
3. The production function is homogeneous of the first order. This means that there are neither advantages nor disadvantages of mass production. There are constant returns to scale.
4. The isoquants intersect at one point. This means that one good is always more capital intensive than the other good. This is the so-called 'strong' Samuelson assumption, which is discussed in detail later.

Assumptions about demand conditions:
5. The demand conditions are identical in both countries:
6. The utility function is homothetic.

Assumption about market conditions:
7. There are no transport costs.

Assumption about the mobility of production factors:
8. The production factors are internationally immobile. There is thus no scope for international movements of capital or international movements of labour.

Factor proportion theory needs these additional assumptions in order to reach precise results or theorems.

Factor proportion theory is often called the Heckscher-Ohlin model, since it was two Swedish economists, Eli Heckscher (1949) and Bertil Ohlin (1933) who first drew attention to this theory of trade which can be deduced on the basis of the neo-classical model with the assumptions referred to above. Many other economists, not least Paul Samuelson, have contributed to the development of factor proportion theory.

Factor proportion theory consists of three theorems. The first theorem is a trade theorem which states that it is factor endowment that determines the patterns of international trade. The second theorem states that, through international trade, factor returns will be the same, unless, after international trade, there is a total product specialisation. If there is a product specialisation there will only be a partial equalisation of differences. The third is the Stolper-Samuelson theorem which states that in a country it is the relatively plentiful production factor which will benefit from international free trade and the scarce factor will lose.

These three theorems will be discussed below. However, before that, two central points must be clarified. The first is a clarification of the concept of factor intensity. The second is the identification of the precise correlation between relative final good prices, relative factor prices and factor intensities in production which apply in factor proportion theory.

6.2 Factor intensity

A given good is produced by means of labour L and capital K. The ratio between the amounts of L and K used is called the factor intensity in the production of the good concerned.

In Figure 6.1 an isoquant is drawn for the production of a unit of a given good. T_1T_1 is the isocost line when the price of capital is r_1 and the price for labour is w_1. The optimal factor use is shown by point A. The slope of the line OA shows the relationship between L and K, which shows the relative use of the two factors.

If the price of capital is unchanged while the price of labour falls, there is a new isocost curve, T_2T_2. It touches the isoquant at point B. The slope of the line OB gives the new relationship in the use of L and

K. The production is said to be more labour intensive. This is the natural result of wages falling compared with the price of capital.

Figure 6.1: Illustration of factor intensity

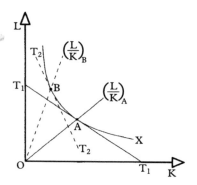

How much the factor intensity will changes will depend on the properties of the isoquant, and thus the properties of the production functions. Changes in factor intensity as a result of changes in relative factor prices can be described by using a measure called the substitution elasticity E_s, which is defined as

$$E_s = \frac{d(L/K)}{L/K} \Big/ \frac{d(r/w)}{r/w}$$

Substitution elasticity is associated with the curvature of the isoquant. Figure 6.2 shows different production functions with different substitution elasticities. In Figure (a) there is a production function with fixed technical coefficients, which means that substitution elasticity is zero. If the production function is linear, as in Figure (b), there will be full substitutability, which means that substitution elasticity will tend to infinity. In Figure (c) there is a Cobb-Douglas function $X = A L^{\alpha} K^{1-\alpha}$, where it can be shown that overall the substitution elasticity is equal to one. Figure (d) shows the CES (constant elasticity of substitution) function, where overall substitution elasticity is the same, but not equal to one.

In Figure 6.3 there are two isoquants which relate to the different production functions for each good. With relative factor prices which correspond to the slope of the tangents A_1 and B_1, the factor intensi-

Figure 6.2: Different kinds of production functions

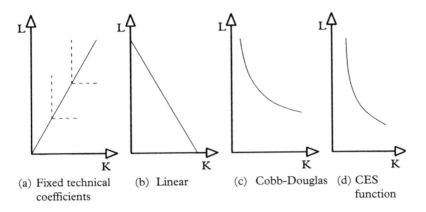

(a) Fixed technical   (b) Linear   (c) Cobb-Douglas (d) CES
    coefficients   function

ties for good a and good b are the same. If the relative factor prices
change, corresponding to the slope of tangents A_2 ans B_2, good a's
factor intensity will be changed more. The same applies if the relative
factor prices correspond to the slopes of the tangents A_3 and B_3. Here
too good a's factor intensity will be changed more. It can thus be seen
that good a, which has less curvature, has greater substitution elasticity than the good with the isoquant with greater curvature. The less
curved isoquant has greater substitution elasticity than the more
curved isoquant.

Figure 6.3: Production functions with different substitution elasticities

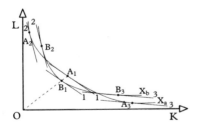

It is now assumed that the two goods have production functions with
the same elasticity. In other words the two isoquants have the same
curvature. It can be shown that this means that the two isoquants
intersect at one point. In Figure 6.4 two isoquants are drawn for a

product unit of good a and good b respectively. The substitution elasticities are the same for both goods.

Figure 6.4: Production functions with uniform substitution elasticities

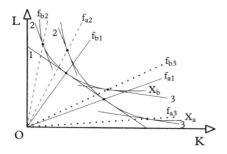

With relative factor prices corresponding to the slope of tangent 1, good b's and good a's labour intensity will be f_{b1} and f_{a1} respectively. Good b is more labour intensive than good a.

If the price for capital increases there will be relative factor prices corresponding to the slope of the tangents 2. The labour intensity in the production of good b and good a will be f_{b2} and f_{a2} respectively. Good b is again more labour intensive than good a. However, if the price of capital falls there will be relative factor prices which correspond to the slope of tangents 3. The labour intensity in the production of good b and good a will be f_{b3} and f_{a3} respectively. Again, good b is more labour intensive than good a.

It is thus shown that, regardless of the relative factor prices, good b will always be more labour intensive than good a when one unit is produced of each good. If the production functions are homogeneous, this will be the case regardless of the extent of the production of the two goods, i.e. regardless of where the isoquants are positioned in the co-ordinate system.

However, this is not the case when the substitution elasticities for the two goods are different, as illustrated in Figure 6.3. At points A_1 and B_1 the two goods have the same factor intensity. With relative factor prices where A_2 and B_2 are the optimal combinations of factors, good a will be more labour intensive than good b. Conversely, at points A_3 and B_3 good a is now more capital intensive than good b.

Where the substitution elasticities of the two goods are different, it is not possible to say unequivocally that good b is more labour intensive than good a. This depends entirely on the relative prices. The assumption that the production functions have uniform substitution elasticities, which means that the isoquants only intersect at one point, is called the 'strong' Samuelson assumption. This assumption means that one good will always be more labour intensive than the other good, regardless of the relative factor prices.

6.3 Final good prices, factor prices and factor intensity

In Section 6.1 three conditions are laid down for the production factors. When these conditions are met it is possible to derive a clear correlation between the relative final good prices and the relative factor prices in a country which produces both goods. It is also possible to derive a clear correlation between the relative factor prices and the factor intensities in the production of the two goods.

The link between final good prices and factor prices

To illustrate this, the isoquants for the two goods are drawn in Figure 6.5. The volume of production associated with the two isoquants is one unit of production.

To find the optimal combination of factors, it is necessary to draw in the isocost curves. An isocost curve can be described by an equation of the following kind:

$$L \cdot w + k \cdot r = Z$$

where w and r are the given factor prices and L and K are the combinations between labour L and capital K, which give constant costs which are equal to Z.

The isocost function can be rewritten as:

$$L = - r/w \cdot K + Z/w,$$

which shows that the slope of the isocost curve is $- r/w$, and the line segment on the L axis is Z/w.

It is now assumed that the relative factor prices are r_1/w_1. It is possible to draw a whole set of parallel isocost lines with the slope $- r_1/w_1$. Isocost line 1 is the lowest lying isocost line which touches both isoquants at A_1 and B_1.

Figure 6.5: Factor prices and final good prices

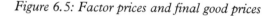

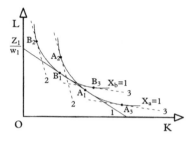

Isocost line 1 intersects the L axis at Z_1/w_1. Z_1 is the total cost connected with this isocost line. Since the isocost line touches the isoquants for both a and b, the total costs for producing a unit of good a and a unit of good b are the same. This means that the final good prices P_a and P_b are the same, if there is perfect competition. When there is perfect competition the price will be the same as the production costs. P_a/P_b is thus equal to 1.

It is now assumed that the price of capital increases from r_1 to r_2, with unchanged wages w_1. This means that it is possible to draw two isocost lines labelled 2. These isocost lines touch the isoquants at A_2 and B_2. The isocost line at A_2 intersects the L axis higher than the isocost line at B_2. This means that Z_2/w_1, which is intersected on the L axis, is greater for good a than for good b. Since the denominator w_1 is constant, this means that the production costs for good a have increased more than the production costs for good b. Once again, the total costs are equal to the price of the goods when there is perfect competition. Therefore one can conclude that P_a/P_b is now greater than 1.

If the price of capital falls to r_3, while wages remain unchanged at w_1, there will be two isocost lines labelled 3 which touch at A_3 and B_3. As the line through B_3 cuts off a greater portion on the L axis than the line through A_3, the total production costs at B_3 fall less than at A_3. This means that the relative final good prices P_a/P_b are now less than 1.

The correlation derived from this can be drawn as in Figure 6.6, which shows the correlation between the relative final good prices P_a/P_b and the relative factor prices r/w.

*Figure 6.6: Related variations between relative factor prices and relative
final good prices*

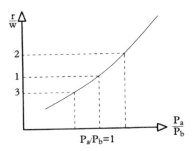

In Figure 6.6 the numbers 1,2 and 3 on the vertical axis correspond
to the relative factor prices r_1/w_1, r_2/w_2 and r_3/w_3. The corresponding
final good prices are shown on the horizontal axis. As shown above,
the result will be a curve which rises from left to right.

The link between factor prices and factor intensity

In Figure 6.4 there are two isoquants for the good a and good b.
Figure 6.4 can be used to show the related variations between relative
factor prices and factor intensities. With relative factor prices corresponding to the slope of line 1, the factor intensity in the production
of good a good b will be the slopes of f_{a1} and f_{b1} respectively.

If the price of capital increases so that the relative factor prices
correspond to the slope of the tangents 2, then good a's and good b's
factor intensities will be the slopes of the dashed lines f_{a2} and f_{b2} respectively. However, if the relative price of capital falls so the slope of
the tangents 3 shows the new factor prices, the factor intensity will be
the slope of the dotted lines f_{a3} and f_{b3} respectively.

These related variations between factor prices and factor intensity
are now drawn in Figure 6.7. With relative factor prices corresponding
to line 1 there will be factor intensities of f_{a1} and f_{b1}, as drawn in Figure 6.7. Good b is more labour intensive than good a. This applies to
all factor prices. With the relative factor prices corresponding to the
slopes on line 2 there will be greater labour intensity in the factor use
for both goods. With relative factor prices corresponding to the slopes
on line 3 there will be less labour intensity in the factor use.

Figure 6.7: Related variations between relative factor prices and factor intensity

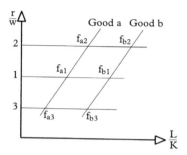

The link between final good prices, factor prices and factor intensities

Figure 6.6 shows the related variations between the relative final good prices and relative factor prices. Figure 6.7 shows the related variations between factor prices and factor intensities. It is now possible to put the two figures together, as shown in Figure 6.8. This figure can be used to illustrate the situation before and after trade. There are two countries A and B, where the production functions are the same for each of the two goods in both countries. In country A the relative prices before trade are equal to P_a/P_b at point A. This means that the relative factor prices r/w correspond to A on the vertical axis. There are a pair of factor intensities in the production of the goods corresponding to point A, which can be seen on the L/K axis. In country B, before trade, there are relative prices equal to P_a/P_b at point B. Corresponding to this there are factor prices r/w as shown at point B on the vertical axis.

After the introduction of trade there will be uniform relative final good prices, as shown by point H on the horizontal axis. This means that there will be uniform relative factor prices corresponding to H on the vertical axis. Corresponding to these relative factor prices there will be uniform factor intensities in each of the two manufactures in country A and B. This analysis shows that, with trade, which gives uniform final good prices, it is also possible for relative factor prices to be uniform. However, this is not always the case, as will be shown later, in the section on factor price equalisation.

Figure 6.8: Relative final good prices, relative factor prices and factor intensities

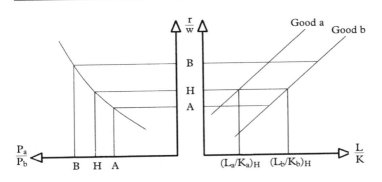

6.4 The trade theorem

There are two countries A and B, which each have a given quantity of the two production factors, capital K and labour L. By means of these two production factors each country can produce the two final goods, good a and good b. The trade theorem states that it is the relative endowments in the two countries of the two production factors K and L that determine the pattern of trade. It is assumed that country A has a relatively large capital stock and that country B has a relatively large labour force. The following therefore applies:

$$\left(\frac{L}{K}\right)_A < \left(\frac{L}{K}\right)_B$$

The relative factor endowment determines the relative factor prices. In country A, with a large capital stock, the price of capital is relatively cheap, and in country B labour is relatively cheap. The following therefore applies:

$$\left(\frac{r}{w}\right)_A < \left(\frac{r}{w}\right)_B$$

The relative factor prices determine the relative final good prices. When good a is always the capital intensive good, the following will apply:

$$\left(\frac{P_a}{P_b}\right)_A < \left(\frac{P_a}{P_b}\right)_B$$

The capital intensive good a will be relatively cheaper in the country in which capital is relatively cheap, because this production factor is relatively plentiful in this country. This is the situation when the two countries have closed economies, without trade. If trade is now introduced, country A will export the capital intensive good a, which is relatively cheap in country A. Conversely, the labour intensive good b will be relatively cheap in country B, which will therefore export this good. After the introduction of international trade, the price of each of the two goods will be the same in the two countries. This is the trade theorem, the content of which will be illustrated in the following.

Figure 6.9: Production functions for the two goods *Figure 6.10: Transformation curves for the two countries*

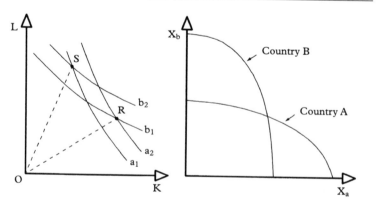

The conditions for production of the two final goods are shown in Figure 6.9 by means of isoquants. For good a there are the isoquants a_1 and a_2, and for good b there are the isoquants b_1 and b_2. The assumptions 2 to 4, as set out in Section 6.1, apply to these isoquants. By drawing these isoquants in a box diagram, as shown in Chapter 2, it is possible to derive the transformation curves of the two countries.

Using Figure 6.9 it is possible to illustrate why the transformation curves for countries A and B appear as they do in Figure 6.10. Good a is the capital intensive good, and good b is the labour intensive good. It is assumed that country A has a factor endowment corresponding to point R in Figure 6.9. Country B has a factor endowment corresponding to point S.

Using the factor endowment in country A to produce exclusively either good a or good b, the country can maximally produce the quantities a_2 and b_1 respectively. Country B can maximally produce the quantities a_1 and b_2 respectively of the two final goods. The country with the greater capital stock can produce more of the capital intensive good, and the country with the greater availability of labour can produce more of the labour intensive good.

The transformation curves from Figure 6.10 are drawn in figure 6.11, and the demand conditions, which are identical in the two countries according to assumption 5 in Section 6.1, are drawn as a single indifference curve.

It can be seen from Figure 6.11 that under conditions of self-sufficiency, good a is relatively cheap in country A (indicated by the slope of P^A) and good b is relatively cheap in country B (indicated by the slope of P^B). Country A produces at point Q_1 and country B at point T_1.

Figure 6.11: Self-sufficiency and trade

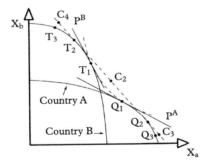

International trade is now introduced, and international terms of trade are indicated, for example, by the slope of the dotted straight line in Figure 6.11. There is then a specialisation of production. After trade, country A which has a large capital stock will produce more of the capital intensive good, which the country has comparatively good conditions for producing at a low cost. The production point for country A moves from Q_1 to Q_2. Country B will move its production point from T_1 to T_2.

In Figure 6.11 there is only partial specialisation, but under certain conditions there can be a total specialisation. However, the question whether or not there is total specialisation does not affect the trade theory, though it is significant for the theory on factor price equalisation, which is considered in the next section.

Finally, it should be made clear that the trade theory does not apply if the demand structure for the two goods is very different in the two countries. If the demand for the capital intensive good a is very high in country A, then the self-sufficiency point may be Q_3. If, correspondingly, the demand for good b is very high in country B, the self-sufficiency point may be T_3.

At point Q_3 the capital intensive good a, which country A has good conditions for producing, is relatively expensive. Similarly, at the point of self-sufficiency at T_3 the labour intensive good b, which country B has conditions for producing, is relatively expensive in country B.

In this situation the introduction of trade will mean that the capital rich country A will consume at point C3 and the country will therefore import the capital intensive good. Similarly, country B, which has a large labour force, will consume at point C4, and the country will therefore import the labour intensive good b. In this wholly exceptional situation, the pattern of trade will not be in accordance with the trade theory.

6.5 The theory of factor price equalisation

The theory of factor price equalisation states that, as long as there is no total production specialisation, then relative factor prices in the two countries will be the same. If, after trade, there is a total production specialisation in at least one of the countries, there will only be a partial equalisation of the relative factor prices which existed before the introduction of trade.

It can be shown that a country's relative factor endowment determines whether, after trade, a country produces both goods or only one good. In Figure 6.12 two sets of isoquants for the good a and good b are drawn. The two sets of isoquants express that the production functions are different for the two goods. When the production functions are homogeneous it means that with the given relative factor prices r/w corresponding to the slope of RR, the expansion path for good a will be f_a and for good b will be f_b, which are straight lines.

After the introduction of trade a set of final good prices, P_a and P_b will be established. The production quantities associated with X_{a1} and X_{b1} are thus chosen so that the value of the production of the two goods is the same, i.e. that $P_a \cdot X_{a1} = P_b \cdot X_{b1}$. There is only one set of factor prices corresponding to the relative final good prices P_a/P_b, which means that it is worth producing both goods. This is the set of relative factor prices corresponding to the slope of R. It is only with this set of factor prices that the costs of producing the quantities X_{a1} and X_{b1} are the same. The costs are equal to the value of X_{a1} and X_{b1}, which are also the same.

If r/w is greater than the r/w which corresponds to the slope of R, it will be more expensive to produce X_{a1}, cf. the arguments linked to Figure 6.5.

If r/w is less than the r/w which corresponds to the slope of R, it will be more expensive to produce X_{b1} than to produce X_{a1}.

Figure 6.12: A country produces both goods

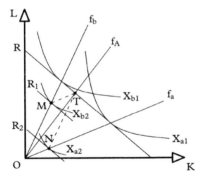

When P_a and P_b are given, there will only be one set of factor prices which make it profitable to produce both goods. This set of factor prices corresponds to the numerical slope of R.

Whether, at these relative factor prices, country A has the possibility of producing both goods depends on the country's factor endowment. If country A's factor endowment is equal to point T, the slope of f_A is an expression of the quantity of L divided by the quantity of K which the country possesses. If T is the country's factor endowment, the country will produce X_{b2} of good b and X_{a2} of good a. M and N show the quantity of factors used in the two manufactures, which, together, give point T.

In Figure 6.13 X_{a1} and X_{b1} as well as the line R are the same as in Figure 6.12. If a country has a factor endowment which is equal to point T, it has been shown above that the country will produce both good a and good b. The quantity of factors used in the production of good b and good a will be M and N respectively. However, if the factor endowment is T_1, there will be less production of good b and more of good a. The use of factors in the two manufactures can now be described by points M_1 and N_1.

Figure 6.13: Different factor endowments in the two countries

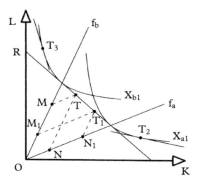

If country A has factor endowment T and country B has factor endowment T_1, for both of which it applies that they lie between f_a and f_b, then both countries will produce both goods, and in both countries there will be factor price relations which correspond to the slope of R.

If, however, one of the countries has a factor endowment which lies outside the limits of f_a and f_b, the country will only produce one product. If one country has a factor endowment corresponding to T_2, it is only worth producing good a, but not good b. The relative factor prices will be equal to the slope of the tangent at T_2. If one country has a factor endowment corresponding to T_3, it will only be worthwhile producing good b. In this case the relative factor prices will be equal to the slope at T_3.

It can therefore be concluded that if the countries' factor endowments L/K fulfil the conditions

$$f_a \leq L/K \leq f_b \qquad\qquad (6.1)$$

for both countries, there will be complete factor price equalisation after trade.

If it is the case for one of the countries that

$$L/K < f_a \text{ or } L/K > f_b \qquad\qquad (6.2)$$

then, in that country there will be production of either good a or good b. In this case there will be different relative factor prices in the two countries after trade. If country A fulfils the conditions of (6.1), the relative factor prices in country A will be the slope of R. If (6.2) applies for country B, then after trade this country will have different relative factor prices.

In the latter case it is also possible to show that, compared with the position under conditions of self-sufficiency, after the introduction of trade there will be a partial equalisation of the differences in relative factor prices, but it will not be total, which would be the case where both countries fulfil the conditions of (6.1).

Moreover, Figure 6.13 shows that the greater the differences in production functions, i.e. the greater the distance between f_a and f_b, the greater will be the probability of factor price equalisation. Figure 6.13 also shows that with the given production functions, the more different the factor endowments of the two countries, the greater will be the probability that there will not be factor price equalisation.

6.6 The Stolper-Samuelson theorem

The link between the relative final good prices and the relative factor prices is illustrated above in Section 6.3. If the price of good a increases relatively, the price for the production factor which is intensively used in the production of good a will increase relative to the other production factor.

The Stolper-Samuelson theorem is a stronger statement, since it states something about the absolute factor returns. The theorem states that, as long as the price of good a increases relatively, then the absolute returns on the factor which is used more intensively in its production will increase. Correspondingly, the absolute returns on the other production will fall.

The link between factor intensity and absolute factor returns

The production function $X = X(K,L)$, which is homogeneous of the first order, is drawn in Figure 6.14, which is equivalent to saying that there are constant returns to scale. Using this assumption, regardless of where one is on a given factor line OE, the marginal productivity of capital $\partial X/\partial K$ will be constant and the marginal productivity of labour $\partial X/\partial L$ will also be constant, see Chapter 2, Section 2.2. In a situation of equilibrium the marginal productivities will also be equal to the real factor returns:

$$\frac{\partial X}{\partial K} = \frac{r}{P} \quad \text{and} \quad \frac{\partial X}{\partial L} = \frac{w}{P}$$

where and w are the nominal returns on capital and labour respectively, and P is the final good price, see Chapter 2, Section 2.3.

It is clear that in moving from OE_1 til OE_2, the real return on factors will change. It has already been established that in moving from OE_1 to OE_2, r/w will rise. The relative return on factors will be changed.

Figure 6.14: Marginal productivities for production factors along factor lines

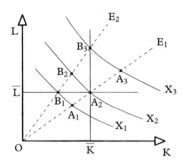

The question now is whether it is possible to state anything about the absolute real return for the two production factors when moving from factor line E_1 to factor line E_2. This is possible when the production function is homogeneous of the first order. This can be illustrated by assuming that the production function is a Cobb-Douglas function:

$$X = A \cdot K^{\alpha} L^{1-\alpha}$$

which is indeed homogeneous of the first order. If the quantity of labour is constant and equal to $\overline{L}$, it is possible to calculate the marginal productivity of capital, with varying capital inputs. In the same way it is possible to calculate the marginal productivity of labour when the amount of capital is constant, for example equal to $\overline{K}$. There is now:

$$X = AK^{\alpha}\overline{L}^{1-\alpha} \tag{6.3}$$

$$X = A\overline{K}^{\alpha}L^{1-\alpha} \tag{6.4}$$

If the equation (6.3) is differentiated with regard to K, and (6.4) with regard to L, the results are:

$$\partial X/\partial K = A\alpha K^{a-1}\overline{L}^{1-\alpha} \tag{6.5}$$

$$\partial X/\partial L = A\overline{K}^{\alpha}(1-\alpha)L^{-\alpha} \tag{6.6}$$

These expression show that when the quantity of one of the production factors is given, the marginal productivity of the other factor will fall when the quantity of the other factor is increased.

Figure 6.15: A given quantity of labour

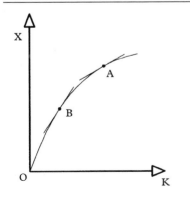

Figure 6.16: Two different quantities of labour

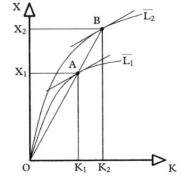

Expression (6.3) can be illustrated in a diagram as shown in Figure 6.15. The slope of the tangents at points B and A indicate the marginal productivity of capital, which is equal to the real return on capital. When there is a given quantity of L, then an increased input of capital will mean that the real return on capital will fall. This corresponds to the situation in Figure 6.14, where there is a given quantity of L and the capital input is increased from B_1 to A_2. In Figure 6.15 it corresponds to moving from B to A, with the result that there is a fall in the absolute return on capital. At B_1 in Figure 6.14 the absolute real return on capital is higher than at A_2.

Similarly, it is possible to give a diagrammatic illustration of (6.4). As shown in Figure 6.14 there is a given quantity of K, and the input of L is increased so there is a move from A_2 to B_3. At B_3 the absolute real return on labour is lower than at A_2.

It has now been shown that if there is a move from E_1 to E_2 in Figure 6.14, the absolute return on capital will increase and the absolute return on labour will fall.

At the start of this section it was said that, regardless of where one is on a given factor line, the marginal productivity of the individual factor will be constant. For example, the return on capital at B_1 and B_3 in Figure 6.14 is the same. This is illustrated in Figure 6.16 where the curve OA represents a given quantity of labour L_1. There is now an increased quantity of labour L_2, which gives a new curve OB, which shows the relationship between K and X. If a straight line OAB is drawn, then K_2/K_1 is equal to L_2/L_1 which is in turn equal to X_2/X_1, because the production function is homogeneous of the first order. The slope of the tangents at B and at A are the same, because the marginal productivity of capital is the same at the two points A and B. B_1 to A_2. In Figure 6.15 it corresponds to moving from B to A, with the result that there is a fall in the absolute return on capital. At B_1 in Figure 6.14 the absolute real return on capital is higher than at A_2.

Similarly, it is possible to give a diagrammatic illustration of (6.4). As shown in Figure 6.14 there is a given quantity of K, and the input of L is increased so there is a move from A_2 to B_3. At B_3 the absolute real return on labour is lower than at A_2.

It has now been shown that if there is a move from E_1 to E_2 in Figure 6.14, the absolute return on capital will increase and the absolute return on labour will fall.

At the start of this section it was said that, regardless of where one is on a given factor line, the marginal productivity of the individual factor will be constant. For example, the return on capital at B1 and at B_3 in Figure 6.14 is the same. This is illustrated in Figure 6.16 where the curve OA represents a given quantity of labour L_1. There is now an increased quantity of labour L_2, which gives a new curve OB, which shows the relationship between K and X. If a straight line OAB is drawn, then K_2/K_1 is equal to L_2/L_1 which is in turn equal to X_2/X_1, because the production function is homogeneous of the first order. The slope of the tangents at B and at A are the same, because the marginal productivity of capital is the same at the two points A and B.

Who wins and who loses with international trade?

Figure 6.17 has a traditional box diagram, representing production of two goods a and b. Good a is the capital intensive product.

In the initial situation there is production at point A. The price for good a is now increased which means that the production point moves to B, where more of good a is produced and less of good b. This means that there is an increase in labour intensity as the slope at O_aB is steeper than the slope at O_aA. This in turn means, cf. the preceding section, that the absolute real return on capital increases, while the absolute real return on labour falls.

The Stolper-Samuelson theorem applies generally to a country but does not necessarily have anything to do with international trade. When the relative demand for two final goods changes, the Stolper-Samuelson theorem becomes relevant. The reason for this can be that there is a change in consumer taste, but can also be related to international trade. If the country imports good b, and if good b is subject to an import duty, then good a will be relatively cheaper than under conditions of free trade.

For example, the country is at production point A in Figure 6.17. Tariff protection for good b is now removed. This means that the relative price of good a increases and production of good a is increased. The country's production will now be at point B in Figure 6.17. The absolute real return on capital will increase and the absolute real return on labour will fall.

The use of the Stolper-Samuelson theorem of international trade shows that in moving from a situation with tariff protection to free trade, one production factor will gain absolutely and the other production factor will lose absolutely.

When country A imports good b, which is labour intensive, then according to the trade theory, it is because country A has a relatively small quantity of labour. When the trade theory applies, country A has relatively plentiful capital. It will thus be the relatively plentiful production factor which will gain by the removal of import duties and the relatively scarce factor which will lose by the removal of import duties.

Figure 6.17: Changes to the composition of production

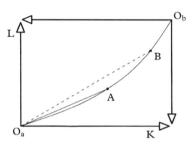

This raises an interesting question as to whether, in terms of Pareto-optimality, it can be said that free trade is better than a situation of self-sufficiency with tariff protection. One production factor receives a poorer return. This means that at least one person is worse off under free trade. This question has already been dealt with earlier in Chapter 4, Sections 4.2 and 4.3. Due to trade the distribution of income will change, and certain groups in society will lose. Therefore the owners of the different production factors can have different attitudes towards free trade. This means that free trade will only improve welfare it it is combined with a change in income distribution.

If one looks at the history of trade policy there are many examples of different groups in society having attitudes to free trade and protection which are in accordance with the Stolper-Samuelson theorem.

One of the causes of the American Civil War 1861-65 was a difference in attitudes to tariff policy. The Southern States had a relatively high amount of land which enabled considerable exports of agricultural products. The Northern States had a dawning industrialisation, but with relatively small capital compared with England. The scarcity of the production factor capital in the North favoured tariff protection while the abundance of the production factor land in the South favoured free trade.

In Denmark, before the Second World War, tariff policy was an area of conflict between the Liberal party and the Conservative party. The Liberal party, which drew much of its support from the agricultural community, was interested in free trade, because Denmark had relatively much agricultural land which made exports of agricultural products possible. The Conservative party was the party of the industrial interests, which was interested in protection. Denmark had relatively little capital and had large imports of industrial goods.

6.7 The Leontief paradox

Leontief's results

Several economists have attempted to show, empirically, whether the existing patterns of trade are in accordance with factor proportion theory. The first and most widely discussed of these empirical analyses was made by W.W. Leontief. Leontief (1953) analysed the capital contents and the labour contents in American imports and exports. The analyses were based on input-output tables for the USA for 1947, and analysis was later made using the 1951 figures. By using input-output analysis for a given good it is possible to calculate how much capital and how much labour is required to produce a given quantity of the final good. This involves using cumulative figures for capital and labour in all the phases of production. The figures thus include the capital and labour which is necessary for producing the raw materials and semi-manufactured goods which are included in the production of the final good in question.

Leontief calculated the amount of capital and the amount of labour which would be released if there was a uniform percentage cut in exports of all goods from the USA. Leontief imagined a re-adjustment of production in the USA so that the USA's exports would be reduced by 5 per cent, for example. Simultaneously, imports would be reduced by the same percentage since the reduced imports would now be replaced by domestic production of goods which had previously been imported. The question was, how much more capital and labour would be required for domestic American production to replace the missing imports.

These calculations gave the surprising result that the USA's exports required relatively high labour in relation to capital, compared with the corresponding figures for the production increases which would be made to substitute its imports. At that point it was clear that it could be assumed that the USA had relatively more capital in relation to labour, compared with the rest of the world.

Leontief's results were thus the exact opposite of what might have been expected. In other words there was a denial of the trade theory which is part of factor proportion theory. Leontief's results prompted a great deal of debate. First, there were questions about Leontief's assumptions in his analysis. Next, Leontief's analyses led to the clarification of the conditions which must be fulfilled for factor proportion theory to apply. It led to the conditions which are referred to above in Section 6.1.

A discussion of the Leontief paradox

Leontief's results are based on a two country model, in which the USA is one country and the rest of the world is the other country. This naturally raises the question whether it is reasonable to treat the rest of the world as one country. If the world is split into three 'countries' (USA, Europe and the rest of the world) it would be possible to see differences between the USA's trade with Europe and the USA's trade with the rest of the world.

Leontief calculated the capital input and the labour input of the USA's imports on the basis of the *technical production coefficients in the USA*. Ideally, these figures ought to be calculated on the basis on the input-output tables for the rest of the world, but these did not exist. Leontief's analysis is implicitly based on the assumption that the production functions in the USA and the production functions in the rest of the world are the same. This is the same assumption which lies behind factor proportion theory, but it does not necessarily apply in practice.

There are great theoretical and practical problems in obtaining figures for the *capital input* of goods. It is possible to obtain an indication of how much capital input there is in a given production by seeing how large a proportion of the production value is due to capital. If the production value is $X \cdot P$ and the costs of labour is W, then the remainder $(X \cdot P) - W$ is allotted to capital.

This value can be calculated for different productions since X, P and W are known. The remainder can be taken as indicating the amount of the capital stock, as long as the capital return in a given production is independent of the volume of production, and if the capital gives the same return on all productions. If these assumptions do not apply, there is a difficulty in using the remainder XP - W as an indication of the amount of the capital stock.

Apart from these criticisms of the practical methods used by Leontief, his results provoked discussion about the conditions which must be met for factor proportion to apply, as well as discussion about whether these conditions are met in practice.

Factor proportion theory is based on *the 'strong' Samuelson condition*, which states that the isoquants for the two production functions may only intersect at one point. This condition is met as long as the substitution elasticities are the same in the two manufactures, cf. Section 6.2 above. If the substitution elasticities are not the same, as illustrated in Figure 6.3, then the good which the USA imports can be capital intensive in the USA, but labour intensive in the exporting country. For example, in Figure 6.3 X_a is the USA's import good and X_b is the USA's export good. Since the USA is well endowed with capital r/w will be small in the USA, which means that the USA will produce at A_3 and B_3, which means that the USA's imported goods are reckoned to be relatively capital intensive. However, in the rest of the world r/w is big, which means that the rest of the world produces at points A_2 and B_2. In the rest of the world the USA's imported good a is more labour intensive than the USA's exported good b. Empirical analyses have been made which show that the substitution elasticities in different business sectors do in fact differ, which puts in doubt the question as to whether the 'strong' Samuelson condition is valid.

Factor proportion theory is based on the idea that *demand conditions are identical* in both countries. At the end of Section 6.4 it is demonstrated that the trade theory does not apply if the demand conditions are very different. In Figure 6.11 it is demonstrated that if the demand conditions are so very different that, under conditions of self-sufficiency, the two countries would produce and consume at points Q_3 and T_3, the country with a plentiful capital endowment will import the capital intensive good. There is undoubtedly a tendency for demand to be relatively stronger for the goods in which the country has some comparative advantages in producing. But it is doubtful whether the differences in demand are stronger than the differences on the supply side.

In factor proportion theory *natural resources* are not included as a production factor along with labour and capital. Natural resources are a decisive factor in agriculture and mining. If productions requiring

natural resources play an important role in trade, it would be natural
to allow natural resources to be included as a third production factor
alongside capital and labour. In industrial countries and in less developed countries, agricultural products require natural resources, but in
industrial countries the natural resources are associated with a large
capital stock, while in less developed countries they are associated
with a large amount of labour. Therefore, if consideration is only
given to the relations between capital and labour, then in less developed countries agricultural products will be categorised as labour
intensive, while in industrial countries agricultural products will be
categorised as capital intensive. The USA has previously been a significant net importer of foodstuffs; from an American perspective these
will be seen as capital intensive, whereas, from the perspective of the
less developed countries these will be seen as labour intensive. Mining
will be considered as capital intensive from the perspective of industrial countries and of less developed countries. The capital involved in
mining in less developed countries will often be the result of foreign
direct investment. Therefore, exports of minerals from less developed
countries will be capital intensive exports, but cannot be explained on
the basis that the less developed countries have plentiful capital. This
is because the underlying natural resources, the existence of minerals,
is an essential condition for the establishment of exports. However,
the capital which is needed for exploiting the minerals is of foreign
origin.

When taking into account the significance of natural resources it is
necessary either to include the natural resources as a production factor
or to test factor proportion theory, which only includes labour and
capital, on a set of products from which products based on natural
resources are excluded. Including natural resources in factor proportion theory is not easy, because natural resources are not a homogeneous stock. There is a great difference between having land in a
temperate climate which is well suited for the cultivation of cereals,
and having land in tropical areas which is well suited for the cultivation of bananas. There is naturally also a big difference between a
natural resource which can be used for agriculture and a natural
resource which can be used for mining, because of the mineral content
of the earth. The significance of natural resources points towards
availability theory, which is dealt with in the next chapter.

In factor proportion theory, where it is said that it is the relative
quantities of capital and labour that determine the pattern of trade, it

must be assumed that *labour and capital are homogeneous production factors*. A unit of labour in the USA and in India are the same. 1 million units of capital invested in the USA and in India are the same. This is one of the most serious objections that can be made against the practical application of factor proportion theory. How is it possible to get figures for labour which take account of the fact that the labour force has different skills in individual countries? How is it possible to get figures for capital which take account of the fact that the capital is invested in different technologies?

Leontief himself was aware that labour is not a homogeneous factor when differences between countries are considered. According to Leontief, because of their better education an American workers are three times as efficient as foreign workers. In other words, the American quantity of labour should be multiplied by a factor of three. According to Leontief, if this is done, the USA will have a relatively large endowment of labour, and thus the Leontief paradox would be solved since the USA, as a country with relatively plentiful labour, will export labour intensive goods. As an argument for using a factor of three Leontief referred to the difference in wage levels between the USA and the rest of the world. Leontief's argument cannot be accepted because he failed to take account of two central problems.

Firstly, a threefold relative difference in wages between labour in the USA and the rest of the world did not express that labour in the USA is three times as efficient because of better education. The higher wages obtained by American labour was an expression of the fact that American workers had a better education, combined with the fact that, per capita, American workers had more and better capital equipment available to them than workers elsewhere. Only that part of the wages difference which was due to the labour force having a better education could be taken as expressing the fact that the labour force was more efficient because of better education.

Secondly, Leontief did not take account of the fact that the labour force in each country was not a homogeneous stock, because different kinds of labour have had different levels of education. For example, in the USA the labour in the high technology industry is, on average, better educated that the labour in the textile industry.

When there are sectoral differences in the levels of education of labour, there are two possibilities. First, it can be decided to introduce the concept of a 'pure' labour force, which has obtained a given low educational level. The education which the labour force has received above that level is considered as human capital, and is added to the physical capital. This procedure is not without its problems. The question is how to measure the human capital. In empirical calculations some economists have started with the difference in wages between better educated workers and unskilled workers. If, for example, it is said that the return on human capital is 6 per cent, which is the reason for the difference in wages, it will be possible to calculate the invested human capital on the basis of the difference in wages. The problem is that wage differences alone cannot be taken as expressing the differences in human capital. Wage differences can also be caused by the availability of a greater quantity of physical capital equipment for each worker. In addition to this, even if there were a reasonable measure for human capital, it is problematic to lump it together with the physical capital. The two types of capital can hardly be substituted for each other.

The other approach is to divide the work force into different categories. For example, it is possible to distinguish between workers involved in research and development, workers with technological know-how, workers with other special know-how, for example to do with administration or marketing. Then there are skilled workers and unskilled workers. If such categorisations are made it becomes possible to examine whether the countries which have a large quantity of labour in research and development and a large quantity of labour with technological know-how have a comparative advantage in the export of high technology products. Conversely, countries with a large quantity of unskilled labour could have a comparative advantage in producing simple labour-intensive products.

Finally, the Leontief paradox could be an expression of the fact that *factor proportion theory cannot explain international trade*. Maybe international trade is due to factors other than the comparative differences in factor endowment, which is the explanation of factor proportion theory. This question will be returned to in the following chapters which analyse other theories.

6.8 Summary

Factor proportion theory is a neo-classical theory which requires a number of conditions, concerning supply, demand and market conditions, to be met before it is applicable.

Factor proportion theory consists of three theorems. The trade theorem states that it is the relative factor endowment of countries which determines the composition of goods traded internationally. The country which has a relatively large capital endowment will export capital intensive goods. The other country, which has a relatively large quantity of labour, will export labour intensive products.

The second theorem concerns factor price equalisation. When there is free trade, the prices of goods will be the same in the two countries. This means that the relative factor prices will also be the same, if both countries continue to produce both goods, after the introduction of free trade. If only one country produces one of the goods after the introduction of free trade, there will only be a partial factor price equalisation.

The Stolper-Samuelson theory is the third step in factor proportion theory. The production factor of which a country has a relatively high quantity of will obtain an absolute increase in return after the introduction of free trade. Conversely, the factor which is relatively scarce will have an absolute fall in its return.

The Leontief paradox raises many questions. Are the methods used by Leontief in his analyses satisfactory? Are the strict requirements which must be met for factor proportion theory to be applicable, in fact met in practice? Or is factor proportion theory not a satisfactory theory for explaining the patterns of international trade and the consequences of trade? This last thought lies behind some of the newer theories which are analysed in the following chapters.

Literature

Heckscher, E.F., 'The Effect of Foreign Trade on the Distribution of Income' in H.S. Ellis and L.A. Metzler (eds.) *Readings in the Theory of International Trade*, Philadelphia, 1949. First published in Ekonomisk Tidsskrift, 21, 1919.

Johnson, H.G., 'Factor Endowments, International Trade and Factor Prices' in H.G. Johnson, *International Trade and Economic Growth*, Cambridge, 1961.

Leontief, W.W., 'Domestic Production and Foreign Trade: The American Capital Position Reexamined', *Proceedings of the American Philosophical Society*, 1953.

Ohlin, B., *Interregional and International Trade,* Harvard University Press, revised edition 1967. First published in 1933.

Samuelson, P.A., 'International Trade and the Equalization of Factor Prices', *Economic Journal* 58, 1948.

Samuelson, P.A., 'International Factor Price Equalization Once Again', *Economic Journal,* 59, 1949.

Samuelson, P.A., 'Price of Factors and Goods in General Equilibrium', *Review of Economic Studies,* 21, 1953.

Stolper, W.F. and P.A. Samuelson, 'Protection and Real Wages', *Review of Economic Studies,* 9, 1941.

7. Increased numbers
of production factors

In factor proportion theory it is assumed that the production function for a particular good is the same in two countries. It is also assumed that there are two production factors which are homogeneous. Altogether, there is a rather restrictive set of assumptions.

If international trade is analysed in practice, it will be natural either to allow that the production function for a particular good is different in different countries or to use more than two production factors in the production function.

The question of the form of the production function and the number of production factors are linked. This can be illustrated by an example. Indian agriculture and English agriculture are very different. If the same production function is used for agriculture in both countries, then either the decisive differences of technology, education and cultivation methods must be incorporated in the method by which labour and capital inputs are calculated, or they must incorporated by the acceptance of more than two production factors.

If, on the other hand, it is accepted that the production functions are different, the differences in technology and education will be reflected in the differences in the production functions. This means that it will be easier to find adequate measures for the inputs of labour and capital.

The differences between countries can be incorporated in the model by accepting that the production functions for a particular good can vary from country to country. Or they can be accounted for by incorporating qualitative differences of capital and labour into the applied measures of the capital stock and the size of the labour force. Finally the differences can be reflected by introducing more than two production factors, which makes it more acceptable to assume that each production factor is homogeneous.

In what follows, first there is an analysis of the 'sector-specific' factor model, which can either be interpreted as a model with three production factors or as a model where the technology is different in the two countries. Next, semi-manufactured goods are introduced as a production factor, and finally there is an analysis of availability-theory, which allows for a number of production factors which are not available in all countries.

7.1 *The specific factor model*

One production factor is sector-specific

Factor proportion theory assumes that there are two production factors, capital and labour, which can be moved from one production sector to another without any problem, in other words, without costs.

However, that is not how the real world works in the short and medium term. The capital consists of buildings and equipment which are specific to an individual industrial sector. The same applies to labour. By not re-investing capital in one sector but by investing it in another sector there can be a gradual 'movement' of capital. Through education and retraining labour can be moved from one sector to another. In other words, there is not full substitutability of the individual production factor in its use in different industrial sectors. What is the result of these new assumptions? For the sake of simplicity it is assumed that labour can be moved from one production to another without any problem. However, the capital stock is sector-specific, which means that the capital stock cannot be moved immediately.

In country A there is production of two goods a and b. In the production of good a capital of type G is used and in the production of good b capital of the type H is used. Both productions make use of labour L. The following production functions apply:

$$X_a = f_a(G, L_a)$$
$$X_b = f_b(H, L_b)$$

where G and H are given quantities $G = \overline{G}$ and $H = \overline{H}$, and where the total given labour $\overline{L} = L_a + L_b$. It is assumed that all production factors are fully used. Figure 7.1 shows how the transformation curve can be derived on the basis of the above information.

In Quadrant III a straight line is drawn which intersects the total labour force $\overline{L}$ on the two axes so that $L_a + L_b = \overline{L}$ which means that the straight line has a slope of -1.

In Quadrants IV the production of good a is shown and in Quadrant II the production of good b is shown as a function of the labour force when the capital stock G and H are given in the two sectors. The curves show that the marginal productivity of labour falls as more labour is used. This is the situation when the production functions are homogeneous of the first order and when the respective quantities of capital are given, cf. the analysis in Chapter 6, Section 6.6.

Figure 7.1: The sector-specific model

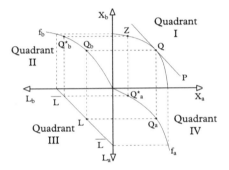

On the basis of the curves in Quadrant III and in Quadrants II and IV it is possible to derive the transformation curve in Quadrant I. If the labour force L is shared between the productions of good a and good b, which corresponds to point L in Quadrant III, there will be production of good a at point Q_a in Quadrant IV and production of good b at point Q_b in Quadrant II. If these two quantities are added together in Quadrant I then the result is production at point Q. If there is a different distribution of labour L between the production of the two goods there will be a different set of quantities of final goods, which can be derived from the curves in Quadrants II and IV, and which can be drawn together in Quadrant I. In this way it is possible to derive the transformation curve.

If the distribution of labour corresponding to point L in Quadrant III is optimal, the marginal product in each of the two productions will be equal to the real wages of the labour. Thus it will be that:

$$f'_a = \frac{w_a}{P_a} \quad \text{and} \quad f'_b = \frac{w_b}{P_b} \tag{7.1}$$

where $f'_a = \partial X_a/\partial L_a$ and $f'_b = \partial X_b/\partial L_b$ the marginal productivity of labour, w_a and w_b are the nominal wages in the two sectors, and P_a and P_b are the prices of the two final goods. It is assumed that there is full mobility in the labour market so that $w_a = w_b$.

The real return differs, depending on whether it is measured in relation to one or the other final good. The real return in relation to the price of good a should be equal to the marginal productivity of labour in the production of good a. At point Q_a the marginal productivity of labour is equal to the slope of the tangent at that point.

When L is the optimal distribution of labour, which means that (7.1) applies, Q will be the optimal point on the transformation curve. The relative prices P_a/P_b will therefore be equal to the numerical slope of the tangent P. The relative prices are determined by the relation of the marginal productivity of labour in the two productions of goods. From the equations in (7.1) it can be seen that:

$$\frac{P_a}{P_b} = \frac{f'_b}{f'_a}$$

The link between final good prices and factor prices

At point Q in Figure 7.1 there is a set of final good prices. There is a nominal wage corresponding to these final good prices which is determined by the marginal productivity of labour at Q_a and Q_b which can be derived from the expressions in (7.1).

The question now is how the factor return changes when the final good prices changes. P_b is assumed to be unchanged, while P_a falls. The slope at P in Figure 7.1 will be less steep and there will be a production point Z on the transformation curve. If horizontal and vertical dotted lines are drawn from Z to the curves in Quadrants II and IV, and further to Quadrant III it will be seen that less labour will be used in the production of good a and more labour will be used in the production of good b.

The new production point for good a will be $Q^\star_a$ in Quadrant IV and $Q^\star_b$ for good b in Quadrant II. At these two points the marginal productivity of labour has risen and fallen respectively, compared with the original situations Q_a and Q_b. This means that, cf. expression (7.1), that a lower price for good a gives a higher w/P_a in sector a, and a lower w/P_b in sector b.

When the production function is homogeneous of the first order, we know from Section 6.6 that a fall in the absolute return on one production factor means that the absolute return on the other factor will rise. It is therefore possible to conclude, in relation to factor returns, that in moving from Q to Z in Quadrant I:

$$\frac{w}{P_a} \text{ rises and } \frac{r_G}{P_a} \text{ falls}$$

$$(7.2)$$

$$\frac{w}{P_b} \text{ rises and } \frac{r_H}{P_b} \text{ falls}$$

where r_G/P_a and r_H/P_b are the real returns on capital in sector a and sector b respectively, calculated in relation to the price for the sector's own good.

In expression (7.2) above, real returns are measured in relation to the price for one good. When the households which receive the factor return consume both goods, a total evaluation of the development of the real return should be seen in relation to the prices of both goods.

For the production factor capital the conclusion on real returns is clear. In sector a the real return falls measured against P_a. If the real return for capital G is measured against P_b, i.e. r_G/P_b, the real return will fall even further because P_b rises in relation to P_a. Regardless of whether the capital in sector a only uses good a or only uses good b or uses a combination of the two goods, the real return on capital in sector a will fall. It is clear that the greater the preference which the capital in sector a has for good b, the further its real return will fall.

In sector b the real return on capital will rise in relation to P_b. If r_H/P_a is measured, it will rise even further than r_H/P_b, because P_a falls in relation to P_b.

However, it is not possible to state definitely how the real return of labour will develop. The real return will rise compared with P_a while real return compared with P_b will fall. How the real return will develop for the individual wage earners will depend on their patterns of consumption. The more that wage earners use of good a, the greater will be their overall chance of an increase in their real return. The converse applies if wage earners have a strong preference for good b.

It can therefore be concluded that in moving from point Q to point Z in Figure 7.1, i.e. in expanding production of good b because it has become relatively more expensive, the real return on capital in sector b will rise. Conversely the real return on capital in sector a will fall because the fixed capital stock will have a poorer utilisation, because of the lower production of good a. However, the real return which the labour receives is, indeterminate, as the real return depends on the consumption patterns of wage earners.

In moving from Q to Z in the factor proportion model, the real return of the factor which is used intensively in the production which increases will always have an increase in its real return. This is so regardless of whether it is measured in relation to P_a or P_b. This is the effect of the Stolper-Samuelson theorem which is analysed in Section 6.6. If labour is the factor which is relatively intensively used in the production of good b, the real return of the wage earners will always rise.

It can therefore be concluded that the Stolper-Samuelson theorem does not apply to the specific factor model.

The quantity of production factors is altered

What happens if the quantity of the production factors G, H or L is increased? For example, it is assumed that the quantity of capital of type H is increased. H is the specific capital which is used in the production of good b. The sector-specific capital in sector a, capital type G, and L are unchanged compared with the initial situation. The effects of this are illustrated in Figure 7.2, which is constructed in the same way as Figure 7.1. In Figure 7.2 the transformation curve TT, the curves f_a and f_b and the line LL are the same as in Figure 7.1.

In Quadrant II the amount of capital is increased. This means that there is a new relation between the input of L_b and X_b which is re-ferred to as f^*_b. The curve f^*_b is higher than f_b, because with a given input of L_b it is possible to produce greater X_b due to the increase in the capital stock.

On the basis of the unchanged production conditions for good a (Quadrant IV) and of the changed production conditions for good b (Quadrant II) and an unchanged labour force (Quadrant III), it is possible to derive a new transformation curve T*T in the same way as the transformation curve in Figure 7.1 is derived.

On transformation curve TT there is a point Q at which the relative final good prices are equal to the numerical value of the slope of the tangent P. If the relative final good prices in the initial situation also apply after there has been an increase in G, there will be a production point $Q^\star$ on the new transformation curve $T^\star T$. Corresponding to $Q^\star$ there are the production points $Q^\star_a$ in Quadrant IV and $Q^\star_b$ in Quadrant II. In the production of good a the marginal productivity of labour increases as one moves from Q_a to $Q^\star_a$.

Figure 7.2: The quantity of capital in one sector is increased

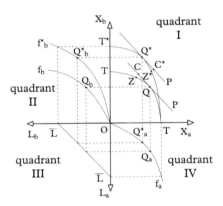

The same applies if one moves from Q_b to $Q^\star_b$ in Quadrant II, since the slope of the tangent at $Q^\star_b$ is greater than the slope of the tangent at Q_b. This can be seen by looking at Figure 6.16 in Chapter 6. When the production function is homogeneous of the first order, the straight line OAB in Figure 6.16 will intersect $\overline{L}_1$ and $\overline{L}_2$ at the two points A and B where the slope of the tangents is the same. This means that the slope of the tangent on curve $\overline{L}_2$ on the section which lies between OB is greater than the slope of the tangent at A. If this is transferred to Quadrant II in Figure 7.2 it is clear that the marginal productivity of labour at $Q^\star_b$ is greater than at Q_b.

Therefore, moving the production point from Q to $Q^\star$ in Quadrant I means that:

$$\text{both} \quad f'_a = \frac{W}{P_a} \quad \text{and} \quad f'_b = \frac{W}{P_b} \quad \text{increase} \qquad (7.3)$$

As the final good prices P_a and P_b are unchanged, this means that the nominal wages increase. At the same time it can be stated that the real wages increase regardless of the consumption combinations of the two final goods by the wage earners.

As the real wage rate increases in both production sectors this means that:

$$\text{both} \quad \frac{r_G}{P_a} \quad \text{and} \quad \frac{r_H}{P_b} \quad \text{fall} \tag{7.4}$$

An increase in the sector-specific capital H means that the real return on capital falls in both production sectors.

If an analysis is made in which H and L are constant, while the sector-specific capital G in the production of good a is increased, the result will be the same.

Figure 7.2 can also be used to analyse the effects of an increase in the work force L. In Figure 7.2 this means that f_a and f_b are fixed and that the straight line $\overline{LL}$ moves to the left in Quadrant III. It is now possible to derive a new transformation curve which is further out in the co-ordinates system than TT at all points. It should be possible for the reader to derive the new transformation curve.

If it is again assumed that the relative final good prices were the same in the two situations with the different labour forces, it is possible to analyse the effect of increased labour on factor returns. It will be seen that an increase in the labour force will give lower real return on labour and a higher return on both of the two sector specific capital factors.

In the foregoing analysis it is the absolute factor return, when there is a movement from Q to Q*, which is derived, cf. the expressions (7.3) and (7.4). When the absolute factor prices are known it is possible to calculate the relative factor prices.

If sector a is considered, it is possible to calculate the relationship between the return on capital G and wages at points Q_a and Q^*_a respectively in Quadrant IV. The outcome is:

$$\left(\frac{r_G/P_a}{w/P_a} \right)_{Q_a} > \left(\frac{r_G/P_a}{w/P_a} \right)_{Q^*_a} \tag{7.5}$$

which follows from the fact that, in moving from Q_a to Q^*_a the numerator falls and the denominator rises, cf. expression (7.3) and (7.4).

In sector b it possible to make a corresponding calculation of the relationship between the return on capital H and wages when moving from Q_b to Q^*_b in Quadrant II. The outcome is:

$$\left(\frac{r_H/P_b}{w/P_b}\right)_{Q_b} > \left(\frac{r_H/P_b}{w/P_b}\right)_{Q_b^*}.$$

It can therefore be stated that in moving from Q to Q⋆ in Figure 7.2, the return on capital will fall in relation to wages. This applies to both types of capital. This is a result which is of interest for the next section.

7.2 The specific factor model in two countries

Above, the specific factor model has been analysed for a single country. Now, there are two countries, A and B, in each of which the capital is sector specific. In both countries there are three production factors: L, which is labour, and G and H which are the sector-specific types of capital used in the production of goods a and b respectively. The two countries A and B have a factor endowment for which the following applies:

$$L_A = L_B$$
$$K_A < K_B$$
$$K_A = G_A + H_A$$
$$K_B = G_B + H_B$$
$$G_A = G_B$$
$$H_A < H_B$$

The two countries have identical factor endowment, except that country B has a greater H, in other words a greater capital stock in sector b. Therefore, country B has a greater total capital stock than country A.

The relationship between country A and country B can be described using Figure 7.2. The production function for good a in Quadrant IV is the same for the two countries, because the amount of G is the same. The labour force in the two countries is the same, so that the line LL in Quadrant III applies in both countries. In Quadrant II f^*_b is the production function for good b in country B, and f_b is the production function for the same good in country A. Country B has more than country A of capital H, which is specifically for the production of good b. Therefore TT can be understood as the transformation curve for country A and T⋆T as the transformation curve for country B.

In a situation of self-sufficiency country A and country B produce at point Z and point Z⋆ respectively. Following the introduction of trade country A produces at point Q and consumes at point C and country B produces at point Q⋆ and consumes at point C⋆. When this is the case, the opening up of trade between the two countries will lead to country A exporting good a and country B exporting good b. It is natural for country B to export good b because country B has more capital H which is used in this sector.

However, the pattern of trade need not coincide with the result arrived at by factor proportion theory. For example, if good a requires more capital intensive production than good b, then country A will export the capital intensive good in spite of the fact that country A has relatively less total capital than country B. This is contrary to the result found by using factor proportion theory.

The theorem of factor price equalisation is part of factor proportion theory. If the capital is sector-specific, the theorem does not apply. In the previous section expressions (7.5) and (7.6) were derived. Points Q_a and Q_b in Figure 7.2 correspond to the equilibrium situation for country A after the introduction of trade, and points $Q^\star_a$ and $Q^\star_b$ correspond to the equilibrium situation for country B after the introduction of trade. The expressions (7.5) and (7.6) can therefore be written as:

$$\left(\frac{r_G}{w}\right)_A > \left(\frac{r_G}{w}\right)_B \quad \text{and} \quad \left(\frac{r_H}{w}\right)_A > \left(\frac{r_H}{w}\right)_B$$

which shows that there will not be the same relative factor prices in the two countries after trade when the specific factor model applies.

This shows that in the specific factor model, which is also a neo-classical model, the three theorems of factor proportion theory no longer apply. The pattern of trade can differ from what would be indicated by factor proportion theory. There is no factor price equalisation, as there would be under factor proportion theory. And it has already been shown in Section 7.1 that the Stolper-Samuelson theory does not apply.

In the specific factor model in this section the two countries are distinguished by having sector-specific capital stocks in each of the two sectors. The model can equally well be used in relation to labour as long as this concerns two different types of labour, for example highly educated labour and unskilled labour which are each used as the only labour in their given sectors.

The model in Figure 7.2 can also be used to illustrate the effects of differences in technology when there are two sector-specific capital stocks. It is possible to imagine that the quantity of labour and the quantity of capital in the two sectors are the same in the two countries. The only difference is that capital H in sector b is more effective in country B than in country A because the technological level of the production of good b is higher in country B than in country A. This can explain why $f^{\star}_{b}$ is higher than f_{b} in Figure 7.2.

7.3 A specific factor model in two countries with the same total capital

In the previous section country A had a smaller total capital stock than country B. It is now assumed that the total amounts of capital in country A and in country B are the same. Capital G and H are still sector-specific, and the composition of the capital in the two countries differs with regard to the industrial sectors. Capital G, which is used in sector a, is greater in country A than in country B. On the other hand, country B has more of capital H which is used in production in sector b. There are now the following relations between the factor endowments in countries A and B:

$$L_A = L_B$$
$$K_A = K_B$$
$$K_A = G_A + H_A$$
$$K_B = G_B + H_B$$
$$G_A > G_B$$
$$H_A < H_B$$

By using a figure corresponding to Figure 7.2 it is possible to derive the transformation curves for the two countries. There will be two transformation curves as shown in Figure 7.3. $T_A T_A$ is the transformation curve for country A, which has more of capital G which is used in the production of good a. $T_B T_B$ is the transformation curve for country B, which has more of capital H which is used on the production of good b. This explains the shape of the transformation curves.

If countries A and B only produce good a, the production of good a
will be greater in country A than in country B. Conversely, country B
could produce more of good b than country A if both countries only
produced this good.

Figure 7.3: Transformation curves where $K = G + H$ *is the same in the two
countries*

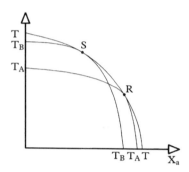

Even if the two countries have the same labour force L and the same
capital stock K, the transformation curves will be different. This is
because the capital is not mobile between the two sectors. If it is now
assumed that capital is fully mobile between sectors, which is the
assumption in factor proportion theory, there will be transformation
curve TT. The two transformation curves without capital mobility will
each be equal to the transformation curve with full capital mobility at
one point. This occurs at points R and S. With relative final good
prices corresponding to the slope of the tangents at R and S, the factor
specific model will give the same production of the two goods in each
of the two countries, which is what will happen if there is full factor
mobility.

It is reasonable to assume that capital is immobile in the medium
term but mobile in the long term. In the medium term the transformation curves $T_A T_A$ and $T_B T_B$ apply in countries A and B respectively.
However, in the long term TT applies in both countries. This applies
when there is a given total capital stock. However, if this is seen dy-
namically, which means that the capital stock is increasing over time,
it can be expected that the capital accumulation will be stronger in the
sector in which the return on capital is greater. If the return on capital
in each of the countries is relatively greater in the sector in which they
have smaller sector-specific capital, the development will be towards

a uniform capital stock in each of the sectors in each of the countries. However, if the real return on capital is greater in the sector in which each country has the greater sector-specific capital stock, the sector-specific differences will increase.

If the conditions are as described in Figure 7.3, it will be seen that in the longer term, where the transformation curves are the same for the two countries, there will not be scope for trade, as long as the demand conditions in the two countries are also the same. This is the conclusion arrived at by factor proportion theory. In the medium term, where capital is not mobile, there will be trade because the transformation curves will be different. This is the response of the sector-specific model, again assuming that demand conditions are the same in the two countries.

7.4 The adjustment process

The specific factor model shows that the transformation curve for a given country will have a different shape, depending on whether medium terms or long term conditions are considered, cf. Figure 7.3. This can be used to analyse the adjustment process which is set in motion by a change in the economy.

In what follows a distinction will be drawn between what happens in the short term, the medium term and the long term. In the short term neither labour nor capital are mobile between the two production sectors in the country. In the medium term capital is still immobile, i.e. capital is sector-specific, but labour is mobile. In the long term capital is also mobile between the sectors. What lies behind these assumptions is that as long as there is a long term equilibrium initially, then a change to the country's economic conditions will only move the country to a new point of equilibrium in the long term. The adjustment from one long term equilibrium to another takes time.

This is a problem which does not occur under factor proportion theory. This is because the theory assumes that when the relative final good prices are changed, there will immediately be new factor prices in the labour market and capital market, because there is perfect competition in these markets. It is also assumed that labour and capital are completely mobile, in other words the production factors can immediately be moved from one sector to the other, as a response to the changes in the relative factor prices.

The adjustment process can be analysed by looking at Figure 7.4. $T_M T_M$ is the transformation curve in the medium term, and $T_L T_L$ is the transformation curve in the long term, when capital is also mobile. In the initial situation the country is at the point of long term equilibrium Q_1 where the relative prices are given by the slope of the tangent P_1. The country is self-sufficient, since the isoquant I_1 touches P_1 at point Q_1.

Figure 7.4: The adjustment process

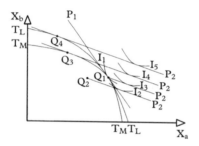

International trade is now introduced. The world market price of good b is equal to the country's domestic price for good b under conditions of self-sufficiency. However, the world market price for good a is lower than P_a under conditions of self-sufficiency. In the short term, when both labour and capital are immobile, there are two new possibilities. If there is perfect competition in each of the two labour markets linked to the two production sectors, but without mobility between the sectors in the short term, the production point will still be Q_1, and there will be consumption where I_3 touches P_2. The welfare in the country will rise because the population will now be able to import good a at a lower price than had to be paid previously under conditions of self-sufficiency.

The second possibility is that there is not perfect competition for labour in the two market sectors. For example, agreements could have been entered into in the labour market which mean that the nominal wages in both sectors are fixed. In this case there will be unemployment in sector a, in which the price of the final good falls. The production point will be Q_2, and welfare will fall because P_2 touches a lower lying indifference curve I_2.

In the medium term there will be changes. In the initial situation, where there is production at Q_1, there will be mobility in the labour market. This means that labour will move from sector a to sector b because the wages of labour at Q_1 are lower in sector a than in sector b. The new production point will be Q_3, and the new consumption point will be where the indifference curve I_4 touches P_2.

In the second situation, where Q_2 is the production point in the short term, it is assumed that the rigidities in the labour market are eliminated and that labour becomes mobile in the medium term. Therefore, in the medium term, the production point will also be Q_3.

In the long term capital will also be mobile between the sectors. This means that there will be movement from transformation curve $T_M T_M$ to $T_L T_L$. The new production point will be Q_4, and the new consumption point will be where P_2 touches the indifference curve I_5. This will be the new long term point of equilibrium.

The example shows that, in the short term, opening up to world trade can lead to a fall in welfare. However, it is not certain that this will occur. In the medium term there will be adjustments in the labour market, so there will be some gains from international trade. In the long term, in which capital also becomes mobile, the gains will be greater.

What happens in the labour and capital markets in the adjustment process is of key importance. It is therefore appropriate to look at what happens in these markets in more detail.

The assumptions should be clearly set out. There are two production functions X_a and X_b, a given labour force L, which is immobile in the short term, but mobile in the medium term, as well as a given capital stock K which is immobile in the medium term but mobile in the long term. There is therefore:

$$X_a = f_a (K_a, L_a)$$
$$X_b = f_b (K_b, L_b)$$
$$L = L_a + L_b$$
$$K = K_a + K_b$$

It is now assumed that the labour in each sector is rewarded according to the value of its marginal productivity. There is therefore:

$$w_a = P_a \cdot \frac{\partial X_a}{\partial L_a} \quad \text{and} \quad w_b = P_b \cdot \frac{\partial X_b}{\partial L_b}$$

which can be written as:

$$\frac{w_a}{P_b} = \frac{P_a}{P_b} \cdot \frac{\partial X_a}{\partial L_a} \quad \text{and} \quad \frac{w_b}{P_b} = \frac{\partial X_b}{\partial L_b}$$

The right hand sides of these expressions show the demand for labour $D(L_a)$ and $D(L_b)$ in the two sectors as a function of the real wages measured in units of commodity b.

In Figure 7.5 the demand for labour is drawn in the upper part of the figure, and a box diagram is drawn in the lower part of the figure. The segment of the line $O_A O_B$ indicates the country's total labour force. At the starting point of O_a, L_a is drawn along the horizontal axis, and the real return in sector a measured in relation to P_b is drawn along the vertical axis. At the starting point of O_b, L_b is drawn along the horizontal axis and real return in sector b is drawn along the vertical axis. Below this, in the box diagram, a contract curve has been drawn, showing the optimal factor combinations when labour and capital are fully mobile.

Q_1 in Figure 7.5 corresponds to Q_1 in Figure 7.4. In the initial situation there is long term equilibrium where there is a set of final good prices P_a and P_b. Trade is now introduced which means that P_a falls while P_b remains unchanged. This means that the demand for labour in sector a falls to the level of the dotted line in the upper part of Figure 7.5. The vertical distance between the unbroken line and the dotted line representing demand for labour is the same in percentage terms as the percentage fall in price for P_a.

In the short term there are two possibilities for adjustment. If the real return on labour falls to a level corresponding to $Q^{\star}_1$ in sector a and continue to correspond to Q_1 in sector b, the employment in the two sectors will continue to be $O_A L_{1a}$ and $O_B L_{1a}$ respectively. The absolute return on labour will be lower in sector a than in sector b. If, because of rigidities in the labour market, the wage demands for labour in sector a remain the same as in the initial situation at Q_1, then the production point in Figure 7.4 will be Q_2, which corresponds to point Q_2 in Figure 7.5. In sector a there will only be employment L_{a2}, which means that there will be unemployment equal to the difference between L_{a1} and L_{a2}.

Figure 7.5: Demand for labour and factor usage during the adjustment process

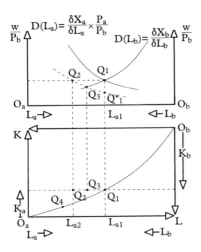

In the medium term wage rigidity and the immobility of labour will disappear, which means that point Q_3 in Figure 7.4 and Figure 7.5 is reached. In the first case it is the wage differences between the two sectors which cause the labour to move. In the second case it is unemployment which ensures wage flexibility and makes it more attractive for labour to move.

At Q_1, under conditions of self-sufficiency, the relative factor return r/w will be the same in both sectors. It will be the case that:

$$\frac{\partial X_a/\partial L_a}{\partial X_a/\partial K_a} = \left(\frac{w}{r}\right)_a \qquad (7.7)$$

$$\frac{\partial X_b/\partial L_b}{\partial X_b/\partial K_b} = \left(\frac{w}{r}\right)_b \qquad (7.8)$$

At Q_1 the relationship between the marginal productivity of the two production factors is the same. As long as there is wage flexibility so that sector b is at point Q_1 and sector a is at point Q^*_1, then (7.7) will also be equal to (7.8). On the other hand, if one moves from the short term to the medium term at Q_3, then (7.7) will be greater than (7.8). In sector a the marginal productivity of labour will increase and the marginal productivity of capital will fall. The reverse will happen in sector b. This therefore means that:

$$\left(\frac{w}{r}\right)_a > \left(\frac{w}{r}\right)_b$$

When w is the same in both sectors, $r_a < r_b$ which means that, in the long term, when capital is also mobile, capital will move from sector a to sector b. In Figure 7.5 this means that, in the longer term, there will be movement to Q_4 on the contract curve in the lower part of the figure. This point corresponds to Q_4 in Figure 7.4.

This model shows that if there is no wages flexibility and if there is not full factor mobility, then the adjustment will take place, if it takes place at all, over a longer period.

7.5 *The production of a good consist of several production processes*

It is well known that the production of a final good consists of a large number of different production steps. A number of raw materials have to be produced. These are included in the production of a number of semi-manufactured products or components which are contained in the production of the final good. In factor proportion theory all this is disregarded since the production of the two final goods is considered being brought about by means of the two primary production factors of capital and labour. The fact that production requires several steps can be illustrated by an example which contains elements which are related to the specific factor model, but which is also reminiscent of availability theory which is analysed in Section 7.6 below.

There are two countries A and B which each produce two final goods a and b. Good a is, for example, an article of clothing which requires a large amount of capital but only a little labour. However, this production requires a third factor, the raw material cotton. Good b, for example furniture, requires relatively little capital, but it does require a large amount of labour. The raw material timber is also necessary.

In country A there is a relatively large amount of capital and only a little labour compared with country B. There is only a small production of cotton, but a large production of timber, compared with country B. A simple application of factor proportion theory would lead to the conclusion that country A, which has plentiful capital, will specialise in the production of clothing, which is capital intensive. Country B which has relatively plentiful labour will specialise in the production of furniture, which is labour intensive.

What factor proportion theory does not take account of is that the production of clothing also requires the production factor of cotton and the production of furniture also requires the production factor of timber.

As long as there is no trade in the semi-manufactures, cotton and timber, the pattern of specialisation can be the opposite of what factor proportion theory would indicate.

Country A has a lot of timber and little cotton. Therefore it is possible for country A to specialise in the production of furniture, even though it is labour intensive and even though country A has relatively little labour. Country B has a lot of cotton but little timber. Therefore it is possible for country B to specialise in the production of textiles which requires a relatively high amount of capital, which country B has relatively little of.

This pattern of specialisation is primarily based on the fact that, in addition to the requirements of capital and labour, which are substitutable, the individual products each require a third production factor, namely cotton and timber, which cannot be substituted by other production factors. Secondly, this pattern of specialisation is based on the fact that there is no international trade in the semi-manufactures of cotton and timber.

If there is a possibility of trading in semi-manufactures, there will be a pattern of specialisation corresponding to that which would apply under factor proportion theory.

This is because country A will import cotton and specialise in capital intensive textile production. Country B will import timber and specialise in labour intensive furniture production.

Depending on whether there is trade in semi-manufactured goods or not, there will be different transformation curves. In Figure 7.6, curve I shows the transformation curve for country A if semi-manufactured goods are not traded internationally. The country exports good b (furniture) and imports good a (textiles). Curve II is the transformation curve when there is trade in semi-manufactures. Here the pattern of specialisation is the opposite of the situation when there is not trade in semi-manufactures.

Figure 7.6: The transformation curve is dependant on whether the inputs are traded

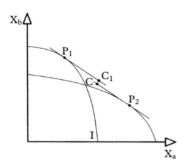

7.6 Availability theory

The content of the theory

If there is one or more production factors which are absolutely essential for a good, only the countries which have such production factors available will be able to produce the good. To grow tropical produce, for example bananas, coffee, tea, cocoa, etc., requires a special climate and particular soil conditions. If the necessary natural resources of climate and soil conditions do not exist, then it is impossible to grow the produce in question. It is equally obvious that fishing cannot be carried on without access to waters with the appropriate kinds of fish. The production of minerals is impossible unless a country has mines containing the minerals in question. The non-availability of climate and soil, fishing grounds and mines makes it impossible to produce certain kinds of agricultural products, fish products or minerals. This is a very simple statement of the concept of availability.

A more complex statement of the theory of availability can be illustrated by an example. There are k countries, k goods and k + 2 production factors. Two of the production factors, for example capital and labour, exist in all k countries and must be used in all k productions. Capital and labour can partially substitute each other. In addition to this there are k different natural resources (raw materials, for example). Each country has one, and only one, of these production factors which none of the other countries possesses. The production of each of the k goods requires a natural resource which is not used in any of the other productions. If it is now assumed that there is demand for all the k goods in all the k countries, then each country will export the good which requires the production factor (natural resource) which the country in question possesses.

Each of the k production factors are in themselves limiting productions factors in the production process. This refers to the production of raw materials where one unit of the final good requires a particular number of units of the production factor. If there are certain possibilities of substitution between the natural resource in question on the one hand, and capital and labour on the other, the possibility of substitution must be very limited if the availability theory is to apply. The technical production coefficient depends on the technology used. A decisive condition for enabling country D to export good f is that country D has availability of the limiting factor without which good f cannot be produced.

The very simple idea that a good can only be produced in a country where all the necessary production factors are present is essential for explaining trade in goods in which natural resources are part of the production process.

It is important to emphasise that natural resources are only decisive in the manufacture of unprocessed raw materials. If the raw material itself is further processed into a final good, then it is the raw material which is the production factor. The natural resource which is necessary for the production of the raw material is no longer a production factor in relation to the final good in which the raw material is included. The essential difference is that the natural resource is physically tied to a geographical locality. Raw materials that are produced by using natural resources, among other things, can in principle be trade internationally. Availability theory relates to the production factors which are physically tied to a geographical locality and which are therefore tied to the country in question. Availability theory is therefore especially relevant when transport costs for the raw materials are high.

Availability theory or factor proportion theory?

There is a question about how much of international trade can be explained by availability theory. Again, it is possible to take an example. There are four countries (A, B, C and D), two final products (food and industrial products), as well as four production factors (agricultural land, labour, capital and know-how). The first three production factors are needed in order to produce the food. The industrial product requires the last three production factors. It is now assumed that countries A, B and C have agricultural land, and countries B, C and D have know-how. All four countries have labour and capital.

In this case country A can only produce food and country D can only produce industrial products. Countries B and C can produce both agricultural and industrial products. The exports of country A and country D can be explained by using availability theory, while the remainder must be explained by using another theory of international trade.

This example can also be used to illustrate that difficulties may arise if factor proportion theory is used without taking all the production factors into account. It is now assumed that only the two production factors of capital and labour are included in the analysis. The industrial products are, for example, capital intensive and the agricultural products are labour intensive. If country A has relatively plentiful capital in relation to labour compared with country D, then the use of factor proportion theory would suggest that country A will export the capital intensive good, i.e. industrial goods, and country D will export the labour intensive good, in other words, agricultural products. As shown above, the pattern of trade will be the exact opposite of this, because the production of industrial and agricultural products require know-how and agricultural land respectively.

7.7 *How much of trade can be explained?*

Just how much of international trade can be explained by availability theory depends on the number of production factors. If a large number of production factors is taken into account, there is a greater probability that availability theory can explain trade. It is possible to imagine that capital and labour can be divided into sub-groups. On the basis that capital and labour are not homogeneous elements, it is possible to divide them into different kinds of capital and labour which will each have greater homogeneity. For example investments in machinery can be divided according to business sectors, and the machine capital can be assumed to be sector-specific. Labour can be divided between unskilled labour, skilled labour with different educational levels, and labour with specialist knowledge, such as technical knowledge, or knowledge of organisational management, marketing or design. In the example used to illustrate availability theory there was a number of natural resources. This is an idea which can be carried further.

If there are a lot of production factors, the possibility of substitution between them will be lessened. At the same time, the likelihood that one country will posses one production factor which other countries do not have is increased. Both these mean that there is an increased probability that availability theory can explain international trade.

Even if it is easier to 'explain' the pattern of international trade when dividing the production factors into several different groups, the question of how much is really explained still remains. A division into many production factors makes it natural to ask what can explain the nature and extent of the means of production which an individual country possesses. A division of 'natural' production factors into a number of natural resources whose extent and geographical location are given does not raise any great questions. However, the division of 'man-made' production functions such as capital and human know-how, can give rise to questions. What can explain why it is that a country has obtained the specific factor endowment which the country benefits from today? The more production factors that are taken into account, the more it becomes necessary to explain a country's factor endowment.

For example, if one is to explain a country's factor endowment today, it is necessary to look at the history of economic development and the forces which have shaped the country's factor endowment. Availability theory can contribute to this. Denmark has a relatively strong position in the food and drinks industry and in the production of specialised machinery for agro-industry. Norway is strongly placed with regard to the fishing industry and Sweden is strong in timber and paper products. There is no doubt that the existence of agricultural land in Denmark, fishing grounds in Norway and forestry resources in Sweden have been of historical importance to the development of this pattern of specialisation. The development of capital stock and educated labour in the business sectors in which the country has natural resources has meant that each country has built up special expertise within these areas. The natural resource base will influence the pattern of specialisation, especially at the start of industrialisation.

7.8 Summary

The specific factor model is interesting because it acknowledges that capital and labour are not homogeneous production factors which, in the short term, can be moved from one sector to another without problems. The specific factor model shows that, even though it is based in neo-classical theory, it does not produce results which accord with factor proportion theory. It is therefore possible that the conditions on which the specific factor model are based are one of the reasons why Leontief's analysis does not support factor proportion theory.

The specific factor model can also be included in a model which shows how the adjustment to new economic conditions takes time. If labour is immobile in the short term and if capital is only mobile in the long term, it will take time before the gains from international trade are realised. If the production factors are not willing to accept a lower return in the sector where production has been affected, there can be losses in the short term when international trade is introduced.

It is important to recognise that the production of a final good takes place in many vertical steps in the production process. If there is no free trade in the semi-manufactures and services which are necessary for production, there will be a new element to the explain trade.

If the production factors are divided into a large number of narrow groups to take account of the fact that capital, labour and natural resources are not homogeneous, this process can cross the boundary into availability theory. It is debatable how much this can explain. It is particularly important to explain why a given country has the given production factors at the given time which are necessary for the given productions. For such an explanation it is necessary to look into the historical factors which have determined the factor endowment which a country has developed.

Literature

Baldwin, R.E., 'Determinants of the Commodity Structure of US Trade', *American Economic Review*, March, 1971.

Jones, R.W., 'A Three-Factor Model in Theory, Trade and History' in J. Bhagwati, R.W. Jones, R. Mundell and J. Vanek (eds), *Trade, Balance of Payment and Growth*, Amsterdam, 1971.

Keesing, D.B., 'Labor Skills and Comparative Advantages', *American Economic Review*, May 1966.

Kravis, I.B., 'Availability and Other Influences on the Commodity Composition of Trade', *Journal of Political Economy*, 64, 1956.

Mussa, M., 'Tariffs and the Distribution of Income: The Importance of Factor Specificity and Substitutability and Intensity in the Short and Long Run', *Journal of Political Economy*, 82, 1974.

Sanayl, K. and R.W. Jones, 'The Theory of Trade in Middle Products', *American Economic Review*, 72, 1982.

8. Economies of scale, firm specialisation and technology

In factor proportion theory it is the differences in the relative factor endowments of countries which determine international trade. A central assumption of the theory is that there are constant returns to scale in production. Thus no account is taken of economies of scale or diseconomies of scale. It is also assumed that each firm produces one good and this is a homogeneous good. Moreover, it is also assumed that both countries use the same production technology.

This chapter will look at what happens when these assumptions no longer apply. Firstly, there will be an analysis of cases where there are economies of scale. Secondly there will be an analysis of the situations in which a firm produces more than one good, which introduces the possibility of firm specialisation. Thirdly there will be an analysis of models in which it is assumed that there are differences between countries with regard to technology and know-how.

In the literature the concepts of knowledge, information and know-how have several different meanings. It is reasonable to look at the different ways in which the concepts are used.

Firstly, the concept of information can be associated with the form of the market. If the individual decision-makers in a market, whether consumers or producers, do not know of each others' existence or of their needs or the products they offer, the market is not transparent. Here the lack of information means a lack of transparency.

Secondly, the concept of knowledge or the concept of know-how, understood as technical skills, can be related to the production function. If there is knowledge about a given number of production processes, but this knowledge is not widespread, there can be a lack of knowledge about a particular production process. Therefore the production function for an individual good can vary from country to country. If there is a dissemination of the knowledge in question, there will be a change to the production function in the country which obtains the new knowledge.

Thirdly, the concept of knowledge and the concept of know-how may be associated with the production factor of labour. If the labour forces in two countries do not have the same education, they do not possess the same knowledge or the same know-how. All things being equal, the country which has the best educated labour will have the highest productivity.

Finally, the concept of know-how can be linked to the ability to develop new products and new production methods. A high level of know-how means that a country is able to adjust its products and production processes to new conditions and to invent new products and production methods. A high level of know-how increases the ability to make economic adjustments. When the concept of know-how means the ability to produce new things, such know-how will be the result of research and development efforts.

8.1 Economies of scale at the firm level

Factor proportion theory is a theory which operates with two countries, two goods and two production factors. The goods are homogeneous goods. It is also assumed that the production function for the individual good is the same in the two countries. If these assumptions are retained but the assumption of constant returns to scale is replaced by an assumption of economies of scale, the transformation curve will be convex instead of concave.

The factor endowment in two countries is the same

If the factor endowment in two countries is the same, the transformation curve will be the same for both countries. The demand conditions in the two countries are also the same, which means that the indifference curves are the same.

These conditions are described in Figure 8.1. In the initial situation the two countries are at point S. When trade is introduced, one country will specialise in the production of good a and the other in the production of good b. The theory does not say anything about which good the individual country will specialise in. Consumption in the country which specialises in good a is shown at point U, and T is the consumption point for the country which specialises in good b.

Even though the factor proportions are the same in the two countries, there will be trade. It is not possible to predict the pattern of specialisation. If the international terms of trade are as shown in Figure 8.1, both countries will gain from trade. Both countries will benefit from exploiting the benefits of economies of scale. Which country will gain most from trade depends on the shape of the transformation curve and the indifference curve as well as the pattern of specialisation, in other words it depends on the location of the production in the two countries. In Figure 8.1 it is clear that the country which specialises at production point P will obtain greater benefits from trade than the country which specialises at point Q.

Figure 8.1: The advantages from economies of scale when the factor endowment in two countries is the same

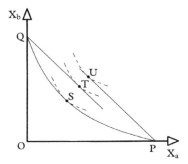

However, the international terms of trade can develop in a way which is disadvantageous for one of the countries, which can mean that the country in question can be worse off after the introduction of trade. Before trade both countries produce at point S (see Figure 8.2). The terms of trade are so much improved for good a that the country which specialises at point P gains all the advantage from trade. The other country's consumption point moves from S to T, which means that the country is worse off.

As long as the advantages from economies of scale are internal economies of scale within firms it is not possible to have perfect competition. Before the introduction of trade there are two producers in each country. After the introduction of trade there is only one producer in each country. It is assumed here that the total average costs continue to fall with the increase in the production volume. In practice there will be economies of scale at smaller volumes of production which will be replaced by constant returns to scale with greater volumes of production. At even greater production volumes there will be diseconomies of scale.

Figure 8.2: A country can lose from trade

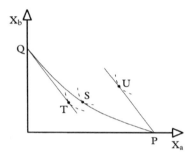

With economies of scale, the total costs C are equal to the fixed costs F and the variable costs which are equal to the marginal costs m, which are assumed to be constant, multiplied by the volume of production X

$$C = F + mX$$

If the price is equal to the marginal costs m, which would be the case with perfect competition, the turnover of the business will be mX, which means that its fixed costs are not covered. The firm will be competed out of business. If the price is to equal the total average costs C/X, there will be an incentive to increase production in one of the firms until the volume of production reaches the total of what can be sold in the market.

The assumptions of economies of scale also affect the returns on production factors. If there are constant returns to scale it is possible to use the theory of marginal productivity as the theory for factor returns. In this case the following will apply to the production function F(K,L):

$$F(K,L) = \partial F/\partial K \cdot K + \partial F/\partial L \cdot L$$

This is Euler's theorem which applies when production functions are homogeneous of the first order. This means that the production value

F corresponds precisely to the sum of the collective return on capital and labour when the production factors are rewarded according to the value of their marginal product.

On the other hand, if there are increasing returns to scale the sum of the return on the production factors will exceed the production value. The theory of marginal productivity can no longer be used as a theory of income distribution. Before a new theory of income distribution is introduced it is not possible to say anything about factor returns when there are economies of scale.

Without introducing a new and exact theory of income distribution, general assessments of the market will conclude that trade will lead to relative factor prices moving away from each other. Under conditions of self-sufficiency, i.e. at point S in Figure 8.1, the demand for the two production factors in the two countries is the same, and the same applies to output. Therefore, it is reasonable to assume that the relative factor prices in the two countries will be the same. After the introduction of trade one country will specialise in the labour intensive good and the other country will specialise in the capital intensive good. As the factor endowments are the same, it must be assumed that the relative factor prices will move away from each other in the two countries.

The factor endowments in the two countries are different

It is now assumed that there are different factor endowments in the two countries. This means that the transformation curves are no longer the same for the two countries, as in Figure 8.1.

The transformation curves in country A and country B will now differ, as shown, for example, in Figure 8.3. A_aA_b is the transformation curve for country A. B_aB_b is the transformation curve for country B. There are now two ways in which specialisation can be undertaken.

First, country A and country B can specialise in good b and good a respectively. This means that country A produces at A_b and country B produces at B_a. Alternatively, countries A and B can specialise in good a and good b respectively. This means that country A produces at A_a and country B at B_b. The model does not indicate which of the two possibilities will be the result. It is clear that the latter pattern of specialisation is to be preferred to the former. In the former case there is a risk that both countries will lose from free trade.

This illustrates that as long as there are internal economies of scale within firms, there will be trade when the demand conditions are the same in the two countries. Internal economies of scale within firms are defined as the conditions under which a uniform increase in the input of all production factors of, for example, 25 per cent gives an increase in production of more than 25 per cent.

Figure 8.3: Advantages from economies of scale for countries with different factor endowments

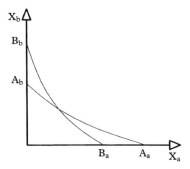

However, such a theory suffers from a serious flaw. It means that in the initial situation, where there are conditions of self-sufficiency, there is only one production unit for each category of goods. This is because when there is total adjustment, i.e. when there is simultaneous adjustment of all production factors, the average total costs will fall steadily as the volume of production increases. Therefore, before the introduction of trade all production will have been concentrated in one firm. Before the introduction of trade between the two countries there will thus be two producers of each good in the two countries. Once trade is established there will only be one firm remaining in each country.

Such a theory is meaningless. It cannot be used to explain the pattern of trade for the whole of society. If the two goods are agricultural products and industrial products it is obvious that there will be many producers in each of the two sectors, even after the commencement of trade.

The theory is so far removed from reality because the internal economies of scale within firms do not continue indefinitely. The production advantages from economies of scale will apply when expanding from small units to large units. After that, the decreasing unit costs will be will be replaced by constant unit costs, because increasing returns to scale will be replaced by constant returns to scale. If production is expanded further then decreasing returns to scale will occur.

8.2 Externalities

In contrast to internal economies of scale within firms, there can also be external economies of scale. These refer to some external advantages associated with a firm being located in an industrial environment. These advantages are called external because they are located outside the firm.

Before discussing this it is appropriate to clarify what is meant by 'externalities'. An externality can be defined as an interaction between different economic agents in a society. The fact that one or more agent initiates an activity will have an influence on conditions for the other agents. The actions of a household or a firm will influence the welfare of other households or affect the production possibilities of other firms. There can be both external economies and external diseconomies.

Examples of externalities

In the private sector there can be four different kinds of interaction between private persons and firms. The first is the interaction between individuals. It is possible that the satisfaction of the needs of one individual depends on the satisfaction of needs of others. If income distribution is very unequal there will be some who live in absolute or relative poverty. Consciousness of or being confronted by the fact that some of one's fellow citizens have a strictly limited capacity to satisfy their needs can reduce the welfare of the citizens who have high incomes. If the owner of a house in a suburb keeps his garden neat and tidy, this will satisfy a need. His neighbour, who can enjoy the garden, also receives satisfaction. Knowing that one's neighbour also derives pleasure from one's own well-kept garden can in itself increase the pleasure or welfare of the owner.

Secondly there can be the influences of firms on individuals. A cement factory emits cement dust from its chimney which leaves a layer of white powder over the neighbourhood. Muck-spreading by farmers affects the air quality of neighbours. A firm which takes un- skilled workers into its work-force and teaches them new skills is helping to create new opportunities for the labour. In brief, a firm can have positive or negative effects on its neighbours through its business activities.

Thirdly, there can be effects the other way round, by individuals on firms. For example an individual can invent something which can be used with advantage by one or more firms.

This can be some new knowledge which can be the basis of new and improved production methods, or it can be new knowledge which leads to the development of a new product.

Fourthly, there can be interaction between firms. A firm's produc- tion and conditions of production depend not only on the firm itself, but are also dependant on other firms. There are three textile firms. Two of the textile firms expand their production. There is thus the basis for greater sales of textile machinery which is produced by the textile machinery manufacturer. This manufacturer can now benefit from the advantages of large-scale production, which means that the price for textile machines falls, including for the third textile manufac- turer even though it has not increased its sales. If the two textile man- ufactures become bigger, there may be new possibilities for the busi- ness sector to initiate research to develop new products or new pro- duction processes which may be to the advantage of all textile manu- facturers.

Relations between firms are often called 'linkages'. Growth in primary agriculture leads to increased production of inputs to primary agriculture. This is an example of backward linkage. Increase in pri- mary agricultural production will lead to growth in the processing sector, such as abattoirs and dairies. This is forward linkage. Finally, increased production in primary agriculture will lead to demand for industrial consumer goods. This is called income linkage.

The four forms of interaction referred to above occur in the private sector. In addition to these there is interaction between the public sector and the private sector. The services of the public sector can be considered as externalities from the point of view of the private sector.

Externalities can be divided into two types, being those whose effect is felt through the market, and those whose effect is not felt through the market. A couple of examples can illustrate the difference.

In an area with relatively little rain there is cultivation of wheat, and there is a given return depending on the input of production factors. If trees are planted in this area, with a view to developing forestry, the forest will contribute to a more rainy climate which will increase wheat production even if the factor inputs of the wheat producers is unchanged. Forestry creates external advantages. A firm which generates environmental problems through its production causes external disadvantages.

What characterises these examples is that there is no market which deals in these conditions. In these circumstances the private economic advantages and the social economic advantages are not the same, just as there are differences between the private and social economic costs.

If a firm can exploit internal advantages of large-scale production in producing capital goods or semi-manufactured goods, the purchasers of these goods will benefit from the advantages of large-scale production through lower prices. This is the example of the manufacturer of textile machinery given above. If a firm is established there will be increased employment generating income. In other words new purchasing power will be generated, leading to increased demand for other products. The establishment of a new firm gives new sales opportunities for other firms. These two examples are illustrations of external advantages which operate through the mechanism of the market.

Even if there is a market mechanism in the area where externalities apply, there will not necessarily be equality between the private economic and the social economic advantages and disadvantages. In the labour market there will be labour with different skills, and these differences in skills will often, though not always, be reflected in the wage structure. There can be problems relating to the training of labour in the workplace. Training of labour can be considered as a private economic investment by the firm. If the training costs of the firm are not reflected in the wages structure of the firm, either by the wages being low during the training period, or by labour agreeing to stay in the firm for a certain period after the end of training, there can be problems. If during the period of training the firm pays a relatively high wage which does not take account of the training costs, and if the newly trained labour leaves the firm immediately on completion of training for better paid jobs in other firms, then the firm has a private economic cost. Society has not only had a cost but also a gain because it has obtained a better labour force through the training costs.

In such a situation there is a risk that private firms will not invest as much in training as would be desirable from a social economic point of view. In such a case it can be reasonable to consider whether the public authorities should not provide support for firms to ensure that the necessary training programmes are put in place.

External advantages of large-scale production

Establishing an industrial environment for a given industry can be considered as an external advantage of large-scale production. Instead of spreading activities over a broader range of industries it can be an advantage to concentrate on fewer industries. By undertaking industrial specialisation there will be greater chances for developing new specialised capital goods, and for developing the necessary specially skilled labour, as well as specialised service providers.

This idea can be illustrated by starting with Adam Smith's theory on the dynamic effects of increased division of labour, cf. Chapter 5, Section 5.2. Adam Smith believed that the size of the market, combined with capital accumulation, was decisive for the extent of the division of labour, which in turn determined labour productivity. Technological development would be promoted through the division of labour.

This means that the transformation curve will be a convex curve, not a straight line, when the situation is looked at from a dynamic perspective, see Figure 8.4. The straight line AA is the transformation curve in the short term, from a static point of view. If a single country specialises, there will be a divisions of labour which will increase productivity. For example, sector a could be an agri-industrial complex based on biological research and know-how, and sector b could be an electronics industry complex, based on special know-how of electronic circuits. There may also be other industrial complexes such as a pharmaceutical industry complex or an information technology complex.

For each producer of final goods within a given complex it is assumed that there are constant returns to scale. It is by achieving external advantages that there are advantages of large-scale production for a given complex. The decisive factors are the better inputs in the form of specially trained labour, specialised machines, specialised semi-manufactured goods and specialised services as well as better technology through research and development. Individual firms have constant returns to scale, but the sector as a whole has increasing returns. This means that in the longer term the transformation curve will be BB in Figure 8.4.

Figure 8.4: Sectoral advantages of large-scale production based on external advantages

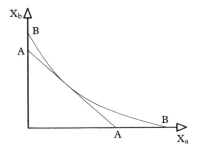

8.3 Firm specialisation

Section 8.1 discussed the traditional advantages from economies of scale at the firm level. It was shown that it is meaningless to use such a theory on economies of scale when the products are homogeneous.

The advantages of firm specialisation

The question now is whether a theory of economies of scale is relevant when there are differentiated products. It is important to distinguish between the traditional advantages of from economies of scale when producing a single product and the advantages of firm specialisation. Firm specialisation refers to the situation where initially a firm produces several product types within a product category. When the firm reduces its product range it will achieve a number of cost savings. This is what is understood by firm specialisation.

The advantage of economies of scale refers to the fact that an increase in a firm's size, measured in the amount of capital and labour, gives lower unit costs. With firm specialisation, with constant inputs of capital and labour, the cost savings are achieved by limiting the product range of the individual firm. By specialising in fewer product types it is possible to have longer production runs. It is possible to obtain special machines, labour can reach higher levels of expertise, and it is possible to improve the organisation of the work. It is also possible to reduce the stocks of finished goods, raw materials and semi-manufactured goods.

In Figure 8.5 the unit costs are plotted against the vertical axis and the production volume is plotted against the horizontal axis. Curve III shows the unit costs for a firm which produces three product types, for example. Curve I shows the unit costs for a firm which has specialised in the production of one product type. If the pattern of the costs is the same for two other firms, which each produce one of the two other product types, it is possible to get a picture of the costs for all three firms together by making a horizontal addition of the unit costs of the three firms, which is curve II. At every cost level curve II is three times further out in the co-ordinates system than curve I. Curve II and curve III intersect each other. To the left of the point of intersection it is best to produce all three product types in one firm. This is because with a small volume of production the traditional benefits from economies of scale are stronger than the benefits of specialisation. However, when production is at higher volumes the advantages of economies of scale will not be as significant as the advantages of specialisation.

Figure 8.5: Unit costs with and without product specialisation

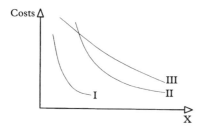

If the firms each produce at a level where the traditional advantages of economies of scale are exhausted, it will be possible to construct two transformation curves with two sectors in one of which firm specialisation has taken place in both sectors, and the other of which it has not taken place. In Figure 8.6 A_1B_1 is the transformation curve where there has not been firm specialisation. Curve A_2B_2 shows the situation for each of the sectors in which there has been firm specialisation.

An example can illustrate the difference between a situation where there has been firm specialisation and one where there has not. For example within the EU each country has a firm which produces 15 product types before trade was liberalised. After the liberalisation of trade, in each country this firm will only produce one product type, and the 14 other product types will be imported from the other countries. Each firm will be the same size, measured by capital and labour, before and after liberalisation. The difference is that after liberalisation there is product specialisation. This is not a randomly chosen example. As we shall see in the next chapter, it is a characteristic of the liberalisation of international trade that product specialisation takes place.

Figure 8.6: Transformation curves with or without firm specialisation

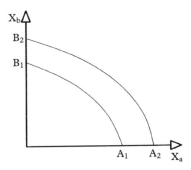

If one considers Figure 8.5 it will be seen that, when there is product specialisation, it is not necessary for there to be a very high level of production before the advantages of large-scale production are exhausted.

Even though there may be exceptions, experience shows that production advantages increase when moving from a small production volume to a larger volume. Then the unit costs remain constant, before increasing with increased production. This expansion of production can give higher costs because there are administrative disadvantages when a firm is already big.

In other words, what appear to be production advantages for big firms are in fact often advantages which can be obtained by smaller firms specialising.

With firm specialisation there is a specialisation within a single industry. If the result is that each country specialises in certain product types within an industry, then it will be possible for each country to export and import goods belonging to the same sector of industry. This is called intra-industry trade as opposed to inter-industry trade where goods from different industries are imported and exported. This is discussed in more detail in Chapters 9 and 11.

The advantages for a firm with several business units

Even though limits to the advantages of large-scale production are usually reached quite quickly, there can well be advantages in having a firm or company which consists of several manufacturing units. There can be advantages for a multi-unit firm with sales, financing, and organisation as well as research and development.

On the *sales side* there can be advantages in market research, in advertising and with distribution. If there are 10 units in one firm rather than 10 independent firms, then the fixed sales costs can be set-off against larger sales with one firm. It is possible to establish common concepts in market research which the firm undertakes, instead of each manufacturing unit going to marketing consultants where the overall costs will be greater. It is possible to advertise nationally or in several countries at less cost, by television for example, with a view to establishing the company's name and brands in the consumers' awareness. It also makes for more rational distribution.

On the *financing* side there is a greater chance that the concern can be self-financing, and if borrowing is necessary it is likely that larger concerns will find it easier to obtain loans and to obtain them on more favourable terms.

In terms of *organisation* there can also be advantages. It is usual to talk of the administrative disadvantages of large-scale production. It is possible to avoid these if there is clear responsibility at the level of the business unit. In respect of its results, each business unit should be considered as an independent unit whose management is responsible for decisions, within the framework of a common management philosophy. Within the concern it is also easier and cheaper to set up personnel development programmes.

Finally the formation of a group of manufacturing units will have advantages with regard to *research and development*, compared with the situation where a number of independent firms are not able, together, to initiate a co-ordinated investment in research and development. The greatest advantage is in the elimination of risk. If 10 firms must choose individually whether to initiate research where the chances of success are 10 per cent, then research activity will be less than if the 10 manufacturing units belonged to the same concern. If the firms are independent only one of them will be successful, while the other 9 will get no return on their research investment. If the 10 manufacturing units are part of one concern, there is certainty that one research project will be successful. The investment in research will not be wasted because the project will be successful. Up to a certain level there are also advantages of large-scale production in research. If the 10 firms are unable to achieve an optimal research unit individually, then research co-operation will be an advantage.

In connection with research and development, the alternative to forming a large concern is for firms to co-operate on research and development. The size of the private economic advantages will also depend to a great degree on what research and development initiatives are taken at industry level, and what initiatives are taken by the public sector. The better the industrial environment is, for research and development, for example by public research and development institutions which co-operate with private firms, the less important it is for the individual firm to be big in order to obtain advantages from research and development. The advantages from economies of scale are external rather than internal for the firm.

8.4 The theory of the technology gap

Factor proportion theory assumes that there is a given production technology which is evident in the appearance of the production function. This technology is given and is available in all countries since it is assumed that the production function is the same everywhere. It is also assumed that the final good has a given form which is not changed.

This view of the world has been rejected by the theory of the technology gap and the theory of the product life cycle. Both theories are based on the idea that final goods as well as production processes change character over time. The core of the theory of the technology gap is that there are temporary differences in a country's know-how about of production technology in a given product sector. At any given point in time there are differences between countries with regard to technology. One or more country has a monopoly in the production of new products and/or in new production methods. It is this monopoly of know-how which affects trade. In time this monopoly comes to an end for the given good because other countries also become able to produce the good in question. However, there is a basis for a technologically advanced country to start the production of a new good. The theory is based on two important assumptions.

Firstly, it is no accident that technological innovations primarily take place in certain countries. Inventions and the production of these inventions take place in countries with high incomes which are technologically advanced.

Secondly, there is not immediate and universal knowledge about the existence of the new products and the new production technology. Demand for a new product comes initially from consumers in the country where the product is introduced, and later from consumers in other countries. As a rule it takes a longer time for other countries to gain knowledge of the new production technology which is necessary for producing the new good.

New goods and new production technology are developed in countries with high incomes

The good is introduced in a country, after which the production expands rapidly, before there is stagnation or a fall in production, cf. Figure 8.7.

When discussing the production of entirely novel products it is reasonable to distinguish between 'invention' and 'innovation'. This distinction comes from J.A. Schumpeter (1934) whose work forms the basis for the theories on the importance of innovation. In order to produce a new product there must be both invention and innovation. An invention is the new scientific knowledge which is necessary before it is possible to think about producing a new product, but which is not in itself enough to make a saleable product. For this, innovation is required; this is the newly developed know-how which makes it possible to turn an invention into a saleable product. While inventions are typically made in research institutes, innovations often take place in firms or in firms in co-operation with public institutions. The invention precedes the innovation. Frequently knowledge about the invention will have been disseminated to many countries some time previously, through scientific journals, scientific symposiums etc., before the innovation takes place.

Therefore, innovations will primarily take pace in countries with the highest per capita income. Three things are relevant here. The potential demand will be in countries with high incomes. Innovation take place in high income countries. Production, likewise, takes place in high income countries.

Firstly, it is in countries with high incomes that there is pressure to find new products. This applies both to consumer goods and to production methods. It is at the highest income levels that the desire for new and better consumer goods is first noticed, and it is in countries with high wages that there is a particular interest in replacing expensive labour with labour saving capital goods.

Secondly, the innovations take place in the countries where the needs for new products and new product technology occur first. Even if the desire for new products arises in the richest countries, there is no necessity for innovations to take place there. It is possible for innovations to take place in countries other than those where the desire for them is felt most strongly. However, there is something else which plays a role. Information about consumer wants will first occur in the firms which have the best knowledge of the market, in other words in firms which are located in the market. In factor proportion theory there is an assumption that there is full information. However, there is not full information about needs and sales potential in all the different markets within an individual firm. A firm's knowledge of the market depends on communication with the market in question. The possibilities of communication are also dependent on geographical proximity. The greater the distance, the more difficult and expensive it is to learn about the market.

The search for information must be considered as part of the decision-making process, so the obstacles to obtaining such information limit the geographical horizons of the firm and thus restrict the scope for activities available to the firm. From this it follows that producers are more aware of the possibilities for introducing new products on their home markets. Since the demand for new products and awareness of this demand will be greatest in the countries with high incomes, it is natural to assume that innovation of new products will take place in these countries.

Thirdly, the production starts in the countries where the needs occur first and where innovations take place. Even if innovation takes place in one country, it is not impossible for production of the good to take place in another country with lower production costs. It is reasonable to suppose that the large number of multinational companies which have production facilities in several countries contribute to such a practice. It is here that the third assumption comes into the picture. In the highly developed countries, where the demand first occurs, there will be specially advantageous conditions for producing the good. This is because of the relationship between demand and production conditions in the introductory phase, cf. the product life cycle below.

Trade is determined by the extent of the technology gap

At the point in time t_0 there is an innovation of a product in country A, see Figure 8.7. The whole of the production is sold domestically until t_1. At that point, information about the new product has spread to country B.

It is reasonable to assume that other highly developed industrial countries will be the first to obtain information about the new product. After that will come the industrial countries with a lower income level, and following that the less developed countries.

Figure 8.7: The theory of the technology gap

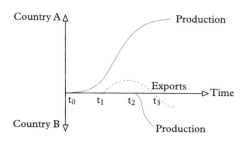

The period $t_1 - t_0$ in Figure 8.7 shows the demand lag. The length of this delay will vary, depending on the country concerned, as discussed above. When the demand lag has passed there will be the basis for export. Export to country B will start at t_1.

With the passage of time the technological knowledge will spread to other countries so that these countries will now be able to produce the product in question. In the case of country B this takes place at t_2. The period t_2 to t_0 expresses the production lag.

There are reasons for assuming that the length of the production lag depends on the development level of a country. The production lag will be shorter for highly developed industrial countries, longer for less wealthy industrial countries, and even longer for less developed countries. The length of the production lag for less developed countries depends on the country's technological state of development, whether it is a Newly Industrialised Country or one of the poorer less developed countries.

Country A's exports to country B, i.e. the exports in the period from t_1 to t_3, are conditioned by country A's advantages in production. The theory of the technology gap puts country A's exports in relation to the technological advantages which country A has in relation to country B. The period $t_2 - t_1$ is used as a measure of these advantages, in other words the difference between the demand lag and the production lag. The longer the period $t_2 - t_1$ is, the greater is country A's technological advantage, and the greater will be country A's exports.

The extent of the technology gap which is expressed by the length of the period $t_2 - t_1$, depends partly on the conditions in country B and partly on the conditions for the production of the good. If country B is a highly developed industrial country which can relatively easily acquire the knowledge necessary for the production of the good, then production of the good will start much earlier than if country B is a less developed country. Besides this, the conditions for producing the good can mean that it is not always easy to achieve competitiveness of the good in country B. For example, the advantages of large-scale production can play a role. If there are considerable advantages of large-scale production connected with the good, this will contribute to reinforcing the technological advance of country A.

When country A's technological advantages have been reduced it can be advantageous to start production in country B. There can be several reasons for this. In country A there can be innovation of new products. There is a focus of interest on these new products. After country B comes into possession of the necessary knowledge, it can be advantageous to transfer production to country B because it will be closer to the then market, and because of simple cost advantages, for example because of cheaper labour.

When country B can start production of the good, country A's exports may not necessarily fall immediately but they will in the longer term. It is also possible that country A's technological advance will be reduced to such an extent that the lower wage costs in country B make it possible to start exporting from country B to country A. This is referred to as low wage cost exports which replace the previous contrary tendency of technologically determined exports. The scope for low wage cost exports from country B will be limited if technological developments are rapid. In the meantime new products will have been developed in country A, which reduces the demand for the old products. If country A retains its technological advance in the relevant product area this will limit country B's low wage cost exports.

If country B exports to a less developed country, these exports will be based on the technology gap. Even though there may be a certain demand for the good in less developed countries, it will take a relatively long time before it reaches any considerable extent. Since it is also difficult to transfer know-how to less developed countries, this is why it takes a relatively long time before production starts in these countries.

The theory of the technology gap ranks countries according to their technological level, in turn this is often related to the country's per capita GNP. The richest countries innovate new products. This monopoly of production is broken down over time. Other countries start production, which means that exports from the innovating country eventually come to an end. If the technology gap is retained, the richest country will develop new products which can then be exported.

Firstly, the theory of the technology gap emphasises the differences in technology between countries. Secondly, it makes allowance for the decisive influence of the time factor. The country which is first to innovate has an advantage by virtue of the fact that it is the first country to produce the good.

8.5 The theory of the product cycle

The theory of the product cycle combines several different elements. The theory combines the principle of the technological gap with differences in factor endowments and the possibility of making foreign direct investment.

Firstly, the theory of the product cycle is based on the idea that a good passes through a certain 'life cycle'. The good is innovated. It then goes through a period of growth before arriving at the stage of stagnation. This process is also encountered in the theory of the technological gap, cf. Figure 8.7 in the preceding section.

Secondly, the theory of the product cycle is based on the fact that the location of production changes while the good goes through its various phases. This is linked to the fact that the production process changes character in its different phases and that countries have different factor endowments. The idea that the production process changes its character conflicts with factor proportion theory. However, the idea that countries have differing factor endowments is in line with factor proportion theory.

Thirdly, the theory of the product cycle is based on the fact that production factors can move across national boundaries. This applies in particular to capital. This movement occurs in the form of foreign direct investment.

In Figure 8.8 the central ideas behind the theory of the product cycle are shown in a three-dimensional diagram. Along one axis are the countries A, B and C, the second axis measures the passage of time, and on the vertical axis production and consumption of the good in question is plotted.

A new product is developed in country A. To start with the production is sold domestically. Later there is demand for the good in country B, which imports it from country A. At a later point, demand arises for the good in country C, which also starts to import the good.

Figure 8.8: The theory of the product cycle

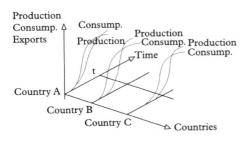

In all countries the good passes through a cycle of growth. In the introductory phase demand increase only a little. This is followed by a growth phase, when there is a strong growth in demand. Finally the stagnation phase is reached, when consumption either stagnates or falls, because new goods are introduced which replace the product.

When trade is initiated country A is the exporter of the good, but its exports decline gradually over time. This is because, in time, the production of the good is moved first to country B and later to country C.

In what follows, the answers to three questions are discussed. What explains the course of production and consumption? What explains the changing location of production? What role is played by direct investment?

The cycle of growth

The fact that a good passes through different phases in its life is known from marketing theory, in which, after the introductory phase, new goods are first sold at an increasing rate and then at a decreasing rate.

Depending on the good concerned, the sales can continue to grow in line with the growth of the number of consumers, and can then hit a ceiling or sales can actually fall if, in the case of consumer durables, there are not enough replacement sales. Finally, in the longer term, production can decline due to the innovation of substitution goods.

The growth curve in Figure 8.8 can be explained not only by demand conditions but also by production conditions. In practice, there will often be some interaction between them. Different mechanisms can apply to both the demand side and the production side.

On the demand side a cause of the growth cycle can be market imperfections in the form of a lack of information about the good. The good is innovated and few people know about it. Awareness of the good spreads gradually and demand grows with it. Awareness about the good first spreads domestically and then it spreads abroad.

Even if there is full information about a product, changes in income elasticity can affect the growth cycle. To start with the country is at an income level which gives low income elasticity. Later a growing level of income will mean that income elasticity will increase. When the market is saturated, then income elasticity will fall again. The fact that exports start later, despite full awareness of the product, can also be due to the fact that the level of income abroad is initially lower. Therefore the income level must rise before there is greater demand for the good.

There will also be a pattern of development on the production side. If there is innovation of a product, the final stage of production technique will not have been developed. Gradually, as the production technique is refined, the price of the final good may be expected to fall. Even if the production technique is given, then the advantages of large-scale production can play a role. The increased use of large-scale production will lead to lower prices and increased sales opportunities.

When operating with growth curves it is necessary to be aware that the shape of the curve will be affected by both demand and production conditions. Different factors on both the demand and the production side are capable of influencing the course of growth.

The location of production

The theory of the product cycle acknowledges the decisive importance of the fact that demand conditions, production conditions and competitive situations are different in the different phases of a product's life. Since the factor endowments of countries differ, different groups of countries will produce the good, according to the phase which the product is in.

In what follows, the growth cycle of the product is assumed to be divided into three phases: introduction, growth and stagnation. What characteristics are associated with each phase? The following description is summarised in Table 8.1.

The introductory phase

In the introductory phase the demand conditions are characterised by uncertainty. It is not yet possible to know how the final good will be in the longer term. It is therefore important to have close contact with the market so that consumer preferences can be noted and can influence the changes to the form of the product which are made over time.

The price elasticity for the new good will be small. The relatively few customers for the good will have a strong desire for it and will therefore be willing to pay a high price. When there is small price elasticity there is weak price competition, which in turn means that the traditional cost considerations do not play a significant role in setting the price. Competition between firms in the market is concentrated on finding the product variant which best meets the wants of purchasers.

There is also uncertainty on the production side. When no one knows how the final good will be in the longer term, it is impossible to know how the production process will develop, or which raw materials or other inputs will be used.

The production possibilities depend on which production factors are decisive. Several production factors are included in the product cycle theory, and it is reasonable to reckon with four types of factors. Apart from the factor of capital there is the factor of labour which can be divided into three type: technical skills, management skills and unskilled labour.

The existence of external advantages in the form of an industrial environment is also important, i.e. whether or not there are surrounding support systems. The existence of a surrounding industrial environment, with sub-contractors and service providers, is often an important pre-condition for being able to produce.

Table 8.1: The characteristics of a good at different stages

	Introductory phase	Growth phase	Stagnation phase
Demand			
The form of the good	Uncertain	Certain	Certain
Price elasticity	Small	Large	Very large
Income elasticity	Small	Large	Very large
Production			
Production process	Uncertain	Certain	Certain
Production factors[1]:			
Capital	0	+	+
Technical know-how	+	0	–
Organisational know-how	0	+	0
Unskilled labour	–	0	+
Industrial environment	+	0	0

1) + = important   0 = not especially important   – = unimportant

In the introductory phase of a good the production factor of technical skills and the existence of an industrial environment are decisive. The technical skills are essential, not only for development of the final good, but for developing the special machines and tools which are necessary. A single firm alone cannot develop both a new product and the means of production that are required. It is important for a firm to be located in an industrial environment where it can buy the necessary support. In the introductory phase price does not play an important role and production runs are small as sales are limited. Therefore capital and unskilled labour are less important.

The conclusion is that a highly industrialised country will innovate and produce new products. The need for new products first arises in rich countries so that innovations will take place in these countries. Likewise, production will take place there since comprehensive information about the market (i.e. consumers, suppliers and competitors) is important for developing the 'right' product and the best and cheapest production technique. The existence of advanced technical skills and an industrial environment are important pre-conditions. On the other hand the price of the good, and thus of the production factors, is not significant since the demand is price inelastic. As long as there is uncertainty about the form of the good and its production, fixing the location and tying up capital will be avoided.

The growth phase

When the good enters the growth phase there is no longer uncertainty about the form of the product or the nature of the production process. In all essentials the product type and the production process are fixed. However, this does not prevent an individual producer from choosing a particular product variant which is targeted at a particular segment of the market when there are consumers with different preferences. The fact that uncertainty about the form of the product and the nature of the production process is greatly reduced means that proximity to the market is not longer of such importance. It also means that it is no longer essential for the firm to be located in an industrial environment. It also means that, once there is an established production technique, firms are willing to invest in greater capital stock.

The demand for the product increases rapidly, among other things because of the fall in price. Price elasticity increases both for the market as a whole and for the individual producer. As a result of the increased price competition, costs become more important than previously.

Production takes place on a greater scale. Because of the stronger price competition it is important to take advantage of existing advantages of large-scale production and/or specialisation. In the growth phase capital and organisational skills are decisive.

The increased production requires investment in greater capital stock. Capital is an important production factor in this phase. Organisational skills are also important in a period when the firm's production is rapidly expanding. The production factors of technical skills and an industrial environment are still necessary, but not of such overwhelming importance.

Which countries are specially well suited to produce the good in this phase? They are countries which have plenty of the required production factors. These will be industrial countries, but not necessarily countries with advanced technology. Such a country must have the possibility of supplying a large market. This may favour larger countries at the expense of the small, especially if there are important trade barriers.

The stagnation phase

In the stagnation phase the characteristics of the product and the nature of the production process are even more firmly fixed. The importance of locating the production of the good close to its markets is thus further reduced.

Demand grows relatively slowly. The slower growth, combined with the greater uniformity of the product, leads to price competition. Firms are therefore highly cost conscious. To counteract the strong price competition firms try to create preferences through marketing initiatives such as building up brands, advertising etc. The market for toothpaste is an example of this.

The production requires considerable capital because it is mechanised. On the other hand there is not a need for highly educated labour in the production process itself. There is no need for great technical know-how. The demand for management skills is also less, compared with the growth phase. Management skills are particularly necessary when a firm grows. Since the product, the production process and the necessary semi-manufactured goods are precisely defined, there is no great problem in obtaining the semi-manufactured goods needed through imports, if they are not available in the country producing the final good. Therefore a well developed industrial environment is not necessary, even if there must be a basic infrastructure in the form of transport and the provision of services. However, it is important that there should be cheap labour to maintain competitiveness.

Which countries are specially well suited to produce the good in the stagnation phase? In this phase cheap labour and cheap and plentiful capital are decisive factors. While less developed countries do not have the ability to innovate products, nor particularly good conditions for producing them in the growth phase, they should have relatively good possibilities for producing them in the stagnation phase. This is especially true if the basic infrastructure functions well.

Less developed countries have plentiful cheap labour. While they themselves have only limited capital, it can be transferred without much difficulty from industrial countries. Capital can be obtained either by a government loan abroad or through foreign direct investment. In contrast to human capital, i.e. knowledge obtained through education, physical capital is highly mobile across national boundaries.

In order to be price competitive in the stagnation phase, there must be large-scale production. The market for the product must be sufficiently big for this. Apart from the large developing countries and from the regional trade groupings, sales possibilities in less developed countries are often limited. In many cases it is only possible to reach a sufficient turnover by exporting to industrial countries. At this stage a number of trade barriers become relevant, in the form of the tariff policies of the industrial countries, quotas, non-tariff barriers and transport costs. These barriers can be quite substantial, since the less developed countries are often at some distance from the markets where the goods are sold, and there is stiff price competition. The policies of the industrial countries can therefore be a barrier which limits the ability of the less developed countries to exploit their comparative advantages.

Foreign direct investment

Finally, the third element in theory of the product cycle is foreign direct investment. Factor proportion theory's explanation of trade disregards capital movements between countries. This is a weakness of the theory since foreign investment has become increasingly important.

In the theory of the product cycle, foreign direct investment is one of the methods by which know-how is transferred from one country to another. When production is started in another country it can be done in several ways:

1. The country's own firms can produce the good on the basis of know-how which is already publicly available (after the expiry of patents) or on the basis of the results of independent research.
2. The country's firms can enter into know-how agreements, by which know-how is bought from foreign firms.
3. As already referred to, foreign firms can set up production units in the market.

Apart from the technologically more advanced developing countries, it is probably the last of these possibilities which is most often realistic for developing countries. Foreign direct investment is discussed in more detail in Chapter 14.

8.6 The applicability of the theory of the product cycle

Factor proportion theory is a strictly formalised theory in which the quantity of production factors sets the limit to how much can be produced. Factor proportion theory is a general equilibrium theory. Compared with it the theory of the product cycle may be said to be more vague. As has been shown, there are several factors which can be the driving force behind the growth process. Equally, several explanations can be given for the pattern of location of production. The limits to capacity of an economy are not included in the theory of the product cycle. The theory of the product life cycle is a partial equilibrium model.

The product cycle theory is not so concise. This is because the theory works with different assumptions from factor proportion theory. On the other hand, when considering certain industrial goods, the assumptions of the product cycle theory are more realistic than factor proportion theory. Besides this, the theory includes some elements which it is necessary to define in more detail. This applies to a) the definition of a good, b) the definition of a new product, c) the shape of the growth curve through time and the boundaries of the phases of the cycle.

The definition of a good

It is the growth path of a good which is the basis for the theory. The theory is based on the idea that the good changes its character with the passage of time. This applies both to the characteristics of the final good and to the production process. If a slightly broader concept of a category of good is to be used in the theory, one category of goods if often distinguished from another by using cross-elasticities. Large cross-elasticities are an expression of substantial possibilities for substitution. Where a product category has a jump in cross-elasticity with other products, from large to small elasticity, that is where there is the boundary between the two categories of the good. It is not possible to use such definition in the current situation. The cross-elasticity for a good in the introductory phase and for the same good in the stagnation phase is generally very little, even though it can be said that the good belongs to the same product category in the different phases.

If a very narrow definition of a good is used, for example a specific type of textile, then at a given point in time there will only be production of the good in one of the phases. In other words, a textile product being produced in all three phases is not one product but three products. If a wider definition of a good is used, for example corresponding to the traditional division of the main industries, then the same good will be produced in all phases simultaneously. As stated, a very specific kind of textile will only be produced in one phase at a time, whereas textiles in general covers so many different variants that textiles in general will produced in all phases simultaneously. There will be new fashion goods introduced in the market. There are more traditional textiles and articles of clothing, which are bought by the greater part of the public, and there will, for example, be very simple product types, such as homogeneous cotton goods.

Definition of a new product

Firstly, a product can be considered as new if technological developments mean that a new production process is used in the manufacture of a product which is a near substitute for a pre-existing product. Here the emphasis is put on the new production process.

Secondly, a new production process can lead to the production of an entirely new product which has no substitutes. The number of entirely new products is relatively limited. Examples of such products are radios, cars etc. Here the emphasis is on the entirely new product.

Thirdly, a new product may merely be a step in ordinary product development. The production process can be more or less new. The same can be said of the product. It is usual that there is an ongoing product development within a business sector. The number of new products, by this measure, is therefore large.

When applying the theory it is necessary to be aware that a new product can mean many different things.

The shape of the growth curve through time and the boundaries of the phases

Production and consumption in three different countries are drawn in Figure 8.8. The differences between the two determine imports and exports.

The trade and the distribution of production between countries which exists at point t, for example, depends on the shape of the growth curve. The curves can be tightly compressed or they can be spread over a longer period. It can be assumed that the shape of the curves will vary from good to good. Several conditions both of the good itself and of the countries will affect this.

In relation to the good, the speed with which technological progress is made can be influential. The possibilities of large-scale production or specialisation in production can also affect the curves of individual countries. For example the production curves will also be influenced by the importance to production of the existence of an industrial environment. The extent of transport costs will also play a role. With the increasing integration of the world economy it can be assumed that the curves will be more foreshortened in time than has previously been the case.

It is difficult to draw sharp limits to the individual phases of a good. As set out above in Table 8.1, there are several characteristics associated with each phase. Passing from one phase to the next does not necessarily take place at the same time for all these characteristics.

The production equipment possessed by an individual country does not necessarily mean that the production possibilities of the country are limited to the phase of the good in which the country has the strongest comparative advantage. The country's production can also be assumed to cover the other production phases to some extent.

What determines the time for changing the location of production? Is the time the same for all goods? What is the decisive factor which determines the movement of production? It is possible to hypothesise that it is the labour intensity in production which is determinant. The production of labour intensive goods should thus be moved more easily to countries with a lower technological level because of the greater importance of cheaper labour. However, it is also possible to hypothesise that it is the elimination of uncertainty about the form of the product and the nature of the production process which determines when it will be advantageous to move the product.

Evaluation

The problems which have been raised here in connection with the theory of the product life cycle are not more serious than the problems which are met with other theories. For example, there are problems in applying factor proportion theory in connection with the definition of production factors, cf. Section 6.7.

It has been argued that the theory on the product cycle and the theory of the technology gap, which was propounded in the 1960's, were more relevant then than today. Then there were clearer differences between countries' GNP per capita, especially in industrial countries. On the basis of GNP per capita the countries were ranked: USA, Northern Europe, Southern Europe, Japan, richer developing countries and poorer developing countries.

Today the differences between the USA, Western Europe and Japan are much reduced and the newly industrialised countries have caught up with the old industrial countries. The theory of the product cycle and the theory of the technology gap can perhaps help to explain this. In addition to this the growth curves are probably more compressed in time due to stronger international integration.

In any case, the dynamic analysis of the course of development which lies behind the theory of the product life cycle and the theory of the technology gap can be said to be an important method of looking at development. Different product types belonging to the same broadly defined industrial category can well be produced in countries with differing characteristics. This leads to trade, and the pattern of trade changes as the production changes character.

8.7 Summary

In this chapter some of the assumptions of factor proportion theory have been discarded. If there are economies of scale at the firm level, factor proportion theory cannot be used, as it is based on constant returns to scale. It is unrealistic to explain international trade for homogeneous goods by introducing economies of scale at the firm level. Economies of scale will lead to the unrealistic result that there will only be one producer of goods in each sector.

On the other hand it is unquestionably correct that by establishing industrial complexes in which there are many firms operating in the same business sector, it is possible to obtain a number of important external advantages for the individual firm, which means that the business sector as a whole obtains increasing returns to scale. This is of decisive importance to the location of production in business centres. This is dealt with in more detail in Chapter 15.

It is important to distinguish between economies of scale at the firm level and firm specialisation. Firm specialisation is an important explanation for the rapid growth in trade between industrial countries as is discussed in Chapter 9.

In spite of their imprecise definitions, the theory of the technology gap and the theory of the product cycle have the advantage that they look at development over time. It is realistic to assume that production technology is not the same in all countries and that the requirements for the production of textiles or electronic products, for example, depend greatly on whether these products are fashion-oriented or are high technology products when introduced, or whether they are traditional products in the growth phase or simple products which are easier to make.

Literature

References relating to economies of scale and firm specialisation:

Chacholiades, M., 'Increasing Returns and the Theory of Comparative Advantage', *Southern Economic Journal*, 37, 1970.

Helpman, E., *'Increasing Returns, Imperfect Markets and Trade Theory'*, in R.W. Jones and P.B. Kenan (eds), *Handbook of International Economics*, vol. I, Amsterdam, 1984.

Melvin, J.R., 'Increasing Returns to Scale as a Determinant of Trade', *Canadian Journal of Economics*, 2, 1969.

References relating to the theory of the technology gap and the theory of the product life cycle:

Hufbauer, G.C., *Synthetic Materials and the Theory of International Trade*, London, 1966.

Posner, M.W., 'International Trade and Technical Change', *Oxford Economic Papers*, 13, 1961.

Schumpeter, J.A., *The Theory of Economic Development*, Cambridge, Mass., 1934.

Vernon, R., 'International Investment and International Trade in the Product Cycle', *Quarterly Journal of Economics*, 80, 1966.

Vernon, R. (ed), *The Technology Factor in International Trade*, New York, 1970.

9. Demand differences

Factor proportion theory is based on the assumption that demand conditions in the two countries are the same. It is also assumed that the utility function is homothetic. Factor proportion theory also assumes that the goods are homogeneous goods. In this chapter there is a discussion of what happens when these assumptions no longer apply.

9.1 Factor proportion theory with different demand conditions

Different factor endowments

It is assumed that the production conditions are different in the two countries A and B. Country A has a relatively large amount of capital and country B has a relatively large amount of labour. Good a is assumed to be capital intensive and good b is labour intensive, and they are both homogeneous goods.

The transformation curves for the two countries are drawn in Figure 9.1. The demand condition for the two countries are very different. This is evidenced by the fact that, under conditions of self-sufficiency country A produces at P_{A1} and country B produces at P_{B1}. The demand conditions in the two countries differ so widely that the capital intensive good a is relatively expensive in country A which has a relatively large amount of capital, and the labour intensive good b is relatively expensive in the country B which has a relatively large amount of labour. After the introduction of trade country A will produce at point P_{A2} and country B will produce at point P_{B2}, and the countries will consume at points C_{A2} and C_{B2} respectively. In this extreme case country A, which has a large amount of capital, will import the capital intensive good a, and country B, which has a relatively large labour force, will import the labour intensive good b.

When demand conditions are different it is possible for the pattern of trade to be the opposite of that predicted by factor proportion theory. Even if the pattern of trade is different, the other elements of factor proportion theory will still apply. The standard of living will rise through trade. Before trade was introduced there was a difference in factor prices. Taking the example in Figure 9.1, capital is relatively expensive in country A, which already has a relatively large amount of capital. In country B, which has a relatively large amount of labour, labour will be the relatively expensive factor. After trade is introduced there will be an equalisation of factor prices in Figure 9.1, as predicted in factor proportion theory.

Figure 9.1: Different factor endowments

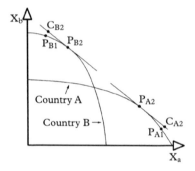

The Stolper-Samuelson theorem says that there will be an increase in the absolute return on the factor which is used most intensively in the increased production of a good. This is still the case here.

Uniform factor endowment

If two countries have the same factor endowment then, according to factor proportion theory, there is no basis for trade. This is based on the assumption that the demand conditions are the same in the two countries. If this assumption does not apply, then there is the basis for international trade. In Figure 9.2 the transformation curve is the same for both countries. Under conditions of self-sufficiency country A and country B produce and consume at points P_{A1} and P_{B1} respectively. After there is trade both countries produce at point P_2. Country A and country B consume at points C_{A2} and C_{B2} respectively.

Figure 9.2: The factor endowments are the same

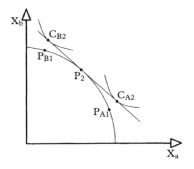

When demand conditions are different there is a basis for international trade, even though the factor endowments of the two countries are the same.

Different factor endowments and large differences of income

In country A there is a large amount of capital which means that it has a comparative advantage in the production of industrial goods, good a. In country B there is a large amount of labour which means that it has a comparative advantage in the production of agricultural products, good b.

It is assumed that country A is a group of industrial countries and country B is a group of less developed countries. Therefore country A's transformation curve is further out in the co-ordinates system than country B's transformation curve BB.

According to factor proportion theory, the less developed countries should export agricultural goods and the industrial countries should export industrial goods. However, demand conditions can lead to a different result. I_B is an indifference curve for country B and I_A is an indifference curve for country A. Demand conditions in the two countries are the same in the sense that when country B reaches country A's income level, then I_A will also correspond to country B's indifference curve. In Figure 9.3, what characterises the demand conditions is that the utility function which lies behind the indifference curves is not homothetic. If the utility function were homothetic, this would mean that the income elasticity for the two goods would be equal to

1. In Figure 9.3 it is clear that the income elasticity for the industrial good is greater than 1 and for the agricultural good it is less than 1.

Figure 9.3: Different factor endowments and uniform demand

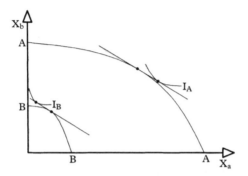

The condition that the utility function should be the same in both countries is fulfilled, but the condition that the utility function should also be homothetic, which is also a condition of factor proportion theory, does not apply.

What this leads to, as is shown in Figure 9.3, is that country B, which has a comparative advantage in agricultural production, imports food. Country A, which has a comparative advantage in industrial products, exports food. Figure 9.3 can help to illustrate the phenomenon which has been seen in recent decades when the less developed countries' net exports of agricultural products has been falling steadily. It is reasonable to assume that the industrial countries will be net exporters of agricultural products in the longer term.

9.2 Demand conditions for differentiated products

The difference between homogeneous goods and differentiated products

In the above it was assumed that the goods a and b are homogeneous goods. The analyses above show that one should not ignore differences in demand conditions, even for homogeneous goods. However, for homogeneous goods the differences between countries are more on the production side than on demand side. The converse is the case with differentiated products.

The question is, what is meant by homogeneous goods and differentiated products? In price and competition theory and in marketing theory the distinction is clear. A homogeneous good is a good to which no preferences are attached. Whereas a differentiated product is a good which is found in different varieties, to which preferences are attached. The development in the post-war period has clearly moved away from homogeneous goods and towards more differentiated products.

It is also possible to use the terms 'homogeneous products' and 'differentiated products' in relation to production. Homogeneous products can be defined as goods that are associated with a production sector. For example agricultural goods and industrial goods are associated with the agricultural and industrial sector respectively, which each produce a homogeneous good. Another example could be the difference between production in different industrial sectors. For example there is the food and drink industry, the textile and clothing industry, the chemical industry, the engineering industry, the electronics industry and so on. It could be said that each of these industry sectors produces a homogeneous good. Nevertheless, within each of these business sectors there is a multitude of differentiated products.

If the world is looked at in this way, a homogeneous good will be a good which is produced by one industrial sector, as opposed to another homogeneous good produced by a different industrial sector. A differentiated product will be a product with different varieties which is produced within the same industrial sector. Trade in 'homogeneous goods' will be trade between industrial sectors, whereas trade in 'differentiated products' will be trade in goods within a single industrial sector.

In this situation the classification of industrial sectors is of great importance. It is appropriate here to distinguish between different complexes of needs. Each consumer has a need for food, clothing, household articles, means of transport, etc. Each industrial sector produces an assortment of goods which is aimed at a complex of needs. Each homogeneous good is aimed at its specific complex of needs, while differentiated products, within the various industrial sectors, are aimed at the corresponding complex of needs. Food, which covers a broad spectrum, is a homogeneous good, and textiles are similarly a homogeneous good. Within each of these two sectors a great range of differentiated products are produced which are each aimed at the same complexes of needs.

The concept of 'quality' is complex

A homogeneous good does not necessarily have uniform quality. Oil, coal and wheat are examples of homogeneous goods. Different kinds of oil can have different energy outputs and different sulphur content. Different kinds of wheat can contain different quantities of energy, protein and water. What characterises a homogeneous good is that it is possible to describe the quality of the good in question by using a number of objective criteria.

The term 'quality' is much more complex when it is used in relation to differentiated products. Quality has several dimensions. The quality of a good is not solely dependent on its physical quality, but also the style of the good. Each of these elements is in turn composed of a number of sub-components. This way of looking at quality comes from Lancaster's theory of consumption (1979).

Figure 9.4 illustrates an evaluation of the quality of a car, consisting of a number of elements where the length of each of the arrows indicates the extent to which the car meets the demands made on it. It is possible to distinguish between the physical qualities of the car and its style. The physical qualities relate to its fuel consumption, the expected maintenance costs, the driving characteristics of the car (for example acceleration and speed), the durability of the car, driving comfort, and the car's safety in accidents. The style of the car depends on the design and the image associated with the particular make of car.

It is very complicated to give an overall evaluation of the different elements that make up the physical qualities of a good, and the evaluation will vary from person to person, because different weightings are given to the different elements. If the style of the good is included in the total picture, as in the total concept of quality, the task is complicated further.

However, this does not prevent most consumers having an idea about the ranking of the quality of a good. For example, if the car manufacturers BMW, Volvo, Toyota and Lada are considered, many will judge BMW and Volvo as being of higher quality than Toyota, which in turn will be judged better than Lada. Even though BMW and Volvo differ on the individual quality indicators, many will undoubtedly place the two makes on the same level, since personal preference will determine whether one make is preferred to the other. The design of BMW may be preferred, while Volvo may be judged a safer car.

Figure 9.4: Quality is a multi-dimensional concept

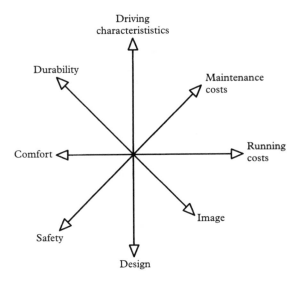

The example illustrates that, with a ranking by quality it is possible to distinguish between vertical and horizontal product differentiation. When a person assesses a BMW as being better than a Toyota, which in turn is assessed as being better than a Lada, this is referred to as a vertical product differentiation. When this same person then judges a BMW and a Volvo to be different, even though they belong to the same quality category, this is referred to as horizontal product differentiation.

9.3 The ideal product variety

In a society, different consumers consider different product varieties to be ideal. What an individual considers to be the ideal variety, for example the ideal car, will depend on taste, relative prices and income.

In a country, different consumers have different tastes and different opportunities for consumption. This means that a supply of vertically and horizontally differentiated choices increases the chances for the individual consumer to obtain his ideal variety of the product. The more different the consumers are in a country, the more differentiated the supply of goods must be if everyone is to find his ideal variety.

It is assumed that there is a number of products which are horizontally differentiated across a scale of characteristics. Consumers have different preferences for individual types of goods. The individual consumer buys only one product variety. The consumer wants to buy his ideal product variety, but whether this happens depends on its price and his income. The idea behind such a model comes from Lancaster (1980). Below there is first a discussion of consumer behaviour and then of production conditions. Finally the conditions are compared before and after the introduction of trade.

The consumers

The product category under consideration is assumed to have two characteristics, Z and Q. In Figure 9.5, the segment of the line AB indicates the product spectrum. Varieties close to B have a large Z/Q. In moving from right to left the quality element Z is reduced and the quality element Q becomes increasing important. Close to A the product variety has a small Z/Q.

Figure 9.5: Different product varieties

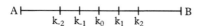

For a given consumer the product variety k_0 is the ideal product variety. As the consumer moves away from k_0 his preference falls. There is assumed to be a symmetry in preference, so that k_1 and k_{-1} give the same fall in preference, and k_2 and k_{-2} give an equal further fall in preference.

These preferences are expressed in the demand for the different product varieties. This can be illustrated as in Figure 9.6. There is a certain total number of consumers for whom k_0 is the ideal variety. Where k_0 is the only variety on the market which these consumers are interested in the demand is equal to the line Dk_0.

At a lower price there will be more who will demand the ideal variety because consumers with lower incomes will enter the market.

If variety k_0 does not exist on the market, but variety k_{-1} does exist, then consumers who ideally want variety k_0 will have demand for k_{-1} which is Dk_{-1}. Even if the consumers' incomes are the same, at a given consumer price there will be less demand for k_{-1} because preference for this variety is lower. For product variety k_{-2} the demand line Dk_{-2} is even lower because this variety is even further from the ideal variety.

If there is only the product variety k_0 on the market, it is possible to find the total demand for this variety. It is assumed that consumers are equally divided between those who prefer k_{-2}, k_{-1}, k_0, k_1, and k_2 as their ideal variety. For each group of purchasers which has an ideal product variety the incomes distribution is identical. Dk_{-1} can now be interpreted as the demand for k_0 which derives from each of the purchaser groups which has k_{-1} and k_1 as its ideal variety. Correspondingly, Dk_{-2} shows the demand for k_0 from those purchaser groups whose ideal varieties are k_{-2} and k_2. In this case the total demand for variety k_0 is equal to $X_1 + 2X_2 + 2X_3$ when the price is P, as shown in Figure 9.6.

Figure 9.6: Demand for different product varieties

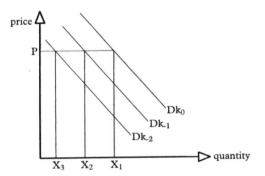

This example is based on the fact that the only variety on the market which has consumers' interest is k_0. If there are multiple product varieties on the market it is obvious that the total demand for each variety will be less. The more varieties there are on the market the more demand will be dispersed since, all things being equal, consumers will choose the variety which is closest to their ideal.

Relative prices also come into the picture. The lower the price of product variety k_{-1} in relation to the price of the closest substitute varieties the greater will be the demand for variety k_{-1} and the less will be the demand for the neighbouring varieties.

The producers

On the production side it is assumed that the production costs for each variety is the same. Each firm has a set of fixed costs and some variable costs which, for example, are linear according to the extent of production. In each firm the total average production costs fall as production increases. The individual firm can choose to produce whichever product variety it wants. When there are advantages for the individual firm in specialising, each firm will only produce one variety and the different firms will choose different varieties.

There is open access to the market for new firms. Firms which do not cover their total costs will leave the market. This means that the price is equal to the total average costs. There is no scope for super-normal profits. If a firm puts its prices down it will attract new consumers whose ideal variety is further from the variety which the firm produces. In this way the firm can sell more units. This will affect the other producers. There will be an equilibrium for the whole market which is as described in Figure 9.7.

For an individual firm the situation will be as shown in the Figure 9.7. The costs are the same for all producers, regardless of which product variety the firm chooses. This is shown by the average total cost curve. Regardless of the product variety, each firm has the same sales curve when there is a situation of market equilibrium. Firstly, this is because, regardless of which product variety is regarded as the ideal, each group of consumers has a demand which can be derived on the basis the curves in Figure 9.6. Secondly, it is because the consumers are spread evenly throughout the range of product varieties AB, as regards the variety which they consider ideal. If each firm has a sales curve D_1, the price of each product variety will be P_1 and a quantity of M_1 will be produced of each product variety. An alternative equilibrium would have the price P_2 and the quantity M_2 if each firm had a sales curve of D_2.

It is now possible to compare the number of firms in the two equilibrium situations. The total demand for all varieties at price P_1 divided by the quantity M_1 which each producer supplies will determine the total number of firms. The same calculation can be made in the other situation, where the price is P_2 and the volume produced by the individual firms is M_2. Whether the number of firms rises or falls depends on the percentage increase in the total demand as a consequence of a fall in the price from P_1 to P_2, compared with the percentage increase in production from M_1 to M_2 which is made by each firm. If the production increase in each firm is proportionately greater than the percentage increase in demand for the different varieties, then the number of firms in the latter situation, with price P_2, will be less than in the former situation with the price P_1.

Figure 9.7: Production costs

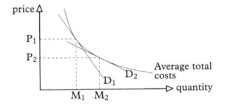

Figure 9.8: The production of multiple product varieties before trade

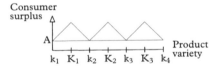

The situation before there is trade

There are two countries which are identical. It is assumed that in each of the countries there are three producers. In Figure 9.8 the straight line shows the spectrum of the product varieties. There are three firms which have chosen, K_1, K_2 and K_3 as product varieties. The range of product varieties is divided in three parts, and each firm chooses the product variety which lies in the middle of each part. There is thus an optimal distribution of customers, evenly spread across the whole spectrum of product varieties.

The consumer surplus for the consumers who have the different product varieties as their ideal is drawn on the vertical axis. The consumers who have product varieties K_1, K_2 or K_3 as their ideal product varieties obtain the greatest consumer surplus. These varieties are available on the market. The further a consumer's ideal variety is from these three product types, the less will be the consumer's surplus. The consumers who have product types k_1, k_2, k_3, k_4 as their ideal product varieties have the smallest consumer surplus, as shown in Figure 9.8. at A. This small consumer surplus is determined by the level of the production price.

The situation illustrated in Figure 9.8 applies in each of the two countries when they do no trade with each other.

The situation with trade

Trade is now introduced between the two identical countries. This means that the market for the individual firm will be doubled. This means that there is scope for more product varieties. It is now assumed that altogether there are four product varieties in the two countries and these are available to consumers. It is assumed that demand is not affected by the fact that trade has been introduced.

In Figure 9.9 the unbroken lines describe the situation prior to trade. This is the same as in Figure 9.8. After the introduction of trade the curve with the dotted line applies.

Figure 9.9: Production of product varieties after trade

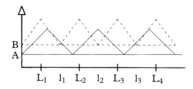

The minimum consumer surplus is increased from A to B, because the price of the product varieties falls after the introduction of trade. Before there was trade there were three producers in each country. After the introduction of trade there are four producers in the two countries together. What happens can be shown by using Figure 9.7. Before the introduction of trade there is a situation of equilibrium in each of the two countries, in which the price corresponds to P_1 and the quantity to M_1. After the opening up of trade two firms in each of the countries produce at a price level P_2 and with sales of M_2. The prices of the product varieties fall. This in turn means that the maximum consumer surplus for those groups of consumers that can obtain their ideal product varieties L_1, L_2, L_3 and L_4 is higher than the consumer surplus for the ideal product varieties under conditions of self-sufficiency. Certain groups of consumers will lose by the change. This applies to those groups of consumers which have, for example, l_1, l_2 and l_3 as ideal product varieties.

Consumers as a whole will gain by the opening up of trade. The area which lies beneath the broken zigzag line which shows the total consumer surplus is greater than the area which lies beneath the unbroken zigzag line.

If welfare is measured by the surplus, it is necessary to look at producer surplus as well as consumer surplus. The producer surplus, both before and after there is trade, is equal to zero, because in both situations the price of the good is equal to the average total costs.

In each of the two countries, which are identical in the initial situation, there will be production of two product varieties after there is trade, where previously there had been three varieties. The theory of the ideal product variety can explain why there should be trade in products which belong to a given product category which consists of horizontally differentiated products. However, the theory cannot explain which products the individual country will specialise in.

The model of the ideal product variety is often called a neo-Hotelling model. Hotelling was one of the first economists to deal with the issue of the factor of distance as an influence on the location of a firm. The theory of the ideal product variety is similarly a 'distance' model as it shows the 'distance' between the product varieties produced.

9.4 Consumers demand multiple product varieties

In the above examples the individual only consumes one product variety. In other cases an individual consumes several different product varieties. The utility for an individual increases with the number of varieties it is possible to buy. The individual good must satisfy a variety of wants. The more varieties there are of the good, the better will the complex of needs be covered.

For example, food must be safe and nutritious. For this there must be calories, protein, vitamins and so on in a suitable combination. The individual food varieties can satisfy these needs in different ways.

Food shall also be tasty and provide an aesthetic experience. Foods are also consumed in a social setting, and individual food varieties can be more or less appropriate for satisfying social needs.

Peoples' desire for strong drink can be met by gin, whisky, cognac, ouzo or snaps. These varieties are not complete substitutes for each other because traditionally they are consumed in different circumstances. The possibility of consuming the 'right' variety in the 'right' circumstances is assumed to increase welfare.

Clothes must satisfy the purpose of covering the body in comfort, keeping the body at a comfortable temperature, as well as satisfying the desire of giving the appropriate appearance and looking good in given situations. The possibility of satisfying all these wants will be increased as more varieties are available.

It is a characteristic of rising standards of living that an individual's consumption of a given good is more and more differentiated. With a higher standard of living there is demand for more varieties. It is assumed that the different product varieties are horizontally differentiated, even if, in practice, they are often both horizontally and vertically differentiated at the same time. The basis of the model discussed below which covers consumption of multiple product varieties, is to be found in Krugman (1987).

The consumers

It is assumed that all product varieties are included symmetrically in the utility function for the representative consumer. The individual consumer consumes n product varieties. A utility function $u(c_i)$ applies for each of these varieties, where c_i is the consumption of variety i. $u' > 0$ and $u'' < 0$. apply for the utility function. There is a falling marginal utility with increased consumption of each individual variety.

The total utility for the whole product category is assumed to be:

$$\mu = \sum_{i=1}^{n} u(c_i) \tag{9.1}$$

This means that consumption of a new variety gives greater utility than increased consumption of another variety which is already included among the varieties consumed. The individual consumer will therefore demand a wide range of varieties rather than concentrating on just a few. Each consumer will consume the same quantity c of each variety.

The total utility µ will therefore be:

$$\mu = n \cdot u(c)$$

The producers

The production will take place using the production factors labour and capital. Each firm, each producing one variety, has the same capital stock f and the costs per capital unit are r. To produce one unit of each variety a unit of labour is needed, which means that the necessary labour force l_i for producing x_i of variety i is:

$$l_i = a\, x_i$$

The total costs $g(x_i)$ for each firm are:

$$g(x_i) = f\, r + w\, a\, x_i$$

where w is the wage rate.

When it is assumed that firms can freely enter and leave the market, there will be no supernormal profit or deficit. The price p_i will be equal to the average costs. Therefore:

$$p_i = \frac{f r}{x_i} + wa$$

which shows that the price of each variety will fall when the production volume increases.

Each firm will produce the same quantity of the chosen product variety which means that $x_i = x$. The labour used by each firm is the same, i.e. $l_i = l$, and the price of each product variety is the same, i.e. $p_i = p$. The number of varieties n produced depends on the total labour force L. The total n is equal to L/l.

The situation after the introduction of trade

If there are two countries in which the situation is identical, and as described above, the utility µ in each society will be as shown in the identity (9.1) above. If trade is introduced the consumers will have the possibility of consuming 2n varieties. There will be an adjustment of the assortment of products so that only one firm produces any given variety. The prices and the costs of each firm will still be the same in the two countries. The only thing that happens is that each consumer now consumes half as much of each variety while the number of product varieties is doubled. In each country the total utility after the introduction of trade will be:

$$\mu = \sum_{i=1}^{2n} u(\tfrac{1}{2} c_i)$$

The individual country will export half of its production. At the same time this country will import half the production of the other country. The model can show that there will be both imports and exports within a given product category. However, the model cannot predict which product varieties an individual country will produce.

Models of this kind are often called neo-Chamberlain models, after E. Chamberlain who was the first to deal systematically with monopolistic competition for differentiated products in 'The Theory of Monopolistic Competition' (1933).

9.5 Vertically differentiated products

The two preceding theories, the theory of the ideal product variety and the theory of multiple product varieties, are concerned with horizontally differentiated products. There are two countries where the conditions of demand and production are the same because the income level is the same.

It is now right to look at vertically differentiated products. It is no longer assumed that the conditions of demand and production are the same in the two countries. The countries may have different income levels. First there is a discussion of a theory which emphasises the demand side, and then there is a discussion of a theory which concentrates on the supply side.

The demand side

The central elements in the theory on vertically differentiated products which emphasises the demand side originates with Linder (1961). As an example of product varieties that are vertically differentiated one can look again at makes of cars. It is assumed that, using a quality index, it is possible to rank different product varieties according to quality. The ranking list for 6 types of car is drawn in Figure 9.10, with the quality indicator on the y axis. Average income is measured along the x axis. It is assumed that there is a correlation between the average incomes in different societies and the kind of quality of car which is most in demand in the country in question. This correlation is shown by the line OT. In country A, which has an average income of A, quality Q_3 is most in demand. The 'representative' demand is directed towards quality Q_3. In country B, which has a somewhat higher average income B, the car make which is most in demand is Q_4, which is of better quality than Q_3. It is assumed that the 'representative' demand varies from country to country, depending on the average income in the country.

Even if the car with quality Q_3 is the car which is most in demand in country A, it is not the only make of car which is in demand. Consumers have different preferences which mean that some will buy a car which is generally regarded as being better or worse than Q_3. There is also an income distribution between consumers which means that some can afford to buy a better car while others can only afford to buy a lower quality car. This means that in both countries there is a potential demand for cars within a range of qualities. In country A this is assumed to span from Q_1 to Q_5 and in country B from Q_2 to Q_6.

Figure 9.10: Vertically differentiated products

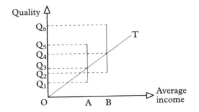

The next step in the analysis concerns the assumption that the demand conditions in the country determine the product types the country will produce. It is assumed that it is the demand conditions in the home market which determine production. The producer knows the conditions of the home market better than the conditions abroad. Because of the physical and mental barriers, for example differences of language and culture, there is much better knowledge about the home market. Therefore producers react to the conditions of the home market rather than the conditions abroad. In country A the producer will choose quality Q_3 because demand for this quality is strongest there. In country B, which is wealthier, the producer will choose to produce a better quality, which will be Q_4.

Whether there are possibilities of trade once production has been established, depends on demand conditions. If the demand conditions overlap and the two qualities which are produced in each of the countries are within the common range of demand, there will be trade.

In Figure 9.10 there is a common range of demand for qualities from a range from Q_2 to Q_5, which includes the qualities Q_3 and Q_4. In this case there is a basis for trade. The wealthier consumers in country A will import cars of quality Q_4 from country B. Conversely the less wealthy consumers in country B will import cars of quality Q_3 from country A. Since the weight of demand will be concentrated around the product variety for which there is most demand, the more similar the demand conditions, the more intense will be the trade.

The incomes in the two countries can be so different that there is no common range where the demand in the two countries overlaps. In such cases there is no basis for trade. If there is a common range of potential demand, the potential demand will not give rise to trade if the range does not include the product varieties produced in the countries. This means that in Figure 9.10 the common range of varieties must include Q_3 and Q_4 if there is to be bilateral trade.

The theory explaining vertically differentiated products requires that it is possible to rank the different product varieties according to their quality. This assumes that the countries have different levels of average incomes around which there is income distribution.

The theory prompts two questions to which it gives the answers. What determines which product quality an individual country will produce, and which it therefore has the possibility of exporting? What determines whether there will be trade, and how much trade there will be if there is trade?

To the first question the theory gives the answer that the average income determines the 'representative' demand in society and it is this demand which determines which product quality the individual country will produce, and possibly export. Briefly, the demand conditions determine what the country produces, and thus what product variety an individual country can export.

The answer to the second question is that there will only be trade as long as there is an overlap in the range of demand in relation to quality, and this overlap covers the product varieties produced in both countries. The larger the area of overlap the more trade there will be. Briefly, the extent of trade depends on how similar the demand conditions are in the two countries.

The first part of the theory is a home market theory which says that the domestic demand determines domestic production. In the past, when national economies were not so integrated and there were larger trade barriers, this was a realistic theory. The question is whether it still applies now that there is much greater integration. If, for example, the British home market is expanded so as to cover Northern Europe it is still possible that the theory is relevant.

The supply side

The central point in the model above is that it is only differences in the level of demand which determine the pattern of specialisation. Production conditions are not included in the model, even though the prices of the different product varieties differ. It is assumed that the prices of horizontally differentiated products are very similar. However, if vertically differentiated products are considered, the price will be higher for the better quality product varieties, and therefore the richer countries will have demand for the better quality products.

In contrast to this there are theories in which the differences in factor endowment are considered to be of decisive importance in explaining the differences in production costs, which in turn play a central role in determining the pattern of specialisation.

The theory of the product life cycle shows how different product varieties which are vertically differentiated require different factor inputs. The textile industry and the electronics industry produce product varieties which belong to different phases of the product life cycle. There are products which are advanced in terms of technology and design, there are more traditional products and there are cheap low-priced products. Depending on the factor endowment of a country, it has a special aptitude for producing a product type which is in a particular phase of the product life cycle.

There is another model which also ascribes a central role to factor endowment in the location of production for vertically differentiated product varieties, cf. Falvey (1981).

The model is based on the traditional assumptions that there are two countries A and B, two homogeneous production factors which are

labour and capital, and two industries. In the first industry a homogeneous product X_a is produced and this product is labour intensive. In
the other industry a differentiated product, X_b, is produced.

Labour is fully mobile between the two industries. This is not the
case with the capital which is sector specific, cf. Chapter 7, Section
7.1. The product varieties in the industry which produces the differentiated products are, for example, two product varieties k_1 and k_2. The
first variety k_1 is of poorer quality and the demand for it comes from
lower income groups. The other variety k_2 is of higher quality and the
demand for it comes from higher incomes groups. The production
costs are different because the quantities of the necessary production
factors needed differ for the different product qualities.

For the sake of simplicity it is assumed that in order to produce one
unit of any of the varieties requires one unit of labour. There is also
a requirement for v units of capital. v varies according to the quality
of the product variety, so that a better quality requires a higher
amount of v. This means that the amount of capital required per unit
produced, expressed as v, can be used as an indicator of quality.

The costs of producing one unit of product quality v in country A
are as follows:

$$C_A(v) = w_A + vr_A \qquad (9.2)$$

where w_A is the level of wages and r_A is the return on the sector specific capital in country A.

Correspondingly, the costs in country B for one unit of product
variety v are as follows:

$$C_B(v) = w_B + vr_B \qquad (9.3)$$

If $w_A > w_B$ and $r_A < r_B$ then country A is the country with more capital
and country B is the country which has relatively more labour. This
means that the per capita income is greater in country A than in country B.

For a given product quality v_f the costs are the same in the two
countries. In this situation:

$$w_A + v_f r_A = w_B + v_f r_B$$

which means that:

$$v_f = \frac{w_A - w_B}{r_B - r_A} \qquad (9.4)$$

On the basis of the equations (9.2), (9.3) and (9.4) it is possible to calculate the differences in the production costs for a given product quality v, as follows:

$$C_B(v) - C_A(v) = \frac{w_A - w_B}{v_f} (v - v_f)$$

The difference in the production costs in the two countries is determined by the difference in the wage levels and the product variety's quality in relation to v_f. Country A has a comparative advantage in the production of quality v, when $C_A(v) < C_B(v)$. When $w_A > w_B$ then $v > v_f$. Before the introduction of trade it is assumed that country A, which is the country with greater capital endowment, produces product variety k_2, for which it applies that $v > v_f$. Country B produces k_1, which is of lower quality, and in respect of which $v < v_f$. When trade is introduced, country A will export product variety k_2. This assumes that there is demand for both product varieties in both countries.

If the production of the homogeneous good in industry X_a is labour intensive, country B will export both the homogeneous good and the lower quality product variety in industry X_b. This is the trading pattern which is recognisable in trade between industrial countries and newly industrialised countries. The advantage of trade is not merely that there is a better factor allocation, but also that the different income groups have better access to the product variety that they prefer.

In the model which has been analysed here it is the factor endowment which determines the pattern of trade. As factor proportion theory plays a central role in explaining the pattern of trade, this model can be called a type of neo-Heckscher-Ohlin model.

9.6 Trade in differentiated products

Section 9.3 discusses the theory of the ideal product variety. In Section 9.4 the theory of multiple product varieties is explained. In both of these, the discussion was concerned with horizontally differentiated products. Section 9.5 dealt with vertically differentiated products, where one model started from the point of view of demand conditions and the other model started from the point of view of the production conditions.

This section summarises what these theories can explain. A distinction is drawn between two situations. In the first situation the countries have the same income levels. The second situation considers countries with different income levels.

Countries with the same income levels

The significance of the structure of needs

It is possible to distinguish between macroeconomic and microeconomic consumer preferences and production conditions. The macroeconomic relates to sectors, for example two sectors, which together constitute the country's economy. The microeconomic relates to the different product varieties within a sector.

When two countries have the same income levels it is natural to assume that the macroeconomic consumer preferences and production conditions are the same. According to factor proportion theory this will not result in trade in the goods that belong to the different sectors.

If the microeconomic consumer preferences and production condition are also the same, the theories in Section 9.3 and 9.4 can explain how it is that there will be trade in *horizontally differentiated products*. However, the theories cannot predict which goods one country will export and which goods the other country will export.

However this is possible if it is assumed that the microeconomic consumer preferences are different. This can be illustrated by an example. In France they drink cognac, in Britain they drink whisky and in the Nordic countries they drink snaps. This pattern has developed because each product was developed in the country in question more or less by chance. First, each product was developed in its country. The demand structure fitted the product to the market. In the old days trade was slight because of trade barriers and because the lower level of welfare did not enable the consumption of many product varieties.

Once the pattern of production is established, and the countries have become better off, allowing for the consumption of multiple product varieties, then the horizontally differentiated spirits will be traded internationally. The course of development sketched here applies to many foods. Knowledge of foreign specialities is promoted through tourism, for example. Foreign goods are integrated in the demand structure through the 'discovery' of foreign specialities. This can be referred to as a kind of international demonstration effect.

Differences in the demand structure can also explain how trade arises when there are *vertically differentiated products*. Furniture and clothing include both horizontally and vertically differentiated product varieties. Trade in horizontally differentiated products can also be explained by means of differences in demand conditions. Differences in the demand conditions can also explain the pattern of trade for vertically differentiated furniture and clothing.

In Northern Europe there is a tradition for emphasising furnishing and interior decoration. In Southern Europe (France and Italy) there is greater emphasis on clothing. The proportion of spending which goes to furniture in Northern Europe is greater than that in Southern Europe. It is the opposite with clothing. This can explain why the industry for fashionable and modern furniture exists in Denmark, and not in the southern countries. Correspondingly it can explain the French and Italian dominance of the fashionable clothing industry. The differences in consumer preferences are drawn in Figure 9.11. The curves show a distribution of preferences in the two areas, Northern and Southern Europe. Even if it is assumed that the areas have the same standard of living and the same income distribution, there is such a difference in the 'average' preferences that Northern Europe produces fashionable furniture and traditional clothes while the reverse is the case in France and Italy. The preferences of the consumers in the two areas overlap, and this gives a basis for trade.

Figure 9.11: Differences in consumer preferences

All the above examples concern consumer goods. It is also possible to find examples relating to capital goods. If a country has a particular preference for improving the standard of its housing or its hospitals there will be demands in these sectors which will lead to a shortage of labour. Therefore there can be development of new capital goods in the country in question. Construction work can be mechanised and new apparatus for use in hospitals may be developed. If a country

introduces strict standards for safety at work, it is possible that new
machines may be developed to meet these requirements.

Thus, demands at different points in the economy or various legal
requirements can mean that different countries develop special capital
goods in a particular sector. These capital goods can be exported,
while more traditional goods can be imported.

The significance of income distribution

Even if the demand structures are the same in the two countries, and
even if the levels of average incomes are the same, the 'representative'
demand can nevertheless be different. This can be because of differences in income distribution. This is shown in Figure 9.12 where the
average incomes in country A and country B are the same, but the
'typical' resident in country A is better off than the 'typical' resident
in country B.

Figure 9.12: Differences in income distribution

In this case the 'representative' demand in country A will be towards
a vertically differentiated product variety, which will have a better
quality than the product variety in country B. Country A will produce
a better product variety and country B will produce a poorer product
variety. The demand conditions in the two countries overlap so there
will be trade.

Countries with different income levels

If there are significant differences of income between countries then
the theories in Section 9.5 can explain how trade in vertically differentiated products can arise. The better off country will produce better
quality goods and the worse off country will produce poorer quality
goods. The pre-condition for the existence of trade is that the demand
conditions in the two areas should overlap.

The theory of the product life cycle can also help to explain trade in vertically differentiated products. The electronics industry is one in which there are many very different kinds of products. There are advanced high-technology products, there are traditional products which have been on the market for several years, and there are simple highly standardised products. The theory of the product life cycle is based on the idea that comparative advantages between countries vary according to which type of product is concerned. The textile sector is another example. In the textile sector there are relatively 'advanced' products, which are associated with design and quality. There are more traditional products and there are basic products. Western European countries export more advanced products and they import more traditional products belonging to the same sector.

9.7 Inter-industry and intra-industry trade

A distinction is made between inter-industry trade and intra-industry trade. Inter-industry trade means trade in products consisting of goods from different sectors. Intra-industry trade means trade in products which belong to the same sector or industry.

In this chapter Section 9.1, which relates to factor proportion theory, illustrates inter-industry trade. There are two sectors which each produce a homogeneous good. As a result of trade there will be inter-industry specialisation.

The other sections of this chapter deal with differentiated products within the same sector or industry. There are imports and exports of goods belonging to the same sector in each country. In other words there is an intra-industry specialisation of production in the sector concerned. The question of intra-industry trade was also referred to in Chapter 8. This was in connection with limiting the product assortment with firm specialisation. This was a key issue in the theory of the technological difference and the theory of the product life cycle.

The development has been towards more and more product areas having differentiated goods. With such differentiated products it is possible for there to be both inter-industry and intra-industry specialisation. Empirical analyses indicate that in the post-war period intra-industry trade has become more significant and inter-industry trade has become less significant.

In the post-war period there have been two sets of empirical analyses which have had a special influence on theoretical developments.

The first set of analyses started with Leontief showing that factor proportion theory should be questioned, see Section 6.7. The other set of empirical analyses points out the great importance of intra-industry trade. One of the first analyses that pointed out the importance of intra-industry trade was made by J.P. Verdoorn (1960), which identified that the establishment of Benelux as a customs union had led, first and foremost, to intra-industry specialisation between the countries. Since then a number of empirical analyses have illustrated the extent and nature of intra-industry trade.

The question is how inter-industry trade and intra-industry trade should be measured. There are several methods for doing this, but the most commonly used index is the expression:

$$\frac{|X_i - M_i|}{X_i + M_i}$$

where X_i and M_i are exports and imports of goods in sector i. If there are only either exports or imports of the products of the sector in question, then there is only inter-industry trade. In such a case, the above indicator, which shows the numerical difference between exports and imports in relation to the sum of the two, will be one. A number close to zero indicates a large degree of intra-industry trade, while a number close to one indicates a large degree of inter-industry trade. It is possible to construct an aggregate measure of the overall level of intra-industry trade. After having calculated an index for each sector, as shown above, the indices can be weighted using for example the sector's relative importance to the country's international trade as a basis for weighting.

There is one overridingly important question in connection with measuring whether the trade pattern is inter- or intra-industry. This is the question of defining where the boundaries of the sectors lie. Industrial statistics usually operate with 20-25 industrial sectors. These data give figures which say something about the importance of intra-industry trade. If more narrow categories are made with more sectors, then more trade will be classified as inter-industry and less will be considered as intra-industry. It is therefore necessary to be aware that the number of sectors into which business is categorised can have an influence on measurements of the importance of intra-industry trade.

The volume of the inter-industry trade has to do with developments in consumption and production in individual countries. If there is a country in which consumption and production develops in parallel in each sector, there will be no inter-industry specialisation and inter-industry trade will not grow. If, nevertheless, there is a much stronger growth in trade than in consumption and production, this will be due to a growth in intra-industry trade.

In the industrial countries there has been a clear trend for the patterns of consumption and production to develop uniformly in all countries. In all countries the growth pattern among sectors is the same. Everywhere the same sectors are expanding and the same sectors are stagnating. The agricultural sector and the textile and clothing sectors are examples of sectors which everywhere are growing only slowly. The chemical industry and electronics industry are examples of sectors which are growing rapidly everywhere. This development is naturally linked to the different nature of the development of demand for the products of these sectors, and this development is very similar in all Western European countries. Since it can be noted that trade has grown much more rapidly than production in the Western European countries, the explanation is that the increased trade must be an expression of the strong growth in intra-industry trade.

Literature

Falvey, R.E., 'Commercial Policy and Intra-Industry Trade', *Journal of International Economics*, 11, 1981.

Greenaway, D. and C.R. Milner, *The Economics of Intra-Industry Trade*, London, 1986.

Grubel, H.G. and P.J. Lloyd, *Intra Industry Trade*, Macmillan, London, 1975.

Lancaster, K., *Variety, Equity and Efficiency*, Oxford, 1979.

Lancaster, K., 'Intra-Industry Trade and Perfect Monopolistic Competition' *Journal of International Economics*, 10, 1980.

Linder, S.B., *An Essay on Trade and Transformation*, New York, 1961.

Kierzkowski, H., 'Models of International Trade in Differentiated Goods' in D. Greenaway (ed), *Current Issues in International Trade*, Macmillan, 1996.

Krugman, P., 'Increasing Returns, Monopolistic Competition and International Trade' in J. N. Bhagwati (ed), *International Trade: Selected Readings*, Cambridge, Mass., 1987.

Krugman, P., 'Scale Economics, Product Differentiation and the Pattern of Trade' *American Economic Review,* 70, 1980.

Verdoorn, P.J., 'The Intra-Block Trade of Benelux' i E.A.G. Robinson (ed), *Economic Consequences of the Size of Nations,* London, 1960.

10. Market imperfections

In traditional neo-classical factor proportion theory it is assumed that there is perfect competition in the market for goods and in the factor markets. In Chapter 8, on economies of scale, firm specialisation and technology, and in Chapter 9 on demand conditions for differentiated products, the assumptions on which these chapters are based are not compatible with perfect competition. There is assumed to be a form of monopolistic competition. However, monopolistic competition is a market form which does not have a central role in explaining trade in these chapters. Other conditions are considered important. In a market with monopolistic competition there are preferences. This means that an individual firm's sales curve falls from left to right in a price/volume diagram. However, it is assumed that there are so many suppliers in the market that power over the market is weak as there are so many suppliers producing so many product varieties that can be substituted in consumption.

If the market can be described as a monopoly or an oligopoly, there are either only one or only a few large suppliers in the market. In this case the nature of the market plays a totally different, and central role in explaining trade.

In this chapter a number of models will be analysed in which there is either one or a few large suppliers in the market. In these models the form of market is much more important than is the case with monopolistic competition, where there are assumed to be many suppliers.

10.1 Monopoly

The standard assumptions which have been used previously are assumed to apply. There are two countries A and B, in which the supply and demand conditions are identical. The transformation curve, which is identical in the two countries, is drawn in Figure 10.1.

In country B there is perfect competition in the market for both goods. This means that under conditions of self-sufficiency country B is at point B, and the relative final good prices are indicated by the slope of the tangent P_B.

Figure 10.1: Monopoly before there is trade

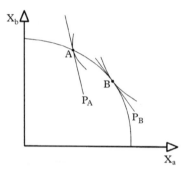

In country A there is perfect competition in the market for good b, whereas there is a monopoly in the market for good a. Country A produces at point A and the relative final good prices are indicated by the slope of the tangent P_A.

The slope of the tangent to the transformation curve at point A indicates the relationship between the marginal costs in the production of the two goods. The marginal rate of transformation MRT is equal to the relationship between the marginal costs, which in turn is equal to the relative final good prices under perfect competition.

Therefore:

$$MRT = \frac{MC_a}{MC_b} = \frac{P_a}{P_b}$$

It is known from monopoly price theory that:

$$MR_a = P_a \left(1 + \frac{1}{e} \right)$$

where MR_a is the marginal income from the production of good a and where e is the price elasticity, which is negative. The optimal price P_a^m will be obtained when MR_a is equal to MC_a which means that:

$$MC_a^m = P_a^m \left(1 + \frac{1}{e}\right)$$

which therefore means that:

$$P_a^m > P_a = MC_a > MC_a^m$$

where P_a and MC_a are the price and marginal costs with perfect competition, and where P_a^m and MC_a^m are the price and marginal costs with the optimal price under a monopoly. The relative final good prices of goods a and b are therefore further apart with a monopoly than they are with perfect competition:

$$P_m = \frac{P_a^m}{P_b} > \frac{P_a}{P_b}$$

Therefore the slope of P_A in Figure 10.1 is greater than the marginal rate of transformation at point A.

Trade is now introduced, which is illustrated in Figure 10.2, where points B and A are the initial situations before trade. B and A are the same points as in Figure 10.1. It is assumed that the relative prices on the world market P_W are positioned between the relative final good prices which existed in countries A and B before the introduction of trade. Therefore:

$$P_M > P_W > P_B$$

After the introduction of trade the relative price of good a will fall in country A and will rise in country B. Therefore, after trade, country B will produce more of good a and country A will produce more of good b. In Figure 10.2 the new supply point for country B is point C and the new supply point for country A is point D. The slope of the two straight lines through these points is the same; they are equal to the relative world market prices P_W.

Country A will export good b and country B will export good a. In Figure 10.2 welfare will rise in country B and fall in country A. Thus, with the conditions illustrated in Figure 10.2, country A, which has a situation of monopoly in the supply of good a, will lose by the introduction of trade. Even if the supplier of good b in country A maintains a certain power of monopoly after the introduction of trade, it is not certain that country A will lose. This is apparent in Figure 10.3.

Figure 10.2: Monopoly after trade where country A loses

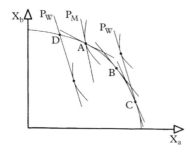

Figure 10.3: Monopoly after trade where country A gains

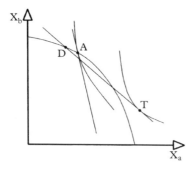

In this case the new consumption point T, after the introduction of trade, is on a higher indifference curve than consumption point A, which was the situation before there was trade. Whether the result is as shown in Figure 10.2 or as shown in Figure 10.3 depends on how much the production point changes, how much the relative final good prices change, and the structure of consumption as described by the indifference curves.

In this analysis the assumption has been that the firm in country A which produces good a still has a certain power of monopoly after trade is introduced. After the opening up of trade price elasticity e is numerically greater than it was under conditions of self-sufficiency. There is a possibility that the monopoly will break down when trade commences. If the introduction of trade means that there is also the establishment of perfect competition in the production of good a in country A, then there is a completely new situation.

In Figure 10.2 country A's production point does not move from A to D. The production point will move from A to B. The relative prices in country A will now be identical to the relative prices in country B, when there is perfect competition in both countries.

When supply and demand conditions are the same in country A and country B, there is no basis for trade. The mere prospect of trade means that there is no longer a monopoly in country A. In this case country A will obtain a gain in welfare because the existence of the possibility of trade. The fact that the mere existence of international competition changes the nature of the market to become more competitive is a considerable advantage of trade.

10.2 Monopolies in both countries

In the above it is assumed that in country A there was a monopoly in the supply of good a and perfect competition for good b. In country B there was perfect competition for both goods. It is now assumed that there is a monopoly in the supply of good a in both countries. This means that after trade is opened up between the two countries there will be a duopoly, i.e. two large suppliers of good a.

Before analysing the conditions of a monopoly in both countries, it is necessary to look at behaviour under a duopoly, because it is significant.

Behaviour under a duopoly

An oligopoly is a form of market in which there are few large suppliers in the market. A duopoly can be considered as a special kind of oligopoly in which the number of suppliers is limited to two. Therefore the analysis given below is not merely relevant to cases of duopolies, but is also of great importance to oligopolistic markets.

In an duopolistic market it is essential to distinguish between autonomous and conjectural business behaviour. Autonomous behaviour means that, when a firm changes its production volume or its price, it does not expect the other firm to make any changes. In other words, the first firm does not expect that its own actions will have any influence on what the other firm does.

Conjectural behaviour means that a firm which is considering changing its production volume or price, will take into consideration that this can lead the other firm to implement changes as well. The firm acts on the basis that its own behaviour will affect the behaviour of the other firm.

The sales curve of a firm depends on whether it acts autonomously or conjecturally. There are two firms, each of which produces a differentiated good. The sales curve of one firm is shown in Figure 10.4.

Figure 10.4: The sales curve with autonomous and conjectural behaviour

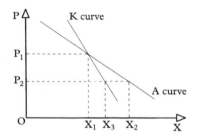

In the initial situation there is an equilibrium where the firm produces X_1 and obtains the price P_1. The firm now puts its price down to P_2. If the firm behaves autonomously it expects that the other firm will keep its price steady. This means that the firm can increase its sales to X_2. As a result of the price reduction, which the competitor is not expected to follow, there will be increased sales, partly because there will be demand for the good from new consumers when the price is lowered, and partly because the firm will take sales from the other firm.

However, if the firm behaves conjecturally, a firm which is considering putting its prices down will take into consideration that the competitor will follow it down in price because the competitor will not want to lose sales. In such a case the first firm will only increase its sales to X_3 if it puts its prices down to P_2.

If, on the other hand, the firm wants to set its prices up, autonomous behaviour will mean that it will expect a larger fall in sales than if it expects that the competitor will also set its prices up.

The A curve is the firm's sales with autonomous behaviour and the K curve is shows the sales with conjectural behaviour. With conjectural behaviour the price elasticity of the sales curve is less than with autonomous behaviour.

In general it can be said that the expected behaviour depends on the structure of the market. The more competitors there are on the market, the less significant to the others is the behaviour of a single firm. This means that it is easier to imagine autonomous behaviour when there are many suppliers in the market compared with a situation where there are only few large suppliers in the market.

In the present example, the firm changes its price which means that it is the market which determines how much can be sold. This is how firms usually act. However, it is possible to imagine the alternative in which a firm determines the production quantity, so it is the market which determines the price of the good.

In the case of a duopoly there will be different equilibriums, depending on whether the firms change the price and let the market determine the quantity, or whether the firms changes the quantity so that the market determines the prices. The first case, where the firms change the prices because they want to gain a greater profit, is called Bertrand competition (named after the French mathematician who was the first to analyse duopolies when there is a change in prices). In the second case, where the firms change the production volumes, this is called Cournot competition (named after the French mathematician who was the first to analyse duopolies when there is a change in the production quantities).

A general analysis

We will now return to the analysis based on a general equilibrium where there is a monopoly in the supply of good a in both countries. In the supply of good b there is perfect competition in both countries. Each of the two goods are homogeneous goods.

In Figure 10.5 the conditions are the same in both countries under conditions of self-sufficiency. The two countries produce and consume at point R. The supply and demand conditions are identical in the two countries.

Trade between the two countries is now introduced. This means that there are two suppliers of good a in the market. The national monopoly is now replaced by a duopoly. As discussed above, the effect of this on prices and volumes under duopoly conditions depends on the behaviour of the firms. It is assumed that each of the two firms behaves autonomously. The firm in country A assumes that the volume produced by the firm in country B is constant, regardless of the volume which it produces itself. The firm in country B behaves in the same way with regard to the firm in country A. The two firms change their volumes of production in order to obtain the greatest possible gain. This is a case of Cournot competition.

Figure 10.5: Monopolies in both countries

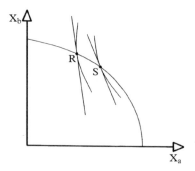

Before there is trade, each of the two countries is at point R. After there is trade the international duopoly in the supply of good a means that the price of this good will fall, compared with the initial situation. S will be the new consumption point, where there is an increase in welfare.

In what follows there is a closer examination of what happens in the market. The total production in the two countries is $X_{aT} = X_{aA} + X_{aB}$, see Figure 10.6. In the initial situation each of the two countries has half of the total market. The demand conditions for good a are the same in country A and country B. It is assumed that the demand curve is a straight line. This assumption is not significant and it is only chosen to simplify the presentation of the argument.

In Figure 10.6 curve MX_A is the demand curve in country A, and since the demand curve in country B is identical to it, then the curve $MX_{A \cdot B}$ will be the curve for the total market, i.e. the sum of the markets in the two countries.

P is the applicable price. PU and UV are the sales in the two countries. The price elasticity at U and at V is the same. The price elasticity is UX_A/MU. If country A puts its price down, in relation to P, then the dotted line UU_1 will be the sales curve which the supplier in country A assumes will apply, since the supplier in country A assumes that country B will only produce the quantity UV after the price is lowered. The supplier in country A sees a possibility of exporting, as long as the price is lowered. When country A has a possibility of exporting, the demand elasticity is therefore greater than if country A can only sell in its home market.

Figure 10.6: Conditions under a duopoly

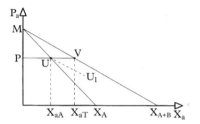

The marginal income in country A is the additional income obtained by producing one extra unit of good. The marginal income is equal to the price of the extra unit sold, less the loss arising from lower price on the original quantity sold because the price of the good has to be reduced in order to sell the extra unit.

The marginal income for country A is:

$$MR_{aA} = P_a + X_{aA} \cdot \frac{dP_a}{dX_{aT}} = P_a + X_{aA} \cdot \frac{X_{aT}}{X_{aT}} \frac{P_a}{P_a} \cdot \frac{dP_a}{dX_{aT}} =$$

$$P_a + X_{aA} \cdot P_a \cdot 1/X_{aT} \cdot \frac{dP_a/P_a}{dX_{aT}/X_{aT}}$$

If country A's share of the total market is X_{aA}/X_{aT}, then S_a is obtained when:

$$MR_{aA} = P_a \left(1 + \frac{S_a}{e} \right) \quad \text{where} \quad e = \frac{dX_{aT}/X_{aT}}{dP_a/P_a}$$

e is the price elasticity when the markets of the two countries are taken together. This elasticity is equal to the elasticity in country A when there are only sales on the home market, i.e. the elasticity at U when the unbroken line MX_A applies.

If country A can also sell in country B while country B's production is constant, then the elasticity for country A will be equal to e/S_a. This is the case when country A's sales curve is assumed to be the dotted line. After trade is introduced, the elasticity is e/S_a, which is greater than the elasticity e before trade, since S_a is less than 1. In the case illustrated in Figure 10.6 S_a is equal to ½.

The introduction of trade means that the nature of the market changes. With the assumption that the competitor in country B will have unchanged production, regardless of what the firm in country A does, the firm in country A will now be faced with a market which has a 'numerically' greater elasticity. This means that at the moment when trade is introduced, MR_{aA} is greater than MC_{aA}.

Before the introduction of trade the production volumes X_{aA} and X_{aB} will fulfil the requirement that the marginal income should be equal to the marginal costs. As a result of the two firms both behaving autonomously, each will experience the marginal income on their sales to the foreign market as being higher than on their sales to the home market. This means that each firm will begin to export to the other country. This means that the total production of the two firms will increase and as a result of this the price level will fall.

At point S in Figure 10.5 there is trade between country A and country B. This is a special form of trade, since both countries export and both countries import the same good a, even though the good is a homogeneous good. The exported volume is equal to the imported volume. Here the advantage of trade is not the exploitation of the advantages of specialisation. Here the advantage of trade is that it changes the nature of the market to become more competitive.

The reason that there is trade, even though the good is a homogeneous good, is that the marginal income, which each of the firms finds that it can obtain by selling on the foreign market, is greater than on the home market. Therefore both countries can see an interest in exporting to each other's markets. Seen from the point of view of the firms, they will be able to obtain the optimal situation if they are able either to establish a joint monopoly or to establish an agreement to share the market, i.e. a cartel, which would in effect operate as if the two countries were self-sufficient in the good.

A partial analysis

The above analysis is general in the sense that it analyses the connection between the two productions of goods a and b. It is now appropriate to supplement this with a partial analysis of the production conditions for good a on its own. In this way it is possible to obtain a deeper understanding of how an equilibrium can be established on the market for good a.

In the above analysis, no account was taken of the transport costs associated with international trade. In the following partial analysis it is assumed that in the internal trade, within a country, there are no transport costs. However, there are transport costs associated with international trade. The following model is based on the work of Brander and Krugman (1983).

In each of the two countries A and B there is a supplier of a homogeneous good. The supply conditions are identical. The cost functions for the suppliers in country A and country B are:

$$C_A = f + m (X_{AA} + X_{AB})$$
$$C_B = f + m (X_{BB} + X_{BA})$$

where f is the fixed costs and m is the marginal costs. X is the production, where the first subscript index symbol refers to the country of production and the second subscript index symbol refers to the country of consumption. X_{AA} is thus the production of country A which is sold in country A. X_{AB} is the production of country A which is sold in country B, i.e. it is country A's exports.

In each of the two countries there is a falling demand curve which is the same in each country:

$$P_A = a - b (X_{AA} + X_{BA})$$
$$P_B = a - b (X_{BB} + X_{AB})$$

The price in the individual country is a function of the country's own production for its home market (X_{AA} for country A), plus the imports to the country (X_{BA} for country A).

The transport costs are assumed to be $(1 - t)$ of the export volume produced. This means that $(1 - t)$ of the export volume 'evaporates' before it reaches the country of consumption. t is the percentage of the total export production which is in fact sold abroad. The remainder of the 'production' is in fact used to cover the transport costs. If t is 0.9, then the transport costs are 0.1 or 10 per cent. This is a technically convenient way to treat transport costs. Thus, for country A to supply exports of X_{AB} to country B, country A must produce X_{AB}/t.

On the basis of the cost conditions it is possible to establish profit functions for the two firms. The profits M_A and M_B for each of the two firms are the sales revenues less the costs:

$$M_A = [a - b (X_{AA} + X_{BA})] X_{AA} + [a - b(X_{BB} + X_{AB})]X_{AB} - f - m(X_{AA} + X_{AB}/t)$$

$$M_B = [a - b(X_{BB} + X_{AB})] X_{BB} + [a - b (X_{AA} + X_{BA})] X_{BA} - f - m(X_{BB} + X_{BA}/t).$$

The production functions show that there is a mutual strategic dependence between the firms. In the actual case there is a duopoly where the equilibrium which is established depends on the way in which the individual firms react.

It is assumed that the two firms behave autonomously, and that they choose the production volume which gives the optimal profit when the other firm has settled on a given production volume. These assumptions mean that this is a Cournot model. The firms behave autonomously and the firms adjust their production volumes.

Therefore the profit function must distinguish between production for the home market and for export for each of the two firms in each country. There are the following relationships:

$$\frac{\partial M_A}{\partial X_{AA}} = -2bX_{AA} - bX_{BA} + a - m \tag{10.1}$$

$$\frac{\partial M_A}{\partial X_{AB}} = -2bX_{AB} - bX_{BB} + a - m/t \tag{10.2}$$

$$\frac{\partial M_B}{\partial X_{BA}} = -2bX_{BA} - bX_{AA} + a - m/t \tag{10.3}$$

$$\frac{\partial M_B}{\partial X_{BB}} = -2bX_{BB} - bX_{AB} + a - m \tag{10.4}$$

The equations (10.1) and (10.3) are entirely symmetrical with equations (10.2) and (10.4). The first set of equations relates to sales in country A's home market. The second set of equations relates to sales in country B's home market. Since the conditions in the two countries are assumed to be the same, it is no surprise that there is symmetry.

Equation (10.1) indicates how the profit changes for the firm in country A when the firm changes its sales on the home market following a given import of X_{BA} from country B. The maximum profit is obtained where (10.1) is equal to zero. This gives the following expression:

$$X_{BA} = \frac{a - m}{b} - 2X_{AA} \qquad (10.5)$$

which should be read as $X_{AA} = f_1(X_{BA})$, where X_{BA} is the independent variable.

If equation (10.3) is equal to zero, the result is:

$$X_{BA} = \frac{a - m/t}{2b} - \tfrac{1}{2}X_{AA} \qquad (10.6)$$

which should be read as $X_{BA} = f_2(X_{AA})$, where X_{AA} is the independent variable.

In other words, there are two equations which show the reaction of one firm when the other firm's sales on the market are fixed.

The first equation (10.5) shows how much it is worth the supplier in country A offering on the home market when the supplier in country B supplies a given quantity X_{BA} in country A. Correspondingly, the other equation (10.6) shows the optimal quantity for the firm in country B to export to country A when country A's supplier provides a given quantity X_{AA} on its home market.

These two reaction equations can be drawn in a diagram, as shown in Figure 10.7. With the respective production quantities X_{AA} and X_{BA} there is a Cournot equilibrium, or more generally it is called a Nash equilibrium. Such an equilibrium is characterised by the fact that if one party continues to supply, for example, X_{BA}, the other party cannot obtain a better result than by supplying X_{AA}. Conversely, the optimal supply of the first party will be X_{BA} if the other party supplies X_{AA}.

Since the conditions in country A and country B are the same, an analysis of the conditions in country B's home market will be precisely as shown in Figure 10.7. The quantities X_{AA} and X_{BA} on the axes should merely be replaced by X_{BB} and X_{AB} respectively.

The greater the transport costs, in other words the smaller the value of t, the further down towards the horizontal axis will be the curve X_{BA}, as shown by the dotted line in Figure 10.7. The new equilibrium means that the home market supplier gets a greater share of the market and imports will be reduced. The higher transport costs mean that supplies to the two countries' home markets will be reduced. This mean in turn that the price level, which is the same in both countries, will be higher, because the total supply will be reduced.

Figure 10.7: Cournot-Nash equilibrium under a duopoly

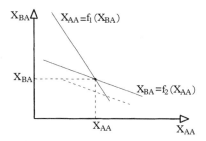

This model is a Cournot model because the firms fix their production quantities, which means that the price adjusts itself. It is possible to construct a corresponding Bertrand model where there is also autonomous behaviour, but where the firms change the prices.

Models with autonomous behaviour can be supplemented by models which assume conjectural behaviour. In most case such assumptions will be more realistic, but the models are more complicated. For example, it is not possible to divide the two markets as in the above example.

The model shows how, when there is an oligopoly, or in this case a duopoly, there can be trade in a homogeneous good. The exported volumes from the two countries are entirely the same. There will be some cross-trading in which the transport costs can be considered as a social economic waste. If welfare nevertheless rises, this is because trade reduces the price of the good in both countries, to the advantage of the consumers. One can naturally ask whether it is not possible for the competition authorities to intervene in the formation of prices so as to obtain the lower prices in the two countries without having to pay the social economic loss involved in the transport of the cross-traded goods.

10.3 Oligopolies and differentiated products

In the previous section it has been demonstrated how trade is possible under an oligopoly (duopoly) even when the product is a homogeneous good. This phenomenon is often called 'reciprocal dumping'. It is clear that an oligopoly with differentiated products will also give rise to trade. Below there is an analysis of a model of the kind used by Shaked and Sutton (1984). The central elements of these types of models are analysed below.

In this case there is a differentiated product with many product varieties. The product varieties are vertically differentiated, in other words, all consumers agree about the ranking of the products in relation to their quality. Different consumers buy different product qualities available on the market because there are different income levels in society.

In Figure 10.8 the product quality is shown on the x axis. The possible qualities range over the spectrum Ok, and the product quality rises from left to right.

Figure 10.8: Costs and incomes for vertically differentiated product varieties

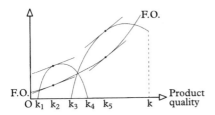

There are fixed and variable costs associated with each product quality. Regardless of the product quality the variable costs are the same. The fixed costs are to a large extent research and development costs, and they increase in line with the rise in product quality. The curve

F.O. shows the fixed costs associated with the production of the different product varieties.

The individual firm must make a number of choices. Firstly, it must decide whether to enter the market as a supplier. Secondly, he must choose the optimal quality, understood as the quality which will give the greatest profit. This choice depends on what suppliers there are already in the market and which product qualities they have chosen. Thirdly, earnings will depend on the price of the product variety, and the volume that can be sold at this price.

In an equilibrium situation there will be a number of suppliers on the market, each of which earns a 'normal' profit as long as there is free entry and exit of suppliers to and from the market. In practice there will be entry barriers to a market of this kind. The size of the entry barriers will depend on the size of the fixed costs.

It is now assumed that there are two firms which enter the market. One supplier is interested in the product range k_1k_4 and the other is interested in the product range k_3k. It is possible to calculate the net revenue (turnover minus variable costs) of the individual product varieties which are the two parabola-shaped curves k_1k_4 and k_3f which are drawn in Figure 10.8. Where the marginal net revenue are equal to the marginal costs, in relation to the varieties of product qualities, there will be the optimal choice of qualities. One firm will choose quality k_2 and the other will choose quality k_5.

How many suppliers there will be room for will depend entirely on the conditions of supply and demand. If the demand for the different product varieties is evenly spread across the range, and if the fixed costs are relatively low, compared with the variable costs, it will be possible for there to be many suppliers in the market. There will only be room for a few suppliers if the variable costs are small in relation to large fixed costs, and if the demand is concentrated on just a few product types. Where there are few large firms an oligopoly market for differentiated products will develop. There is a kind of 'natural' oligopoly which is results from the large research and development costs. The pharmaceutical industry is an example of a sector of this type.

It is now assumed that there are two countries which are identical. In each of the two countries there are two firms whose conditions are as shown in Figure 10.8. Market equilibrium has been established, and is identical in both countries. Trade is now introduced between the two countries, which each have two suppliers in the business sector in question. There are two 'low quality' suppliers and two 'high quality' suppliers, which now compete with each other for a market which is twice the size of that served by each of the suppliers before there was trade.

If competition between the firms is neutralised, the four firms can continue even after the opening up of trade. For example this can be achieved by a more or less unspoken agreement not to intrude on each others' markets. However, it is highly probable that sooner or later there will be price competition, at the same time as an individual firm tries to break into the market of another country. The two suppliers of low quality products and the two suppliers of high quality products will each compete against each other. An equilibrium will be established in which it is possible that there will only be one supplier in each product category remaining. All things being equal, the total costs for one firm will be less than the combined costs of two firms. However it is not possible to say precisely what the new equilibrium will mean. The net revenue curve which the individual firm operates with will take a step upwards because the market is now twice as big. The slope of the new net revenue curve of a given product quality will be steeper, and this means that the chosen product quality which gives the maximum return will be a variety of higher quality. It is also possible that there will be room for three or four firms on the combined market, which is now twice as big as each of the national markets.

The new equilibrium depends on the cost conditions, demand conditions and the behaviour of the firms.

One thing at least is sure, and this is that there will be specialisation of product varieties between countries. This means that there will be a basis for trade of an intra-industry nature. It is possible to explain that trade arises between the countries. When countries and firms are identical it is not possible to explain which product varieties the individual country will produce. It is only possible to explain the pattern of specialisation if the assumption that there are identical conditions is abandoned and if instead differences on the supply side or on the demand side are introduced. The significance of such differences has previously been discussed in Section 9.6.

10.4 Summary

In traditional factor proportion theory it is assumed that there is perfect competition. On the basis of the traditional neo-classical theories it is easy to believe that perfect competition is the ideal form of competition. According to this theory perfect competition will ensure the efficient allocation of the production factors and the efficient allocation of the production and the demand for goods.

This theory is static, since it takes as its point of departure a given quantity of production factors, and given production functions as well as given utility functions. In the real world there will be changes to these conditions. There will be product development which will create new products, and production processes will change. There is no scope for such elements if it is assumed that there is perfect competition.

In truth, perfect competition is more the exception than the rule. Today there is a whole range of differentiated products where there is monopolistic competition, where each supplier has a falling sales curve, but where there is only a certain room for manoeuvre because there is competition between near substitutes. The possibility of making a supernormal profit is limited in time unless there are significant entry barriers to the market, for example in the form of high fixed costs. On markets with monopolistic competition the entry or exit of firms will mean that each firm will, in the long run, only be able to obtain a 'normal' profit.

Monopolistic competition is a pre-condition for the theories on trade in differentiated products, which are reviewed in Chapter 9. In this case other conditions, beside the nature of the market, are of decisive importance.

In this present chapter attention has been focused on market forms where there are just a few major suppliers in the market. This chapter has shown firstly, that as long as there is a monopoly or an oligopoly, the introduction of trade will have the advantage of changing the nature of the market in the direction of potentially greater competition. The number of suppliers will be increased which means that there will be more competition and lower prices.

Secondly, the chapter shows that in a market for homogeneous goods, cross-border trade in homogeneous goods can occur as the result of a duopoly (oligopoly). This is due to the form of the market and the behaviour of the firms in the market.

Thirdly, it has been shown that, in the model for a duopoly in an international market for a homogeneous good, the size of the transport costs will affect the extent of trade. The transport costs are a barrier of distance of which there are many in practice. The existence of barriers of distance, which are dealt with in the next chapter, can be seen as an expression of market imperfection. With this exception, this chapter has not introduced distance barriers, since the concept of market imperfection has been related to the fact that there are only a limited number of suppliers in the market. It has been indirectly presupposed that the market mechanism works perfectly in the sense that there is market transparency and that there are no barriers of distance. Clearly, if there are no markets, or if the markets are 'imperfect', because there are large transport and distribution costs which limit competition, there is a special problem which affects not least the poorer less developed countries.

Fourthly, this analysis shows that if there are differentiated products, where there is a kind of 'natural' oligopoly as a result of large fixed costs, for example in connection with research and development, the nature of the market can give rise to trade.

Literature

Brander, J.A. and P. Krugman, 'A Reciprocal Dumping Model of International Trade', *Journal of International Economics*, 13, 1983.

Greenaway, D., and Chris Milner, *The Economics of Intra-Industry Trade*, Oxford, 1986.

Eaton, J. and G.M. Grossman, 'Optimal Trade and Industrial Policy under Oligopoly', *Quarterly Journal of Economics* 101, 1986.

Eaton, J. and H. Kierzkowski, 'Oligopolistic Competition, Product Variety and International Trade' in H. Kierzkowski (ed), *Monopolistic Competition and International Trade*, Oxford, 1984.

Shaked, A. and J. Sutton, 'Natural Oligopolies and International Trade' in H. Kierzkowski (ed), *Monopolistic Competition and Intertonal Trade*, Oxford, 1984.

11. A multiplicity of theories

In most of the areas of economic theory there has been a common development. This development moves from a situation in which there is only a single theory, or only very few theories, in a given area to a situation in which there is a multiplicity of models. Economic theory has generally changed from being simple to become highly complex. Today, on the basis of different pre-conditions and assumptions there is a multiplicity of models in each of the subdivisions of economic thought. The theory of international trade is no exception. In the preceding chapters the core theories of international trade have been analysed. It is now appropriate to attempt to compare and evaluate these theories.

Theories of international trade should preferably be able to answer a number of questions. Firstly, the theories should be able to suggest which factors determine the pattern of international trade. Secondly, the theories should be able to predict the economic consequences of international trade. What will happen to final good prices? What will happen to factor returns? What will happen to income distribution within an individual country, and what will happen to income distribution between countries? It is possible to consolidate these questions, which are interesting in themselves, in one overriding question: what is the effect of trade on welfare?

The picture which appears from all this is that it is possible to distinguish between a traditional theory of international trade and a newer theory of international trade. The traditional theory of international trade can be said to encompass the theories which are analysed in Chapters 5-7, and the newer theory of international trade encompasses the theories which are analysed in Chapters 8-10.

International trade theory is interesting as a descriptive theory which explains what happens in fact. International trade theory also has great interest as a normative theory which can suggest a basis for the choice of trade policy which an individual country ought to follow. International trade theory lies behind the ideas influencing the shape of international trade co-operation.

In the preceding Chapters 5-10 a number of theories have been analysed which suggest what it is that determines the kinds of goods traded and the extent of trade. Situations of self-sufficiency have been compared with situation where there is free trade. The theories show the consequences for welfare of free trade compared with self-sufficiency.

With certain exceptions, the theories considered have been static. They compare two situations where all the conditions are the same, with the exception that in one situation there is self-sufficiency while in the other there is free trade. It is important to note that growth in itself affects trade and that trade can, in turn, affect growth. Also, cumulative processes associated with growth mean that growth tends to be concentrated in certain centres.

International factor movements, such as capital movements, including foreign direct investment, as well as labour migration, are not taken into account by theories of international trade. These conditions also require analysis, and these are dealt with in Part III of this book.

Before undertaking such analysis, it is right to attempt to summarise the international trade theories which have been analysed in the preceding chapters.

11.1 The traditional and the newer theories of international trade

The theories of international trade which are current and which have been analysed in the preceding chapters can be arranged in a table, as shown in Table 11.1. Theories Nos. 1-4 cover the traditional theories, while theories Nos. 5-13 are the newer theories.

The traditional trade theory is based on the idea of comparative advantage. Comparative advantages can be related to different conditions. In Smith's and Ricardo's theories the advantages are linked to productivity, because of differing production functions in different countries. In factor proportion theory the production function for a given good is the same everywhere, and trade is conditioned by the fact that relative factor endowments differ in different countries. In the specific factor models labour and capital are no longer homogeneous quantities. There are differences between different types of labour and different types of capital.

Table 11.1: Theories of international trade

1	Differences in the production function (Adam Smith and David Ricardo).
2	Differences in factor endowment (Heckscher-Ohlin).
3.	The specific factor model.
4.	Availability theory.
5.	Economies of scale and firm specialisation.
	a. Traditional advantages of economies of scale.
	b. External advantages in the form of an industrial environment.
	c. Firm specialisation.
6.	The theory of the technological gap.
7.	The theory of the product life cycle.
8.	Demand for the ideal product variety.
9.	Demand for multiple product varieties.
10	Demand determines the pattern of production and thus trade (Linder's model).
11	Demand conditions and factor endowment determine production and trade (Falvey's model of vertically differentiated products).
12	Oligopoly where the products are homogeneous goods.
13	Oligopoly where the products are differentiated goods.

Different types of labour or different types of capital cannot immediately be substituted for each other. Availability theory emphasises that the necessary production factors are not present in every country. Only those countries which have access to the necessary production factors are able to produce and export the final goods which require these production factors.

At a given point in time the factor endowment of different countries will differ. This can be a central factor which contributes to the explanation of trade. However, it should not be forgotten that comparative advantages can change over time. If a country has obtained a comparative advantage in the production of a given good, this advantage can either be further developed or it can be diminished. Changes to relative factor endowment can occur through the education of the labour force, through increasing the capital stock and through technological progress.

The traditional trade theories are thus somewhat limited in their ability to analyse problems. Firstly they explain a given trade pattern solely on the basis of the relative production conditions. Secondly, they do not explain how trade both in itself and in combination with a number of other factors can influence economic growth, which can in turn change the relative factor endowment which again can result in a change to the pattern of trade.

The traditional theories explain trade on the basis of the supply side, whereas the newer theories take into account, in varying degrees, the demand side, the supply side and market conditions. In Table 11.2 the different theories are arranged according to the importance which each theory ascribes to the different conditions.

Table 11.2: Theories categorised according to whether supply, demand or the nature of the market is the central element

	Theories in Table 11.1
Production	1, 2, 3, 4
Demand	8, 9, 10
Production and demand	5, 6, 7, 11
The form of market	12, 13

A first set of theories focuses on supply conditions. This applies to the traditional trade theories. A second set of theories focuses on demand conditions. This applies to the theory of the ideal product variety, and the theory of demand for multiple product varieties to satisfy a given complex of demands. This includes the theory which states that demand is critical in explaining production and trade (Linder's theory). A third group of theories combines conditions of supply and demand. Some of these theories look on trade as part of a pattern of development. This applies to the theory of technological advantages and the theory of the product life cycle. Others consider trade in a more static context, as in Falvey's model. Finally, the fourth group of theories ascribes decisive importance to the form of the market.

11.2 What types of trade can the theories explain?

There is a tradition for analysing trade between two countries, which each produce two goods by means of two production factors. Such a model is relatively simple on the basis of which it is possible to derive a number of distinct statements (theorems), cf. factor proportion theory. It deals with the most simple conceivable case. To expand the model to k countries, m goods and n production factors can give a more realistically shaded picture of the pattern of trade, but there is often a question about how much additional knowledge is obtained at the cost of the vastly increased complexity of the model. It is not possible to generalise on this. When the very basic factors for explaining trade are concerned, a model with few countries and few goods will be sufficient. However if it is a case of an empirical description, it will be necessary to make a much more detailed model with many countries or regions and many product groups. To expand the model with a number of goods is not so problematic. To expand the model with more than two countries makes it possible to describe an individual country's bilateral trade relations, which can give different results than if the country's total international trade is considered. However, it can be problematic to include more than two production factors in the model, because the concept of factor intensity loses its clarity.

If the analysis is concentrated on two countries and two goods, there is naturally a question about which characteristics should be included in the model to describe the two countries and the two goods.

As for the two countries which are included in the analysis, the question is how the countries can best be described. It is possible to divide countries according to per capita GNP. Even though this measure is far from perfect, it is often used as an indicator for how similar or how different countries are. If a distinction is made between cases where countries are the same and cases where countries are different, then, without making an absolutely sharp distinction between the two instances, it can generally be said that the closer the per capita GNP of the two countries, the more similar the two countries are. Correspondingly, the greater the difference in per capita GNP, the greater the dissimilarity of the countries.

As for categories of goods, it is usual to distinguish between homogeneous goods and differentiated goods. These definitions are well established in price and competition theory. Homogeneous goods are goods with which no preferences are associated, as opposed to differentiated products, where the sales curve for the individual firm falls from left to right, as the result of preferences.

Categories of goods are often related to business sectors. For example, one good is an agricultural product and the other good is an industrial product. It is also possible to distinguish between industrial goods, for example, textile products on the one hand and electronic products on the other. What is decisive is that two different categories of goods are considered, in which it is assumed that each of the two goods are homogeneous goods. If the concept of the goods is linked to different sectors, the result will be an analysis of trade in goods from different sectors. In other words there will be inter-industry trade. However, if the analysis is concentrated on the individual sector within which differentiated goods are available, there will then be product varieties within the same sector which have different characteristics. If the concept of goods is linked to different product types within the same sector, the result will be an analysis of intra-industry trade.

Table 11.3: Theories arranged according to the characteristics of countries and goods

Countries Goods	The countries are the same	The countries are different
Homogeneous goods	3, 12	1, 2, 3, 4
Differentiated goods	5, 8, 9, 10, 13	5, 6, 7, 10, 11

Therefore, distinguishing between homogeneous goods on the one hand and differentiated goods on the other will in practice also lead to a distinction between cases where there is trade in goods from different sectors, and cases where there is trade in goods within a given sector.

In Table 11.3 the theories are classified according to categories of countries and categories of goods. A distinction is made between trade between countries which are relatively similar and countries which are dissimilar. A distinction is made between goods which belong to different sectors since it is assumed that each sector produces a homogeneous good and differentiated goods which are produced within the same sector.

The traditional theories in Table 11.1 are numbered 1 to 4, and in Table 11.3 they are placed in the category in which the countries are different and the goods are homogeneous goods. The core of Ricardo's theory is precisely that one country may be better, in absolute terms, at producing all goods, but that in spite of this there will be a basis for trade. The countries are at different levels. In factor proportion theory one country has a relatively large amount of capital and the other has a relatively large amount of labour. All things being equal, the country which has a large per capita capital stock will be wealthier than a country with a small per capita capital stock. The specific factor model is placed both in the category of countries which are the same and in the category of countries which are different, since it can help explain the conditions in both categories of countries. Something similar could be said about availability theory, but it has traditionally been used to explain trade where there are natural resources in the form of a special climate or raw materials present in some countries but not in others. Therefore today it is more noted for explaining trade between less developed countries and industrial countries than for explaining trade between industrial countries, where a product's dependence on the existence of raw materials etc. plays a less important role. The traditional theories typically consider trade in goods which belong to different sectors and which are assumed to be homogeneous goods.

The newer theories, which are numbered 5 to 13 in Table 11.1, primarily deal with trade in differentiated products. This can either be trade in horizontally differentiated products or vertically differentiated products. Trade in horizontally differentiated products takes place mainly between countries with the same income level. Trade in vertically differentiated products often takes place between countries with different income levels. For this reason, the theory of the ideal product variety and the theory of multiple product varieties are in the same category which relates to similar countries. By contrast, the theory of the technology gap, the theory of the product life cycle, and Linder's theory and Falvey's theory, which are all concerned with vertically differentiated products belongs in the category where countries are different. However, it is also reasonable to put Linder's theory in the category of similar countries. The theories which emphasise economies of scale based on external advantages as well as firm specialisation can help to explain trade both between countries which are similar and countries which are dissimilar.

There remain the theories which ascribe a central role to the nature of the market. They can explain trade in both homogeneous and differentiated products between countries that are similar.

11.3 The problems with the traditional theory

The traditional paradigm for explaining international trade is the theory of comparative advantage. This was originally formulated by Ricardo, but since then the idea has been incorporated in the neo-classical factor proportion theory, in which it is the factor endowments of countries which determine the pattern of trade. Neo-classical factor proportion theory was developed in the period up to about 1960. Since 1960 there has been development of the newer international trade theory.

The reason why the new international trade theory has been developed since 1960 is that factor proportion theory had encountered some problems.

Empirical analyses

As previously referred to, there are two sets of empirical analyses which have had a special influence on theoretical developments.

At the beginning of the 1950s Leontief carried out a number of analyses of the USA's foreign trade. As has been noted, he came to the conclusion that the USA imported capital intensive goods and exported labour-intensive goods. Even though there was no existing calculation of the factor endowment of the USA and the rest of the world, it was reasonable to assume that the USA had a relatively large stock of capital. This is why this is referred to as the Leontief paradox because his results conflicted with factor proportion theory. Leontief's analysis also gave rise to a number of theoretical speculations which showed that a large number of restrictive conditions had to be satisfied before factor proportion theory could apply.

Around 1960 Verdoorn carried out his analysis of the internal trade of the Benelux countries, and he found that that the strong growth was overwhelmingly due to intra-industry trade, i.e. trade in differentiated products belonging to the same sector. Consequently a large number of studies were undertaken which confirmed that trade between industrial countries, which has grown strongly, has primarily been intra-industry trade.

Factor proportion theory explains trade in homogeneous goods, but not trade in differentiated goods. This is a problem in itself, as the trend in post-war development has been towards a much smaller proportion of production being of homogeneous goods, and a steadily increasing proportion being differentiated products.

Why trade and factor movements take place simultaneously

Factor proportion theory does not make allowance for trade and factor movements taking place at the same time. If trade is to explained, it must be based on the assumption that there are no cross-border factor movements in the form of capital movements or labour migration. As a result of trade there will be the same factor returns in the two countries. When the returns on capital and labour are the same there will be no scope for factor movements, even if they are allowed. There is no incentive to move abroad, either for capital or labour.

In a factor proportion theory model, if in the initial situation there is a possibility of factor movements, without there being trade, then capital will flow to the country with a low level of capital and labour will go to the country with a relatively small amount of labour. In this way there will be an equalisation of factor prices, which means that there will be no scope for trade when this is allowed. Factor price equalisation creates uniform final good prices, so there will be no incentive for trade.

Factor proportion theory can therefore either explain trade or factor movements. However this is unsatisfactory as there has been a strong growth of both trade and foreign direct investments in the post-war period.

The explanation of trade

According to factor proportion theory, the greater the differences in the factor endowments of two countries, the greater will be their trade. If the relative factor endowment is the same while the demand structure is the same, there will not be a basis for trade.

If countries are divided into two groups, between industrial countries and developing countries, then factor proportion theory cannot explain world trade. According to the theory, there should be a large amount of trade between industrial countries and developing countries, while trade between industrial countries with the same income level should be small. In fact, trade between industrial countries and developing countries is small compared with the trade between industrial countries. What has happened has been that trade between industrial countries has grown far faster than trade between industrial countries and developing countries.

The explanation of foreign direct investment

According to factor proportion theory, the differences in factor endowment between countries means that the factor return differs between countries. If, again, countries are grouped into industrial countries and developing countries, then capital e.g. in the form of foreign direct investment should be located in the developing countries. Conversely, there should not be scope for foreign direct investment between industrial countries because the factor returns are the same.

Here again, the conclusions of factor proportion theory are not confirmed in practice. Direct investments by industrial countries in other industrial countries is greater than the investments by industrial countries in developing countries. Historically, investments by industrial countries in developing countries have been concentrated in the production of raw materials. The growth in investments by industrial countries in other industrial countries has been far greater than the growth of investments by industrial countries in developing countries.

11.4 An extended factor proportion theory

As shown above, factor proportion theory has problems in explaining world trade and foreign direct investments. However, the problem may be because it operates with a two-country model, which is a very considerable simplification of what happens in the real world. When the world is divided between industrial countries and developing countries, there is an implicit assumption that these are two homogeneous groups of countries. This is far from being the case. Among the industrial countries there are differences between the richest industrial countries (Northern Europe, North America and Japan), a middle-income groups (Southern Europe), and a low-income group (Central and Eastern Europe). Among the developing countries there are the newly industrialised countries (South Korea, Taiwan etc.) which can in many respects be considered as industrial countries. There are richer developing countries (Latin America), there are the middle-income developing countries (several of the ASEAN countries), and there are the poorest developing countries (Southern Asia and Sub-Saharan Africa). In Table 11.4 the axis indicates the per capita GNP. As one moves to the right in the figure the per capita GNP increases. The ranking of each category of countries is apparent in the figure.

Factor proportion theory, which is based on a model with 2 countries, 2 goods and 2 production factors, gives a clear answer as to when there will be trade and what the consequences of trade will be. However, the problem is, how to expand the model so that it will fit a world with many countries, many goods and many production factors. This becomes clear when an attempt is made to test the theory in the real world. It might be possible to choose a generalised model where there are n goods, m countries, and k production factors. The problem is not that it is impossible to build such a model consisting of relations between the supply and demand for the different goods in the different countries, and including a larger number of production factors. Nor is the problem that it is impossible to resolve such a model calculation so as to find how much an individual country exports and imports of the various goods. The problem is that it is not possible to make a hypothesis about what the pattern of trade will be. In other words there is no clear theory which it is possible either to prove or disprove.

However, if a less drastic approach is used, successively changing the number of countries, goods or production factors, it will be possible to put forward in advance, before starting the investigation, some presumptions on the basis of the simple 2 x 2 x 2 factor proportion theory. A number of examples are given here.

Table 11.4: Countries grouped according to per capita GNP

				→	per capita GNP
Southern Asia	ASEAN countries	Latin America	Central and Eastern Europe	Southern Europe	Northern Europe
Sub-Saharan Africa			Newly Industrialised Countries		North America
					Japan

First it is assumed that there are three goods, two countries and two production factors. The production factors are capital and labour. The goods can be ranked according to factor intensity, i.e. how much they require relatively of the two production factors. Factor proportion theory will state that after the introduction of trade countries with a relatively large amount of capital will produce and export the most capital intensive goods. The other country will produce the most labour intensive goods. It is not possible to make any prediction about the production and trade in the third good which lies between the other two goods with regard to factor intensity.

Next, if it is assumed that there are three countries, two goods and two production factors, it is clear that the country with most capital will produce and export the most capital intensive good. Conversely, the country which has the largest labour force will produce and export the most labour intensive good. However, it is uncertain whether the two countries will each produce the other good, and there is uncertainty about what the pattern of production and trade will be for the third country which has a factor endowment which lies between the factor endowment of the other two countries.

The idea behind the above models will be recognised from the analysis of Ricardo's theory of the comparative advantage in Chapter 5. Here the model is expanded from 2 goods to n goods, and then the model is expanded from 2 countries to N countries.

Finally, it is possible to illustrate the significance of having several production factors by assuming that there are 2 countries, 4 goods and 3 production factors, which are physical capital (K), human capital (H) and labour (L). Labour means unskilled labour which has a basic education, for example up to secondary school level. Human capital, which is incorporated in the labour force, is the education and knowledge which has been acquired above this level.

The problem with having a total of production factors of more than two is that the concept of a good's factor intensity loses its clarity. In the above example there will be four kinds of goods which vary according to their factor intensity, see Table 11.5.

Table 11.5: Factor intensity when there are three production factors

$\frac{H}{L}$ \ $\frac{K}{L}$	Large	Small
Large	1 Intensive with regard to physical and human capital	2 Intensive with regard to human capital and labour
Small	3 Intensive with regard to physical capital and labour	4 Labour intensive

If one of the countries has a high H/L and a high K/L in relation to the other country, then international trade will lead to the first country exporting good 1 and the other country exporting good 4. It is not immediately possible to say which country will export goods 2 and 3. Good 3 requires a relatively high amount of physical capital, but not much human capital. On the face of it, it would seem that the country with high K/L would have an advantage. However, it is possible that this country has already used its capital in the production of good 1 so that capital is expensive in this country. Even if the other country only has a little capital, it could well be cheaper because the labour intensive good 4 only requires a little capital. Therefore it is not impossible that the country with the large labour force will produce good 3. If the country can import physical capital through capital movements, the possibility of producing good 3 will be greater.

In the above there has first been an increase in the number of goods, then in the number of countries and finally in the number of production factors. None of these models is ideal when it confronts the real world. The most reasonable way to fit factor proportion theory to the real world is to say that there are n goods, k countries and two or only very few production factors. The above example illustrates the problems connected with increasing the number of production factors from two to three. The concept of factor intensity loses its clarity. In the following it is therefore assumed that there are two production factors, capital and labour. There are k countries, which is fewer than n which is the number of goods. All n goods are ranked according to their factor intensity.

In Figure 11.1 good 1 is the most capital intensive good. Good f is more labour intensive than good 1, and good f in turn is less labour intensive than good i. The most labour intensive good is good n. In Figure 11.1 an isoquant is drawn for each of goods 1, f, i and n. Under conditions of international free trade there will be a range of world market prices which, for these four goods are P_1, P_f, P_i and P_n. The production quantities X_1, X_f, X_i and X_n, which are associated with the four isoquants fulfil the conditions:

$$P_1 \cdot X_1 = P_f \cdot X_f = P_i \cdot X_i = P_n \cdot X_n$$

This means that the incomes of the firms are identical when producing the quantities X_1, X_f, X_i and X_n. The firms will therefore only produce the goods where the costs are the same. This idea has already been used previously, cf. Chapter 6, Section 6.5. In this model there are k countries. The slopes of the lines of the lines $(L/K)_1$, $(L/K)_h$ and $(L/K)_k$ indicate the relative factor endowment in the three countries 1, h and k, which have been chosen. In country 1 there is a large capi-

A multiplicity of theories

tal stock. Therefore the relative factor prices are equal to $(r/w)_1$. With these relative factor prices country 1 will produce goods from 1 to f. In country h there are relative factor prices which are equal to $(r/w)_h$ which is greater than (r/w), because country h has relatively less capital. This means that country h produces from good f to good i. Finally there is country k which is the country which has relatively most labour. In country k the relative factor prices are equal to $(r/w)_k$. This means that country k produces from good i to good k.

Figure 11.1: n goods, k countries and 2 production factors

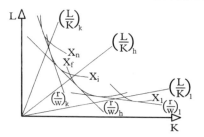

This expanded factor proportion model cannot generally predict which goods the individual countries will produce when there is international free trade. However, the model can predict that the countries which have relatively more capital will produce a range of goods which share the characteristic of being capital intensive. Conversely, the countries which have a relatively large labour force will produce a range of goods in which there is high labour intensity. Countries which have an L/K which lies in-between will produce a range of goods where the factor intensity also lies in-between.

The model also reveals another interesting condition. Both country 1 and country h produce good f, but the production of this good is more capital intensive in country 1 than in country h. Correspondingly, both country h and country k produce good i. The production of this good is more labour intensive in country k than in country h. When this is the case this is because the relative factor prices in the model are not the same in all countries when there is international free trade. In this way the model is much more realistic than the factor proportion theory which is based on a 2 good/2 country assumption in which there is factor price equalisation after there is trade if both countries produce both goods when there is trade.

11.5 A different approach

In Section 11.3 it is shown that there are problems with factor proportion theory when using a 2 good/2 country model. If the model is expanded to include n goods and k countries, the model is more realistic if the n goods are considered as being produced in each of n business sectors.

However, this expansion of factor proportion theory is far from solving all the problems. Factor proportion theory is based on a number of problematic assumptions, such as that the production function for a good is the same everywhere, and that the production factors of capital and labour are both homogeneous both within a single country and between countries. Finally, it is assumed that the goods are homogeneous goods and that there is perfect competition in the markets. In other words it does not allow for differentiated products.

It is therefore proper to acknowledge the limitations of factor proportion theory. An important starting point, which takes account of these problems, is to acknowledge that demand conditions, supply conditions and the barriers of distance are very different in the different groups of countries referred to, for example, in Table 11.4.

Demand

There are marked differences in demand conditions between a poorer society and a richer society.

Firstly, rising incomes mean that there is a relative fall in the demand for agricultural products and a corresponding increase in the demand for industrial products. With further rises in incomes the relative importance of industrial goods will fall, and the demand for services will rise.

Secondly, if there is an increased possibility of consumption, the structure of needs changes and is developed through the purchase of goods. There will be a possibility of satisfying hitherto unsatisfied wants, especially for the highest income groups, which means that there are incentives to develop new products and new production processes in the richer countries.

Thirdly, a higher living standard leads to more differentiated consumption, see Section 9.4. With a low income it is necessary to satisfy a group of needs with a single good or with very few goods. With a high income there is the capacity to consume several product types which each give a higher satisfaction of particular parts of the complex of needs. In a society where there is a varying, and often an increasing number of goods which satisfy a complex of needs, there is particular scope for cross-border trade in differentiated products.

Production

In relation to the surrounding world, a country's production possibilities are not God-given, but are to a great extent subject to man-made changes. If the different economic phases of a country are seen in relation to different epochs or if different countries which are at different stages of development are seen at a particular point in time, the production possibilities will naturally be very varied. This is because the relative quantity of production factors will be very varied.

In countries with a low average income, production will take place using labour and land, understood as a natural resource in the broadest sense, including climate and the existence of mineral resources. The less developed a country is, the more important land is as a production factor, since there will only be a small amount of capital and knowledge available. In such societies to all extents and purposes production consists of agricultural products and raw materials. This disregards the fact that within individual sectors it is possible for foreign investments to establish capital intensive production. Where there is such foreign investment, contact with the other parts of the commercial life of the country in question will often be very limited.

In countries with a middling average income most of the production will take place using a combination of the production factors of labour and capital. In these societies production will mostly consist of simple industrial products.

In the richest countries the most important production factors are capital, labour and knowledge. In these societies production is relatively concentrated around industrial products whose production requires a high level of knowledge, and around the provision of services.

It is important to define the term 'knowledge' as it is often used imprecisely. There are several elements in the expression 'knowledge'. First, knowledge means possession of information about existing technology. Secondly it means that the labour force has a high educational level, both in general and specifically. A high level of general education is necessary for the labour force to be able to adapt to new tasks. Special knowledge is necessary for being able to take part in the production of special products. There must be a labour force which possesses technical knowledge, organisational skills and marketing skills. Thirdly, the word knowledge is used in connection with the ability to develop and create entirely new products. Fourthly, 'knowledge' is used to mean knowing about the market. There must be an overview of the market including where it is possible to buy the special semi-manufactures and services which are necessary to be able to produce and sell the products. It is a characteristic of all these forms of knowledge that they increase as the per capita GNP increases.

In the least developed countries the business structure is concentrated on primary industries. Over time, and as higher income levels are reached, mining and agriculture can give rise to the industrial processing of primary products. Manual crafts will also develop into industries.

It is characteristic of industrial production in the more advanced developing countries and in the least developed industrial countries that it uses simple production processes. The import of raw materials and semi-manufactured goods for the production of final goods is relatively limited.

In the most highly developed countries the products and production processes are so complicated that there are considerable imports of semi-manufactured goods. There is movement towards a situation in which the production process is sub-divided up into a large number of steps.

Distance

Distance operates as a kind of barrier, the strength of which helps to determine the extent and composition of trade. Distance can consist of several elements. There is the physical element, the economic element and the political element.

Physical distance concerns transport costs, extra warehousing costs, and extra financing costs because international trade takes longer.

The economic distance concerns the effectiveness with which the market mechanism works. The market mechanism can be considered as a signalling system which sends messages about what potential opportunities there may be. The more integrated the markets are the better the signalling system works, and the lower the transport and communication costs will be. An effective market mechanism requires:

1. that there is good information about market conditions, or good possibilities for obtaining such information.
2. that business leaders have a broad scope of interests and an ability to make realistic evaluations of risks, on the basis of which they exploit the possibilities for production and sales.
3. that the markets are integrated so that the firms and the labour force can relatively easily adjust to changing market conditions.
4. that the infrastructure and the institutional conditions are such that the costs associated with international trade are not too great.

The last element of distance, which concerns politics, covers all kinds of political barriers in the form of tariff protection, quantitative restrictions, and so on, which either prevent or limit international trade.

11.6 The consequences for trade

The characteristics referred to above mean that there will be different kinds of trade depending on which countries are concerned. Starting with the richest countries, in Northern Europe, North America and Japan, the factor endowments are very similar, demand is strongly differentiated, and there are large areas of overlap with regard to the kinds of goods for which there is demand in the individual countries. Finally, the markets work effectively and are integrated. In this situation there is scope for comprehensive mutual trade in which there will be a high degree of goods belonging to the same business sectors. There will be considerable trade in both horizontally differentiated products and vertically differentiated products. The inter-industry specialisation which will take place is exemplified by the Danish exports of processed foods, the Swedish exports of goods from the paper industry and German exports of chemical products, which are largely due to external advantages in the form of an industrial environment.

If trade between the richer industrial countries and Central and Eastern Europe is looked at, as well as trade with the newly industrialised countries, it will be found that there is also scope for intra-industry trade. This will be dominated by vertically specialised products. There will also be an increase in the trade in goods from different industrial sectors. There will be greater differences in the production possibilities.

If trade between the richer industrial countries and developing countries is considered, it will be found that the overlap of demand is reduced. This reduces the intensity of trade. Trade will no longer be dominated by intra-industry trade, but inter-industry trade will be more significant. In this situation the differences in factor endowment become increasingly important. In many cases availability theory will prevail, for example in connection with tropical agricultural products and trade in mineral products.

The trade of industrial countries will be dominated by intra-industry specialisation. Trade between industrial countries and developing countries, and trade between developing countries will be dominated by inter-industry specialisation. Trade between developing countries will be limited by the fact that the demand conditions are only slightly differentiated and by the fact that 'distance' between developing countries is often great.

11.7 The influence of distance on trade

It is now appropriate to look more closely at the role of distance in international trade. What is the role of distance in the traditional theory and in the newer theory? What is the role of distance in the development of trade patterns? The barriers of distance play different roles in the traditional theory and in the newer theory.

Distance and the horizon of interest of firms

In the traditional theory the physical costs of distance, for example in the form of transport costs, can easily be incorporated in the theory. The transport costs can be considered as a wedge which is inserted between the lower price which the exporting country obtains and the higher price which the importing country must pay.

If the costs of distance are the same for different goods, then they do not affect the pattern of trade, but only its extent. If the barriers of distance vary for different products, then the pattern of trade can be affected.

In the newer theory the costs of distance play a completely different and significant role. This applies to theories 5b, 6, 7 and 10 in Table 11.1 above. What these theories have in common is that proximity to consumers and the possibility of exploiting external advantages in the local industrial environment are highly significant.

In the past the costs of distance were even more significant than now because transport and communications systems were not so well developed. In the past there were no multinational companies and foreign direct investment to help generate greater knowledge within individual firms about conditions in other countries. Also, increased trade resulting from cheaper transport costs, has helped to increase firms' knowledge about foreign markets.

The barrier of distance is also of decisive importance in the home market theory, which is incorporated in theory 10 in Table 11.1. Its starting point is the individual firm. A firm is set up with a view to satisfying some demand on the home market. When the home market has been satisfied, in the sense that it is only possible to increase sales by lowering the price, and damaging profitability, the firm will begin to be interested in export to the nearest markets which it is easiest to obtain knowledge about. Once these markets have been satisfied there will then be interest in more distant markets. In other words, there is a gradual expansion of the horizon of interest of such firms. It can be said that over time the horizon of interest of such firms becomes broader.

In addition to the horizon of interest becoming broader it can also become deeper in a particular market. When a firm considers going into a foreign market, the firm has no export know-how. Therefore it is natural to choose an export agent from its own country to look after exports. If the firm is small it can enter into some co-operative arrangement with other firms with regard to export tasks.

When exports have grown, the firm will want to have greater direct control over its exports which can come about through agreements with sales agents or dealers in the foreign market.

If exports continue to grow, the agent will lose interest in increasing the firm's sales and turn instead to other products were the sales work is easier. At the same time the firm's sales will be sufficiently large to justify the costs of establishing its own sales office.

The next step, for example, is to enter into a licence agreement or an agreement for production co-operation with firms in the countries in question. Finally, the firm can decide to invest in a production unit, and this will usually be the final stage of the development outlined here.

One of the interesting aspects of this theory is that trade and foreign establishment are both part of a process in which the firm becomes gradually more internationally oriented.

This is a process in which the firm increasingly gets bound into a particular market. Investments in the market increase, so the fixed cost element is increasingly important. Among other things, the advantages of being bound into the foreign market is that the distance to the market is reduced as knowledge of the market is increased. The reduced distance means that the costs can be reduced so that the sales possibilities are increased.

The home market theory is more relevant in cases where there are considerable barriers of distance. Distance barriers depend on the physical and cultural distance, the nature of the good and the type of firm. Today cultural barriers are more important than physical barriers. The barriers of distance are more significant for differentiated products than for homogeneous products. The barriers of distance are more important for small and medium sized firms than for large firms or multinational firms. Today there are many more multinational firms and many more internationally oriented firms than previously. It can therefore be asked whether the home market theory had greater value in the past than it does today.

Distance and the pattern of trade

It is natural to ask how it can be that the European countries, for example, have such similar business structures as they have. From a historical perspective it has been the same business sectors that have been either expanding, stagnating or contracting throughout the region. Inter-industry specialisation between the individual countries in Europe has been much less than the inter-industry specialisation between the regions of the USA. In the USA Detroit has been the area for motor car manufacture, while textile manufactures have been concentrated in the New England states.

An explanation for this can be found in the extent of the barriers of distance. Historically the barriers of distance in the USA have been much less of an obstacle than the barriers of distance between the European countries. The USA has been a free trade area while the European countries have each had their trade barriers. In the USA the cultural barriers have been much smaller, among other things because of their common language.

Since the barriers of distance in Europe were so high in the period when industrialisation took place, that industrialisation was home market oriented to a high degree. If several countries have the same level of incomes, the business structure will be the same in the countries in question. Only in cases where there are products in which a production factor determined by nature is decisively important will there be a comparative advantage which is sufficiently clear for the products to be able to overcome the trade barriers. Even if a country has such a considerable comparative advantage that it would be expected that there will be exports to another country, it is not certain that the possibility of trade will be realised. The other country can implement protective measures to ensure domestic production.

As a consequence of barriers of distance, which are in part man-made, the countries of Europe have very similar business structures. It is only after the countries have reached a high per capita income that the barriers of distance are broken down. When the man-made barriers disappear, and when technical developments reduce the other barriers, then there will be specialisation within business sectors. Highly differentiated consumption and the international demonstration effect of foreign travel contribute to this. The adjustment of manufacturing is also relatively easy. Since the changes to production take place through product development and product adjustments within business sectors, there will only be a limited reallocation of production factors.

A liberalisation of trade thus gives rise to increased specialisation within business sectors. There will be the same effect if transport costs fall or if there is increased growth. The specialisation is intra-industrial and to a high degree it is specialisation between horizontally differentiated products.

If the barriers of distance had been eliminated at a time when the per capita income had been lower, the result could have been different. Because of external economies different industrial sectors would develop in different countries. Individual countries would obtain comparative advantages in relation to different business sectors. If the barriers of distance disappeared at an earlier stage of industrialisation, there would be specialisation between countries involving whole business sectors. The pattern of development of specialisation will therefore depend on when the barriers of distance are removed.

Today, the industrialisation of developing countries is taking place in a situation in which the barriers of distance have been reduced. It can therefore be expected that inter-industry specialisation will play a greater role, especially with vertically differentiated products.

11.8 The influence of trade on final good prices and factor prices

The traditional theory of international trade is a general equilibrium theory in which there is full utilisation of all production factors, which are fully mobile within a country. As a consequence of international trade the relative final good prices will be changed. In the country with a larger amount of capital the relative price of the capital intensive good will go up. The relative price of the labour intensive good will fall. There will be the reverse situation in the other country. At the same time there will be a complete or partial equalisation of factor prices in the two countries.

The newer trade theory concentrates on differentiated products where there is monopolistic competition, and where there is the possibility of exploiting the advantages of specialisation at firm level. The theory concentrates on the conditions within the business sector. It is therefore not an equilibrium model for the whole of society, even though it may well be an equilibrium model for the individual sector.

The gains from trade are associated with exploiting of the advantages of specialisation and with the increased competition which comes from the opening up of international trade. Trade in differentiated products therefore means there will be lower prices for the goods that are traded. Therefore the prices of 'international goods' will fall in relation to the prices of 'home market goods', i.e. the goods which are not traded internationally.

This applies to horizontally differentiated goods. On the other hand, if there are vertically differentiated goods, both the price level and the price structure will be affected by trade. If there is a possibility of trade then for vertically differentiated products there will also be a tendency for there to be a generally lower price level than in a situation in which the possibilities of trade are either limited or non-existent. In addition to this, trade will also affect the price structure, since the market for 'advanced' products will be influenced by monopolistic competition where there can be very strong preferences. There will also be foreign competitors in the market sector for advanced products who will come from other industrial countries where the cost levels are high. With more traditional products or basic products which are more homogeneous, the preferences will be weaker. In these cases the foreign competitors will come from countries which will often have much lower cost levels. Both these situations mean that price competition will be much keener for the traditional products, and especially for the basic homogeneous products, than for the advanced products.

In connection with the discussion of the prices of the goods it is important to note that, for differentiated products, the sales and distribution costs constitute a steadily increasing proportion in relation to the pure production costs. Most of the distribution costs are borne by the importing country. This means that a given percentage fall in the price in the exporting country is not reflected in an equal percentage fall of the sales price in the importing country.

How are the factor prices of labour and capital affected? For horizontally differentiated products, where the factors used in the different product types are very similar, there is no reason to believe that there will be any particular changes to relative factor prices. For vertically differentiated products, the 'special' production factors which are used in making the 'advanced' products will obtain a relatively higher return than production factors used in more traditional productions which will include low price products.

How the returns on capital and on labour will be shared within the individual categories of goods will depend on how the wages are fixed. In cases where there is a uniform centralised wage formation, the differences in the returns from the different product groups will be seen in the return on capital. Where there is a decentralised wage formation, which to a large extent takes place within firms, then the differences in returns between different productions will be seen in the returns on both labour and capital. It is clear that the more uniform the wage formation is, regardless of the differences in the returns from the production of the goods, the greater will be the risk that low price production will be competed out of the market in the industrial countries.

The knowledge in which richer countries have a monopoly gives the richer countries better terms of trade than if this knowledge were available to other countries. This is why the question of intellectual property rights relating to such knowledge is assuming an ever more important role in international trade negotiations. The developing countries are interested in a set of rules which limits these intellectual property rights. The industrial countries and their producers would like to keep these rights for themselves.

Intellectual property rights, for example in the form of patents, were introduced in order to encourage firms to initiate research and development programmes for the development of new products and new production processes. An interim monopoly is necessary so that a firm can cover its research costs.

There is a need for a balance. Intellectual property rights must be sufficient to stimulate development, but on the other hand the rules should not be so restrictive as to prevent others from producing which would create competition and prevent monopoly profits.

11.9 The gains from international trade

From the starting point of the neo-classical theory, which lies behind factor proportion theory, the gains from international trade have already been discussed in Chapter 4. According to factor proportion theory there is an advantage to an individual country from a pure exchange of goods as long as the international terms of trade after trade differ from the relative final good prices before trade. In addition to this there will be advantages from specialisation in production, which is linked to the fact that the factor endowments of the countries are different.

Chapter 4 has also referred already to two problems: firstly, the question of income distribution, cf. Sections 4.2 and 4.3, and secondly, the question of factor immobility and imperfections in the factor markets, cf. Section 4.5. Factor proportion theory states, cf. the Stolper-Samuelson theorem, that the production factor which is used most intensively in production, which increases as a result of free trade, will obtain a return which increases in absolute terms. The other production factor will experience a fall in absolute return. In other words, as a result of trade there will be a redistribution of income which means that not all households will gain from trade.

The consequence is that it is only possible to say that free trade is potentially better than self-sufficiency. In order for free trade to be better in fact, then there must be a redistribution of income at the same time as there is free trade, in order to ensure that none are worse-off. As shown in Chapter 4, such a redistribution of income is possible in theory. Whether, in practice, it is politically possible is another matter.

The other problem which has been raised concerns the immobility of factors and the imperfections of factor markets. Section 4.5 shows that if these problems cannot be solved within a reasonable period, it can be problematic to remove tariff protection for an industry, for example. Here it should be noted that even in industrial countries where there is greater factor mobility and the market imperfections are not so great, these problems have meant that industrial countries have protected their own more 'sensitive' areas, such as the agricultural and textile sectors. In developing countries the possibilities for adjusting to new and alternative productions is much more limited. When the adjustment process is brought into the picture, it is necessary to depart from the comparative static assumptions which are the basis of factor proportion theory, and move into the realm of a dynamic theory. Looking at free trade from this perspective, the question of the benefits of free trade are less obvious, especially for the poorer developing countries.

To summarise the conclusions of factor proportion theory, it can be said that: Compared with self-sufficiency, international free trade will give all countries an advantage. Free trade is potentially better, as the question of whether certain groups are worse-off can be solved by a redistribution of income. Factor proportion theory disregards the other questions of factor immobility and market imperfections since they conflict with the pre-conditions of the theory.

If the newer trade theories, which explain trade in horizontally and vertically differentiated products, are considered the question of relative factor endowment in the different countries is only relevant in relation to trade in vertically differentiated products. On the other hand, the gain on the demand side linked to the fact that free trade gives consumers a better possibility of obtaining their ideal product type, and that they have an increased possibility of obtaining a multiplicity of product types, is assumed to increase welfare. On the supply side there are advantages linked to exploiting firm specialisation and to the increased competition which will arise from establishing a bigger market.

11.10 Income distribution between countries

The distribution of income between different groups of countries is very uneven. There has been a change in income distribution. Between some countries there has been a narrowing of the differences in income. Between other countries there has been an increase in the differences in the countries' incomes. In the group of richer industrial countries consisting of North America, Western Europe and Japan, there were considerable differences in per capita income immediately after the second world war. Today these differences have been evened out so that the three regions have roughly the same per capita income. If industrial countries are compared with the so-called newly industrialised countries, there has also been a relative equalisation of incomes as growth in the newly industrialised countries has been much more rapid than in the industrial countries. If, on the other hand, a comparison is made between the poorer developing countries and the industrial countries, it will be seen that the gap has become bigger.

However, the picture is not clear cut. In the mid-1970s a country like China was one of the poorer less developed countries. Since then there has been strong economic growth in China and the income gap has been reduced.

Differences in income are measured in per capita GNP. This is far from being an ideal measure, because it exaggerates differences in income. If, nevertheless, this measure is used it is necessary to distinguish between absolute and relative differences of income. If an industrial country has a low growth rate compared with a developing country, which has a high growth rate, then the relative income difference will be reduced, whereas the absolute income difference can be increased. Low growth on the basis of a large per capita GNP can very well be greater than a high rate of growth on the basis of a small per capita GNP.

The question which it is natural to ask is whether free trade reduces inequalities of income. The theories of international trade which have been analysed in the preceding chapters are not able to contribute much to this question. This is because the theories are comparative static theory. The theories do not look at the process of growth, and they do not indicate how trade affects the process of growth.

If the discussion is restricted to the comparative static analyses, what do the theories of international trade say about income differences between countries?

The traditional theory says that both countries will potentially gain from free trade. Both countries will attain a higher economic level. If there are differences of income between the countries, it is not possible to predict whether the relative inequalities will be greater, unchanged or smaller. This depends on who gains most from the trade. The theory cannot predict with certainty which country will obtain the greatest gains. The theory can only say that, in general, the distribution of the total gains will depend to a high degree on the relative prices under international trade.

If the newer theory of trade is considered, it is necessary to distinguish between trade in horizontally differentiated products and trade in vertically differentiated types of goods. Trade in horizontally differentiated products is typically carried on between industrial countries with approximately the same income level. The theory says that all industrial countries will benefit from specialisation. There is no reason to suppose that the income distribution between countries will be altered.

Certain of the theories on trade in vertically differentiated products explicitly take account of developing countries. For example this is the case with the theory of the product life cycle. The result of this theory is that inequalities can occur with regard to who gets the greatest benefit from trade. Firstly, the theory of the product life cycle says that industrial countries will concentrate on products in their introductory phase and developing countries will concentrate on products in their stagnation phase. All things being equal, this will be an advantage for the industrial countries which will be further reinforced if the industrial countries do not remove trade protection for the types of product which are in the stagnation phase. Secondly, the theory says that industrial countries will obtain advantages in their terms of trade by concentrating on new product types, where the competition is not as keen as it is with more traditional products.

In moving from self-sufficiency to free trade there are a number of adjustment costs. If there is intra-industry trade with differentiated product types, the costs of adjustment are less than if there is inter-industry trade. Since the industrial countries are involved in intra-industry trade to a much greater extent than the less developed countries, the industrial countries have an advantage over the developing countries.

Inter-industry trade involves greater adjustment costs. In many cases such adjustment will be especially problematic for developing countries in which alternative production possibilities are much more limited. In addition to this, the market mechanisms in developing countries are often characterised by more imperfections than is usual in industrial countries.

11.11 Summary

Today there are two sets of theories which explain international trade. There is the traditional theory in the form of factor proportion theory, and there are a number of newer theories.

The distinction between inter-industry and intra-industry trade is a key issue. Inter-industry trade is trade in products from different business sectors. Factor proportion theory is the central theory with regard to homogeneous products, which are produced in different business sectors. It is possible to make factor proportion theory more generally applicable by expanding it to cover n goods and k countries, instead of the usual case of 2 goods and 2 countries. Factor proportion theory starts from the point of view that there is given factor endowment in countries which are different. There are considerable problems in classifying production factors as either capital or labour, since human capital is so important. It is a comparative static theory, which means that it does not take account of the fact that factor endowment is not God-given but is the result of man-made changes in the form of investments. Therefore the theory cannot give an explanation of why an individual country has the factor endowment which it now has.

The newer theories look primarily at trade in products within a single business sector. This can either be trade in horizontally or vertically differentiated products. In these cases demand conditions, firm specialisation, the existence of an industrial environment as well as the form of the market all play a quite different role than in factor proportion theory.

It is reasonable to consider the two sets of theories as being complementary rather than competing. They try to explain different types of trade. Factor proportion theory, which is a general equilibrium theory, tries to explain trade in products from different business sectors between countries with different income levels.

The theories about trade in horizontally differentiated products try to explain trade in products which belong to the same business sector. The theories are partial in the sense that they only cover one business sector, but they can naturally also describe a general equilibrium within that sector. The theories about horizontally differentiated products concern intra-industry trade between countries of the same income level. In contrast with this, the theories on trade in vertically differentiated products are concerned with intra-industry trade between countries with different income levels.

Whether it is better to use one set or the other set or a third set of theories therefore depends on the actual problem under consideration.

The traditional and the newer theories give different answers on how final good prices and factor prices are affected by international trade. The traditional theory says that relative final good prices will change. This means that the return on one production factor will increase absolutely. According to the newer theories there will be a general tendency for the price level of goods which are traded internationally to fall. If there are vertically differentiated products, international trade will also mean a change to the price structure between 'advanced' products and 'low price' products, to the advantage of the former.

Whether there is a basis for gains through international trade will also differ according to which of the two sets of theories is used. In both sets of theories there are advantages in exchanging goods. In traditional theory the exchange of goods is linked to changes in their relative prices. In the newer theories the advantage of exchanging goods is primarily linked to the greater range of goods available. In addition to this there are lower prices on goods which are traded internationally, because of the stiffer competition. In the traditional theory the advantages on the supply side come from the comparative advantage in the production of goods. In the newer theories the advantage comes from economies of scale production and firm specialisation, which are decisive factors in production.

How does international trade affect income distribution in the world? The traditional theory concludes that all countries will gain from free trade. The newer theories, which take account of the barriers of distance, for example in the form of inefficient market mechanisms, especially in developing countries, are somewhat less optimistic. The terms of trade between 'advanced' products and 'low price' products will also develop to the disadvantage of developing countries. By opening up for trade there will be intra-industry specialisation in industrial countries, whereas for developing countries there will be inter-industry specialisation. Inter-industry changes are always more difficult than intra-industry changes, especially in a society with a lower standard of living and with fewer alternative opportunities for employment.

It can thus be concluded that the two theories give different answers to a large number of key questions.

Part III
Economic growth,
factor movements
and cumulative processes

12. Economic growth and trade

12.1 Economic growth

The national product Y is produced by means of the factors of production capital (K), labour (L) and technological know-how (T). It is usual to set up a macroeconomic production function

$Y = f(K,L,T)$.

Economic growth is measured as the increase in national product $\Delta Y/Y$. The level of Y depends on the quantity and quality of the factors of production and the organisation of production.

An increase in the amount of capital and labour will produce a greater Y. This is also the case if the capital stock is improved or if the labour force becomes more skilful. In the production function set out above it appears as if the factors of production, K, L and T are independent of one another, but this is not the case.

Many technological improvements are inherent in the capital stock and the labour force. Newer capital equipment is better than old because more recent technology is built into in the newer equipment but not in the old. If there is an improvement in education the younger workers will acquire skills which the older workers do not have. This is referred to as the vintage effect. Technological progress of this kind is called 'embodied' technological progress.

When new workers enter the labour market they do not have the same skills as the workers who have already been employed for some years. There is a need for learning in the workplace, 'learning by doing'. Here there is also embodied technological progress which is called the year effect because it is linked to the number of years of experience in the labour market.

'Disembodied' technological progress is independent of the capital stock and the labour force. If one acquires new knowledge so the existing factors of production can be reorganised and production can be increased without a change to the factor inputs, there is disembodied technological progress.

For example if a dairy farmer obtains new knowledge about a new feeding method or a new feed that can increase milk production, this is 'disembodied' technological progress. If, on the other hand, by means of a breeding programme the farmer acquires a herd that gives a greater milk yield, this is 'embodied' technological progress.

The vintage effect means that productivity increases when older capital stock and older labour is exchanged for newer. The year effect gives increased productivity because there is 'learning by doing', i.e. learning on the job, and because management is better at combining the factors of production.

Finally one must take into account a third factor, the age effect. As capital stock and the work force age there will be a fall in productivity due to 'wear and tear'.

In developing a theory of growth it is natural to take account of these different effects. In the following, in which we will look at the influence of growth upon trade, we will assume for the sake of simplicity that all technological progress is disembodied.

Economic growth can be described as a process in which individual countries accumulate assets by means of which the country's production capacity is increased. This chapter will look at how growth affects trade. There is an exogenous growth in the quantity of capital, the quantity of the work force and in the quantity of technological know-how. This growth influences consumption, production, trade and prices. Therefore the analyses in this chapter are concerned to show how a given change in production capacity affects the country's economy and thus its international trade. The intention is to analyse how changes on the production side and changes on the demand side affect international trade.

A totally different question is the analysis of the factors that determine economic growth, including the role played by international trade in the growth process. The economic policy, including industrial policy and trade policy, influences not only growth but also the structure of a country's economy. Should a developing country choose a strategy based on exports of raw materials, or based on exports in general, or should the country choose a more or less extended import substitution strategy? Here it is a question of analysing how international trade influences growth and the development process. This question is discussed in another book, *International Trade Policy* by the present author.

12.2 Comparative statics
and the factor proportion model

There is a quantitative change in the use of factors of production. How does this affect international trade? Here the terms of trade play an important role.

The factor proportion theory in Chapter 6 is based on the cases where the countries have a given endowment of production factors. It explains the pattern of foreign trade and its economic consequences at a given point in time. However the theory says nothing about what happens when, due to growth, there is a change to the factor endowment domestically and abroad.

It is possible to introduce economic growth into factor proportion theory by using comparative statics. As will appear from the following, the theory of comparative statics will not give a different explanation of the pattern of trade than the one given by factor proportion theory. The comparative statics method has the advantage that it gives a description of the effect of growth on a number of key variables in the economy.

To start with there is a state of equilibrium, and growth now occurs, due either to capital accumulation or an increase in the labour force or technological progress. These exogenous changes bring the country to a new position of equilibrium. In the model it is possible to describe the influence of growth on the volume of external trade, the terms of trade, factor return and income distribution, as well as the national income of the country.

Economic growth can be introduced into a neo-classical factor proportion model by using a set of equations as shown below. This general equilibrium model is based on the model which is discussed in Chapters 2-4. This model will form the basis for the analyses in this chapter.

Demand

In the two countries A and B the consumption functions for the two goods a and b can be derived from the social indifference curves in the two countries. As stated in Chapter 3, there are problems as to whether it is possible to derive social indifference curves which meet the conditions for transitivity that are necessary for indifference curves to be used. It is assumed that the conditions for deriving the social indifference curves are met.

Figure 12.1: The derived demand curves when there is a general equilibrium

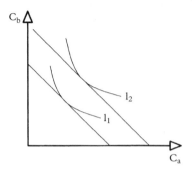

If one knows the national income in countries A and B respectively, Y^A and Y^B, and if one knows the relative prices of the two goods a and b, $P = P_a/P_b$, one can calculate the consumption of the two goods in the two countries. The consumption can be designated by C_a^A, C_b^A, C_a^B and C_b^B, where the lower symbol refers to the good and the upper symbol refers to the country. There are indifference curves, as illustrated in Figure 12.1, for each of the two countries.

This means that there are two equations which describe the consumption of one of the goods in each country, namely:

$$C_a^A = C_A(Y^A, P) \tag{12.1}$$

$$C_a^B = C_B(Y^B, P) \tag{12.2}$$

In the Equations (12.1) and (12.2) consumption of product a is shown. When the relative prices and national income are given it is possible to work out the consumption of product b in the two countries. Therefore the consumption of product b, which is residual, cannot be expressed as an independent equation which is included in the model.

Production

The production conditions can be expressed by means of transformation curves. The quantity of good a which country A is able to produce depends on how much the country produces of the second good b, and of the position of the transformation curve in the co-ordinate system which is assumed to be a function of time t, which is an exogenous factor. The two countries' transformation curves can be described by the Equations (12.3) and (12.4).

$$X^A_a = X_A(X^A_b, t) \tag{12.3}$$

$$X^B_a = X_B(X^B_b, t) \tag{12.4}$$

Figure 12.2: The transformation curve moves out in the co-ordinate system

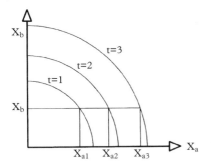

Figure 12.2 shows how the transformation curve moves out with the passage of time. t expresses the economic growth which occurs with time. If X_b is given, X_{a1}, X_{a2} and X_{a3} show how much of good a can be produced at the points in time 1, 2 and 3. When the individual country is on the transformation curve and the assumptions in the Equations (12.3) and (12.4) apply, both societies will have full employment.

Apart from the demand curves (12.1-12.2) and the transformation curves (12.3-12.4), there are some equations based on definitions and some on equilibrium conditions.

Equations based on definitions and equilibrium conditions

The national incomes Y^A and Y^B in the two countries are defined in such a way that the following equations can be written:

$$Y^A = PX^A_a + X^A_b \tag{12.5}$$

$$Y^B = PX^B_a + X^B_b \tag{12.6}$$

The national product of a country is the sum of the value of production of the two products. The price for good b is assumed to be 1, which means that the price for good a is P.

There are further equations based on definitions as follows:

$$X^A_a - C^A_a = C^B_a - X^B_a \tag{12.7}$$

$$X^A_b - C^A_b = C^B_b - X^B_b \tag{12.8}$$

It is apparent from the equations that one country's export volumes are equal to the other country's import volumes.

Finally, there are two equilibrium conditions. The first is that there shall be equilibrium on the current account of the balance of payments for both countries.

For country A the following therefore applies:

$$P\,(X^A_a - C^A_a) = C^A_b - X^A_b \quad \rightarrow$$

$$P\,X^A_a + X^A_b = P\,C^A_a + C^A_b \quad \rightarrow$$

$$Y^A = PC^A_a + C^A_b \tag{12.9}$$

Equation (12.9), which shows that the value of production is equal to the value of goods consumed, is a condition for country A having equilibrium in its balance of payments. When this condition is met for country A, it is also automatically met for country B, when there are only two countries.

The other equilibrium conditions require that the terms of trade shall be equal to the marginal rate of substitution on the transformation curve. The following applies:

$$P = \frac{dX^A_b}{dX^A_a} \tag{12.10}$$

$$P = \frac{dX^B_b}{dX^B_a} \tag{12.11}$$

The model presented here consists of a system of equations where the number of equations is 11 and the number of variables is 12. The twelfth unknown t is precisely the exogenous variable which is changed by economic growth. When t is increased the position of the transformation curve changes since the curve moves out in the co-ordinate system. This can either be due to the change in the quantity of capital, a change in the size of the labour force, or technological progress.

The model can be shown graphically, as in Figure 12.3, where the conditions for country A are illustrated.

There is economic growth in country A which means that the transformation curve moves to the right. In Figure 12.3 the transformation curve $T_1 T_1$ has the same shape as the original transformation curve $T_0 T_0$. The result of this is that, as long as the relative prices of the final goods remain constant, production of the two goods will increase by the same percentage rate. The production point will move from P_0 til P_1. It is a sufficient but not a necessary condition for this that the production functions for the two goods a and b are homogenous of the first degree, and that the capital stock and the labour force increase by the same percentage.

Figure 12.3: The influence of growth upon trade

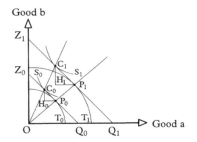

In Figure 12.3 the social indifference curves S_0 and S_1 are drawn, and these are based on a utility function which is homothetic. This means that with unchanged relative prices the consumption of the two goods will increase by the same percentage, since the point of consumption will move from C_0 til C_1. The income elasticity of the two products is equal to 1.

In the initial position the national product is OQ_0 measured in good a or OZ_0 measured in good b. The growth in national product is therefore $Q_0 Q_1 / OQ$ measured in good a or $Z_0 Z_1 / OZ_0$ measured in good b.

When looking at the triangles $C_oH_oP_o$ and $C_1H_1P_1$ it is also seen that imports and exports increase by the same percentage, equal to the growth in production and the growth in consumption.

12.3 The economic effects of growth

The effect on trade

In the above it is assumed that the relative prices of the goods produced remain unchanged after growth. The transformation curve and the social indifference curves are such that growth is neutral with reference to the patterns of production, consumption and trade. The fact that growth is neutral with regard to production and consumption is a sufficient condition for growth being neutral in relation to trade. But it is not a necessary condition, since with unchanged prices the production and consumption pattern can be biased in opposite directions so growth has a neutral effect on trade, which means that exports and imports grow at a rate equal to the rate of growth of the national product.

It is still assumed that prices on the final goods remain unchanged after growth. If the growth is no longer neutral, either in relation to production or consumption, growth can no longer be assumed to be neutral in relation to trade.

It is now assumed that the transformation curve moves out in the co-ordinate system, as shown in Figure 12.3. Production is still neutral in relation to growth. However consumption is not neutral, since the social indifference curves are no longer based on a utility function which is homothetic.

If the social indifference curves move so that they touch the line $Z_1 - Q_1$ in the section Z_1C_1, then growth will promote trade. Growth in imports and exports will be greater than growth in the national product.

Now, the development of the transformation curve is still unchanged, but the social indifference curve touches $Z_1 - Q_1$ in the section C_1P_1. In this case the growth inhibits trade. There will either be a fall in imports and exports, or else there will be a growth in trade at a lower rate than the growth in the national product.

The final possibility is that the social indifference curve touches the line $Z_1 - Q_1$ in the section P_1Q_1. In this case the pattern of trade will change character since good a will now be country A's import good, and good b is the country's export good.

Now, instead of the social indifference curve moving in different ways, it is assumed that the indifference curve moves from S_0 to S_1, while the transformation curve moves in different ways.

If T_1 touches the line Z_1-Q_1 in section P_1Q_1, the new conditions for production will cause a greater increase in trade than in the national product. In other words the growth generates trade. If T_1 touches $Z_1 - Q_1$ in the section C_1P_1, trade will fall relatively, and possibly also absolutely. Here growth inhibits trade. If the transformation curve touches the line $Z_1 - Q_1$ in the section Z_1C_1, good a will be an import good and good b an export good.

The effect on terms of trade

In the foregoing it has been assumed that the relative prices of the finished goods remain unchanged following growth. This assumption is reasonable if country A is a very small country, with little economic significance for its surroundings, i.e. country B is a large country.

On the basis of the general model, as shown in Section 12.2, it is possible to deduce that

$$dP/dt = \frac{[\Delta C_a^A - \Delta X_a^A] - [\Delta X_a^B - \Delta C_a^B]}{N} \tag{12.12}$$

where dP/dt is the change in relative prices of the goods $P = P_a/P_b$, which is equal to the international terms of trade. Δ represents the change in consumption C and production X, which will occur as a result of growth when the relative prices of the goods are constant. The lower symbol a refers to good a and the upper symbols A and B refer to the two countries. The denominator N depends on the elasticity of supply and demand in the two countries.[1]

---

1. It can be shown that N is equal with

$$N = -\frac{C_a^A}{P} \cdot e_a^A - \frac{C_a^B}{P} \cdot e_a^B + \frac{X_a^A}{P} \cdot s_a^A + \frac{X_a^B}{P} \cdot s_a^B$$

where e_a^A and e_a^B are demand elasticities for good a in countries A and B respectively. s_a^A and s_a^B are supply elasticities in countries A and B respectively. The demand elasticities are negative when the two goods are substitutable in consumption, and the supply elasticities are positive. Therefore N is positive and N is small if the numerical elasticities are small.

What Equation (12.12) shows is in fact very simple and intuitively easily understandable. In the initial situation country A has the transformation curve T_0 (see Figure 12.3) and the country produces P_0 and consumes at C_0, because the international terms of trade are given with the slope of the line $Z_0 Q_0$.

Country B has another transformation curve and another set of indifference curves. With international terms of trade P this means that country B imports the quantity $H_0 P_0$ (see Figure 12.3) which corresponds to country A's exports. Country B exports $H_0 C_0$ of good b, which is equal to country A's imports.

It is now assumed that there is growth in both country A and country B. In Equation (12.12) ΔC and ΔX show how consumption and production will change, as long as the relative prices of goods remain equal to P. If this growth in the two countries means that the demand for good a in both countries increases more strongly than production of good a with the given price relation P, then P must necessarily be altered to achieve a new equilibrium. When the total demand for good a in both countries increases more strongly than the total production, P must rise, since P_a increases in relation to P_b.

The above example used in Equation (12.12) means that $\Delta C_a^A > \Delta X_a^A$ and $\Delta C_a^B > \Delta X_a^B$.

This means that the numerator is positive, and since N is positive, dP/dt will be positive, which means that P_a will increase in relation to P_b.

The denominator N, which includes the supply and demand elasticities for good a in the two countries, is always positive. This means that the size of the elasticities does not influence the direction in which the terms of trade develop. However, the size of the elasticities does influence how big the denominator N is. The elasticities express something about the capacity for adjustment (the possibilities for substitution) in consumption and production in the two countries. If the capacity for adjustment is greater, i.e. the elasticities are greater, then the denominator N will be greater and the change in the terms of trade will be smaller. The greater the possibilities of substitution in consumption and production, the smaller the changes in the terms of trade. Smaller possibilities of substitution give greater changes in the terms of trade.

How country A's terms of trade will be affected by growth thus depends primarily on where the growth occurs. Is the growth in country A or country B, or both? Secondly, country A's terms of trade depend on how the growth affects the patterns of consumption and production. It is naturally also decisive whether the good whose relative price falls is an export or an import good. Thirdly, the change to the terms of trade depends on the elasticity of supply and demand.

The effect of growth on factor prices and income distribution

Economic growth can be the result of increase in the labour force, capital accumulation and technological progress. The effects of growth on the volume of trade and the terms of trade are analysed above. These effects are generally applicable when it is known how the transformation curve and the social indifference curve move out in the co-ordinate system. How the transformation curve extends is decisive for how the terms of trade and trade itself are affected. However, the cause of the change is unimportant to the movement of the transformation curve.

Growth affects factor prices and income distribution. It is not possible to analyse how factor prices are affected by using a model such as Figure 12.3. To study the effects on factor prices and income distribution it is necessary to look at the causes of growth.

In this example it is assumed that the quantity of capital in country A increases, without there being growth in country B. This means that the profit per capital unit will fall and wages will rise if, for example, the demand conditions are based on a homothetic utility function. It seems intuitively correct that when there is an increase in one production factor, capital, and there is the same quantity of the other factor, labour, then the price of the factor in plenty will fall. A more detailed examination of this is undertaken in Section 12.4, where the Rybczynski theorem is considered.

If, following growth, the two countries continue to produce the two goods, the factor return in the two countries will remain the same. As the labour force remains constant in both A and B, the income of the labour force, i.e. the sum of the wages, will increase. The return on capital will fall in country B. In country A the profit per capital unit will fall, but the amount of capital will increase.

The effect on national income

The national income will be influenced by the changes in the production possibilities. Here too the element which creates the increased activity is important. Here it is assumed that there is growth in country A but not in country B. If the amount of *capital* in country A increases there will be scope for increasing production of both goods. Since the labour force is unchanged it will seem reasonable to expect that the per capita national income will increase. However, it is possible that there will be a simultaneous worsening in the terms of trade for country A. Country B thus experiences an increase in real income through an improvement in its terms of trade with country A. It is theoretically possible that, after growth in the amount of its capital, country A can be worse off than before. Even though production has increased, the terms of trade can deteriorate so much that they outweigh the increase in production. Such a situation is known as immiserizing growth. This is dealt with in more detail in Section 12.6.

If it is the *population* which grows, the national income in total will grow. Unless it is possible to realise the advantages of economies of scale, the growth in the national income will be lower than the growth in the population. There will therefore be a fall in the per capita national income. However it is possible that the terms of trade could be changed to the advantage of the country so that the per capita national income will rise.

If there is *technological progress*, the national income will also rise. Here too changes to the terms of trade can either give a further increase to the national income or reduce growth to a greater or lesser extent.

The conditions required for growth which is promoted by capital accumulation or by technological progress to cause a fall in the standard of living are relatively strict. It is not sufficient that there should merely be a deterioration to the terms of trade.

It requires that the deterioration should be so great that it more than compensates for the growth which comes from the increase in capital or the technological development.

It can be seen from Equation (12.12) that the conditions of supply and demand can be such that there is a deterioration in the terms of trade. The extent of such a deterioration depends on the denominator, which in turn depends on the elasticities of supply and demand. This can be illustrated by an example. Industrial countries have a tendency to have falling real prices on agricultural products. This is why comprehensive support has been given to the agricultural sector.

The agricultural sector is characterised by having low price elasticity of demand, low income elasticity of demand, and low price elasticity of supply. This is illustrated in Figure 12.4.

Figure 12.4: The conditions of supply and demand in the agricultural sector

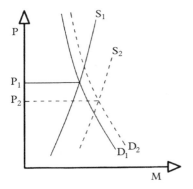

In the initial situation in period 1 the supply and demand curves are S_1 and D_1. The curves are steep because the price elasticities are small. From period 1 to period 2 there is technological progress which moves the supply curve to S_2, while the demand curve D_2 is only moved a little, because of the low income elasticity. This means that the prices of agricultural products fall. The quantity of goods traded increases, but it is possible for the total income to fall.

In the case of a developing country which almost exclusively produces agricultural products or raw materials, the conditions can be as described in Figure 12.4 and there is a risk of there being a significant deterioration in the terms of trade.

It is precisely these observations which lie behind the Singer-Prebisch theory (Singer 1968, UN 1950) which says that there is a long term trend towards a deterioration of the terms of trade of developing countries. Singer and Prebisch assume that industrial countries produce industrial goods and developing countries produce primary commodities. It is central to Singer's and Prebisch's explanations that increased production of primary commodities leads to deteriorated terms of trade because the price and income demand elasticities and price supply elasticities are so small for these commodities. The Singer-Prebisch theory is an argument against developing countries choosing a development strategy based on exports of primary commodities.

12.4 Growth in the capital stock
or the labour force

Changes to the transformation curve

In this section there is an analysis of the effects of economic growth caused by an increase in the capital stock or in the labour force.

There are two countries A and B, and country A has a relatively large capital stock and country B has a relatively large labour force. Country A exports the capital intensive good a and imports the labour intensive good b. The conditions of factor proportion theory are assumed to apply.

There is now a capital accumulation and an increase in the labour force in country A. Against this, there is no development on country B. This means that country A's comparative advantage in the production of good a (the capital intensive good) is either strengthened or weakened.

In Chapter 2, Section 2.5, it is shown how the transformation curve can be derived on the basis of a box diagram in which the length of the axes represents the amount of capital and the size of the labour force which are available to a country. If the capital stock and the labour force increase by the same percentage, there will be a new transformation curve with the same shape as the first, and which moves out in the co-ordinate system, see Figure 12.5.a.

Figure 12.5: Changes in factor endowment

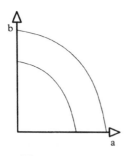 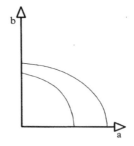 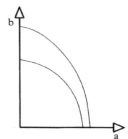

a. The amount of capital and labour increase by the same percentage.

b. The amount of capital increases but the amount of labour is constant.

c. The amount of capital is constant, but the amount of labour increases.

If only the amount of capital is increased, the country which previously had relatively more capital will have its comparative advantage strengthened. In Figure 12.5.b the transformation curve moves to the right in such a way that the possibility of producing the capital intensive good a in particular is improved.

If the country's labour force is increased, without changes in the capital stock, the transformation curve is moved upwards, as shown in Figure 12.5.c. If the country has previously had comparative advantages with regard to capital intensive production, these advantages will be weakened. It is possible that the country will obtain a comparative advantage in the production of the labour intensive good b.

The prices for final goods (the terms of trade)

A closed economy

If it is assumed that country A has an increase in the amount of its capital, which can be a simplification of a situation in which the amount of capital grows faster than the growth of the labour force, the price of the capital intensive good will fall in relation to the price of the labour intensive good. This is the conclusion of the Rybczynski theory (Rybczynski 1955) which is reviewed below.

In Figure 12.6 K_1 and K_2 represent the amount of capital at two different points in time, in a box diagram where the amount of labour is constant. The two contract curves are derived from isoquants which are not drawn in.

For the relative prices on final goods to remain unchanged when moving from time 1 to time 2, the relative factor prices must also remain unchanged. If the relative factor prices are the same, then the factor intensity in the two productions must likewise be the same. For the relative prices on the finished goods to be the same before and after the addition of capital, the two points on the contract curves must lie on the same trajectory from O and on the two parallel trajectories starting from O_1 and O_2.

At the points S and P the relative prices of the finished goods are the same. Since the functions of production are homogenous of the first degree, the extent of the trajectory gives the extent of production. Less of good b is produced at point P than at point S.

The increased amount of capital means that the national income is higher in situation 2 than in situation 1. If P is the new point of equilibrium, then b must be an inferior product since the income elasticity is negative, as the increase in national income gives a fall in demand for the good.

When working with two categories of goods, each of the categories must have a high degree of aggregation. For example they could be agricultural and industrial products. With goods with a high level of aggregation it is unthinkable that one of the groups of products should be an inferior product area. Therefore, point P cannot be the new point of equilibrium. At the new point of equilibrium the demand for good b must be greater than at point S. At the new point of equilibrium Q, which lies to the left of P, there is a greater demand for both good a and good b, compared to point S. At point P the prices of the final goods are the same as for the prices of final goods at point S. At point Q the price for good b will be relatively higher than at point P, as a result of the increased demand for good b and the fall in demand for good a. At point Q P_a/P_b is less than at point S.

The consequences of greater capital stock can also be illustrated by means of transformation curves which can be derived on the basis of the box diagram in Figure 12.6.

Figure 12.6: The Rybczynski theory illustrated by a box diagram

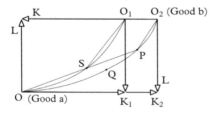

Figure 12.7: The Rybczynski theory illustrated by transformation curves

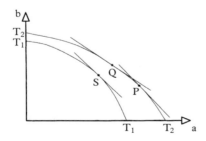

The transformation curve T_1T_1 in Figure 12.7 corresponds to OK_1O_1K in Figure 12.6. Point S in Figures 12.6 and 12.7 correspond to the situation where the relative prices of final goods are equal to the slope of the tangent at point S in Figure 12.7.

The transformation curve T_2T_2 corresponds to OK_2O_2K in the box diagram and point P in the two Figures corresponds to the situation where the relative prices of the final goods at P are equal to the relative prices of the goods at point S. As appears in Figure 12.7, the quantity of good b produced falls. When b is not an inferior good the new point of equilibrium must be further up the curve than P, for example at point Q, where the price of good b will be relatively higher than at point S.

An open economy

The analysis undertaken above is of a closed economy. A similar analysis can be undertaken in the case where there is trade in the initial situation. Again it is assumed that country A increases its quantity of capital, and the labour force is constant. In country B the factor endowment is unchanged. The mechanisms which affect a closed economy will also affect an economy where there is trade.

The development of the relative prices can be illustrated with the help of Equation (12.12). If good a is a capital intensive product, the price will fall if the amount of capital increases. X_a^A will be greater than ΔC_a^A.

With given relative prices of final goods the production of good a will increase by PS/OS per cent, see Figure 12.6. Demand for good a, at given prices, will increase less when it is assumed that good b is not an inferior product. An increase in demand corresponding to the increase in production will mean that good b is an inferior product. As mentioned earlier, the elasticities are relevant to the extent of the changes to the terms of trade.

Factor prices and income distribution

At point Q in Figure 12.6 and 12.7 the demand for both good a and good b is increased. This means that the demands for both labour and capital increase. Since only the supply of capital is increased, the cost of labour will increase in relation to the cost of capital. As a consequence of this there will be a substitution of labour by capital, and at point Q both productions will be more capital intensive.

In country B the production of the capital intensive good will be reduced because of the fall in the relative price of the good. Production of the labour intensive good will be increased. Because of the increased production of the labour intensive good, the cost of labour will also increase, relatively. Therefore less labour and more capital will be used in both productions.

In both countries the distribution of income will change to the advantage of labour and the disadvantage of capital.

National income

It is assumed above that country A is rich in capital and that therefore good a will be country A's export good. If the amount of capital in country A is increased, the country's terms of trade will deteriorate in relation to country B.

However, if country A were to be the country which has a relatively high amount of labour, country A's terms of trade will be improved when the amount of capital increases and the country's imported good falls in relative price.

Under 'normal' conditions the result would be that the national income in country A increases as a result of the increased amount of capital. If country A is already rich in capital, relative to country B, a part of this increase in national income will be neutralised by a deterioration in the terms of trade. Country B gains a share of the growth due to an improvement in the terms of trade.

However, if country A is a country with plentiful labour, the increase in the amount of capital will lead to a strong rise in national income, partly due to the greater capital stock, and partly due to the improvement in the terms of trade. In such a case the growth in country A will harm country B because good a, which is the capital intensive good which country B exports, will fall in price.

12.5 Technological progress

Different kinds of technological progress

In the previous Section economic growth was determined by changes to the amount of capital or quantity of labour.

Economic growth can also be achieved through technological progress. There are different kinds of technological progress. It is usual to distinguish between:

neutral technological progress
capital saving (labour intensive) technological progress
labour saving (capital intensive) technological progress

The traditional method for distinguishing between the three types of technological progress in relation to the production of a given good, is illustrated in Figure 12.8.

In the initial situation a given quantity of goods, X_o, is produced on the basis of the isoquants represented by X^F_o. Following technological development it is possible to produce the same quantity of goods while using fewer factors of production. What distinguished between the three types of technological progress is the way in which the isoquants move.

In Figure 12.8 the different kinds of technological progress are defined on the basis of how the marginal productivity of capital $\partial X/\partial K$ develops in relation to the marginal productivity of labour $\partial X/\partial L$ in connection with the technological progress. This method is usually called the Hicks definition because it was used by J.R. Hicks in his work 'The Theory of Wages', London 1963.

With a given factor intensity, for example OA, the slope of which is equal to L/K, in the initial situation $(\partial X/\partial K)/(\partial X/\partial L)$ will be equal to the slope of the tangents at point A. There will be neutral technological progress as long as the technical progress means that

$$\frac{\partial X/\partial K}{\partial X/\partial L} \text{ is constant}$$

In Figure 12.8.a there is neutral technological progress. After the neutral technological development the slope of the tangent at B equals the slope of the tangent at A. When this applies to all factor intensities this means that the new isoquant has the same shape as the isoquant before the technological development.

In Figure 12.8.b there is capital saving technological progress, which is defined by the fact that

$$\frac{\partial X/\partial K}{\partial X/\partial L} \text{ falls}$$

With a factor intensity that corresponds to the slope OA, at point B the slope of the tangent at B will be shallower than the slope of the tangent at A.

Figure 12.8: Different kinds of technological progress

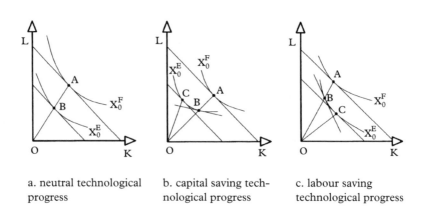

a. neutral technological progress

b. capital saving technological progress

c. labour saving technological progress

Figure 12.8.c shows labour saving technological progress which is defined by the fact that

$$\frac{\partial X/\partial K}{\partial X/\partial L} \quad \text{increases}$$

In this case the slope of the tangent at B, where the factor intensity is the same as at point A, will be steeper than the slope of the tangent at the initial situation A.

With relative factor prices after the technological progress being equal to the relative factor prices before the technological progress, the factor intensities will vary according to the type of technological progress. With neutral technological progress the factor intensity will remain unchanged. With capital saving technological progress the capital intensity will be less than before the technological progress. With labour saving technological progress the capital intensity of the new optimal combination of factors will increase.

The effects of neutral technological progress

Technological progress influences the relative prices of finished goods, which is equal to the terms of trade when there is international trade.

Technological progress also affects the factor remuneration being paid to the production factors of labour and capital.

The following looks at how neutral technological progress influences the terms of trade and factor remuneration, and how the gains achieved through technological progress are shared between the two countries, depending on two sets of circumstances. First, it is important whether the technological progress occurs in the capital intensive or the labour intensive production. Next, it is decisive how the pattern of trade is in the initial situation, which is determined by the relative factor endowment before the technological progress.

Country A is assumed to have large capital stock compared with country B. This means that country A exports capital intensive goods. There is now neutral technological progress within the capital intensive sector in country A, but there are no technological changes in country B.

Figure 12.9 is a box diagram showing the situation for country A, where a's isoquants can be drawn with their starting point at O, and b's isoquants with their starting point at O_1.

Figure 12.9: Neutral technological progress in the capital intensive sector

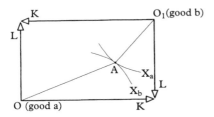

In the initial situation A is a point of equilibrium, with which there is associated production of good a, which is for example X_a = 100, and production of good b which is for example X_b = 50. There is now neutral technological progress for good a. It could be that with a given combination of factors it is possible to produce 20 per cent more of good a. This means that at A after the neutral technological progress X_a = 120.

At point A the factor prices before and after the technological progress are the same. The total cost of producing X_b = 50 is unchanged so that P_b is constant. The total cost of producing X_a = 100 before the technological progress is the same as the total cost of producing X_a = 120 after the technological progress. If the price for the good a is 6 before the technological progress, the price will be 5 after the technological progress, when there is perfect competition in the market for the goods. This means that the price of good a will fall by $1/6^{th}$.

It is possible to derive the transformation curves which are shown in Figure 12.10. on the basis of the box diagram.

Country A's transformation curve in the initial situation is T_0T_0. After the technological progress in the production of good a, which involves an increase in productivity of 20 per cent, the new transformation curve T_0T_1 will move to the right so that with a given production of good b it is possible to produce 20 per cent more of good a. At point A_1 20 per cent more of good a is produced than at point A_0. The slope of the tangent at A_1 is $1/6^{th}$ shallower than the slope of the tangent at A_0, because the production costs of producing good a have fallen by $1/6^{th}$ per unit.

In the initial situation country A finds itself in a position where there is production at point A_0 and consumption at point C_0. The transformation curve for country B is given to the right in Figure 12.10. Here, before the technological progress in country A there is production at point A_0 and consumption at point C_0. After the technological progress in country A, country B will produce at point A_1 and consume at point C_1, (see the right hand half of the figure).

The result is that part of the gain from the technological progress goes to country B in the form of improved terms of trade, since the imported goods fall in price. Country A gets a gain as a result of the technological progress, but the technological progress in the export sector worsens country A's terms of trade.

The fact that in Figure 12.10 the production points will be A_1 following the technological progress is naturally an assumption which involves a relative fall in the price of good a by $1/6^{th}$. If it is assumed that the relative prices of the goods are equal to the relative prices before the technological progress, the production point for country A will be A_2, where the slope of the tangent is equal to the slope of the tangent at point A_0.

At A_2 with unchanged terms of trade it is unlikely that there will be a new point of production. With unchanged terms of trade the quantities of exports and imports will be the same as in the initial situation, because country B, with unchanged terms of trade, will export and import the same quantities as before the technological progress. For country A this means that A_2 can only be a point of equilibrium if the income elasticity for good b in country A is negative.

Figure 12.10: The transformation curves with neutral technological progress in the capital intensive sector

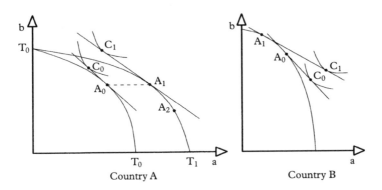

Country A   Country B

If the income elasticity for good b in country A is positive, then the relative price for good a will fall, but it can fall by less than $1/6^{th}$. In that case the new production point will lie somewhere between A_1 and A_2 in Figure 12.10 (see the left hand side of the Figure).

This analysis can be repeated for cases where there is neutral technological progress in country A in the production of product b, which is the country's import good. In this case the price of good b will fall. This means that country B will suffer a loss in the form of a deterioration in terms of trade, which reduces welfare. Country A will gain a double advantage both in the form of the technological progress and the improvement in its terms of trade.

How is factor remuneration affected? This can be illustrated using Figure 6.8 in Section 6.3 in the chapter on factor proportion theory. This figure is repeated in Figure 12.11 in which the left hand side shows the relationship between the relative prices of the final goods and the relative factor prices, and the right hand side shows the relationship between the relative factor prices and the factor intensities.

The curve Z_0Z_0 applies to both countries in the initial situation, since the functions of production are identical in both countries. It is assumed that international trade creates relative prices for final goods which are equal to A. This means that the relative factor prices correspond to point E. This in turn means that the factor intensity for good a and good b are F and G respectively.

There is now a neutral technological progress for sector a in country A. This means that the relationship between the relative prices of final goods and the relative factor prices moves from $Z_0 Z_0$ to $Z_1 Z_1$. It has been shown, on the basis of Figure 12.9, that if before or after the technological progress country A finds itself at point A, the relative factor prices will be unchanged, but the relationship between the relative prices for final goods P_a / P_b will fall by $1/6^{th}$ if there is a productivity increase of 20 per cent within the sector. If this is carried over into Figure 12.11, this means that with unchanged factor prices at E, P_a / P_b will fall by $1/6^{th}$. This means that the new curve $Z_1 Z_1$ moves horizontally to the right by $1/6^{th}$.

Figure 12.11: Factor remuneration with neutral technological progress in the capital intensive sector in country A

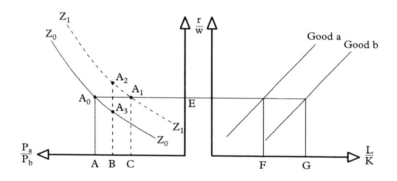

In country B there are no changes. The functions of production are the same as before, which means that the curve $Z_0 Z_0$ will still show the relationship between the relative prices for final goods and the factor prices in country B.

Immediately after the technological progress the relative prices for final goods in country B will be at point A, and the relative prices for final goods in country A will be at point C, when the relative factor prices are unchanged corresponding to point E.

Of course, these differences in the relative prices of the final goods cannot be maintained when there is free trade. Trade ensures that in both countries the prices of finished goods are the same, and correspond, for example, to point B. This means that the relative factor prices in the two countries A and B will be different. Point A$_2$ *shows the relative factor prices in country A, and point* A$_3$ the relative factor prices in country B.

Compared with the initial position this means that, relatively speaking, capital wins and wage earners lose in country A. Conversely, in country B wage earners win and capital loses.

How does this affect the absolute return on the production factors? In country B the wage earners' real income will increase overall and the real return on capital will fall. This is in accordance with the Stolper-Samuelson theorem, cf. Section 6.6.

In country A the absolute earnings will increase both for capital and for wage earners, as long as the factor prices are unchanged. However, the factor prices are not unchanged, since wages fall by comparison with returns on capital. These two effects, working together, mean that the real return on capital increases. It is not possible to generalise as to whether the relative fall in the wage earners income is greater or less than the progress which is due to technological progress. It is possible that the wage earners' real income will rise, but it is also possible that it will fall.

If there is neutral technological progress in the labour intensive sector b in country A, then country A's terms of trade will be improved if country A imports this good. In Figure 12.11 this means that the curve Z_1Z_1 for country A will lie to the left of Z_0Z_0. The effect for factor remuneration will now be that wage earners gain both relatively and absolutely. Capital will lose relatively, and there is also a risk that the real return on capital will fall.

In this section the effects of neutral technological progress on terms of trade and factor remuneration have been analysed. Correspondingly it is possible to analyse the effects of capital saving and labour saving technological progress.

12.6 Growth can be immiserizing

In the foregoing the discussion has concerned economic growth where the production potential increases. Growth can be due to increased accumulation of factors in the form of greater capital stock or a larger population. This can also be through technological progress. There is no certainty that an improvement in the basis for production will give a higher standard of living. Examples of this will be given below.

Population growth

It is clear that if the population grows while the capital stock remain constant and there is no technological progress, then there will be a growth in production capacity. However, it would not be correct to describe this as real growth if the per capita consumption of goods falls.

In Figure 12.12 in the initial situation production is at X_1 and consumption at C_1. Good b is the labour intensive good. The quantity of labour increases and the country's transformation curve moves from T_1T_1 to T_2T_2. The new production point is X_2 and the new consumption point is C_2.

Figure 12.12: Population growth

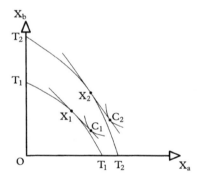

In the production of both goods relatively more labour is applied and L/K rises. Because of the falling marginal productivity of the labour force the rate of increase in production of the two goods from X_1 to X_2 will be lower than the rate of increase of the labour force. When, at the same time, there is a deterioration of the terms of trade for the country's export good, the growth in consumption in the move from C_1 to C_2 will be less than the growth in the population.

The result will be that the per capita consumption will fall.

Deterioration of terms of trade

As shown above in Section 12.3, growth will often lead to changes in a country's terms of trade. Growth can lead to a deterioration in a country's terms of trade.

The question which now arises is whether growth can so deteriorate the terms of trade that the total effect of growth is that the standard of living is lowered. The answer to this is that it is possible.

There are two groups of countries: industrial countries and developing countries. There are two goods: raw materials (primary products) and industrial goods. The developing countries have a comparative advantage in the production of raw materials, and the industrial countries have a comparative advantage in the production of industrial goods.

If the income elasticity for the raw materials is very small, and if the price elasticity for supply and demand is very small, then an expansion of raw material production will give a relative fall in prices for raw materials. A growth in the raw materials sector in all developing countries could therefore cause such a deterioration of the terms of trade that the developing countries could end up being poorer as a result of growth.

If the growth in one country can affect terms of trade, that country is an economically significant country whose conditions affect the world economy. This also means that the country can affect the terms of trade through its tariff policy, cf. the theory on the optimal tariff which is discussed in the author's book *International Trade Policy*, Copenhagen, 2001.

In the above example this means that if all developing countries acted together, for example by forming a cartel, they could prevent the deterioration of their terms of trade by imposing an export tariff on the raw materials. By imposing the optimal tariff the growth would not be immiserizing. Alternatively it could be possible to introduce a quota system for each country participating in the cartel, as has happened for example with OPEC.

12.7 The supply of factors is not constant

In factor proportion theory it is assumed that the supply of factors is constant, irrespective of the prices of the factors of production. In the real world factor supply is not constant. The supply of labour is assumed to vary according to the level of real incomes, as shown in Figure 12.13. With low real earnings the supply of labour will increase when real earnings increase. Above a certain level an increase in real earnings leads to a fall in the supply of labour. The higher real earnings lead to the labour force wanting more free time. This change in assumptions also means that the traditional conclusions do not necessarily apply.

Figure 12.13: The supply of labour is dependent on real earnings

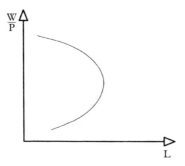

The first conclusion to be drawn from the traditional model is that when the price of one good increases in relation to the price of another good, the production of the first good rises. There are two goods, a and b. Good a is a capital intensive good and good b is labour intensive. The traditional transformation curve shows that when P_a/P_b falls, the production of good b will rise.

This is no longer necessarily the case when labour supply is on the upper part of the curve in Figure 12.13. When the price of good b rises, the real earnings will rise. This follows from the Stolper-Samuelson theorem. The higher real earnings mean that the supply of labour will fall. This means that with given relative prices for the goods, production of good b, which is a labour intensive good, will fall, and production of good a will rise. This accords with the Rybczynski theorem.

There are now two conflicting tendencies in play. The fact that the price of good b rises will of course mean that it will be more profitable to produce good b. There will be a transfer of production factors from good a to good b. On the other hand, the reduced supply of labour will first of all affect the production of good b. With the given relative prices of final goods, production of good b will fall. It is not possible to say which of the two effects will generally be the stronger. A rising price on good b can lead to a fall in the supply of good b.

The other conclusion that can be drawn from the traditional model is that if good a is the country's import good, a relative fall in price will mean that imports of good a will increase. In Section 4.7 in Chapter 4 the so-called offer curve for a country was derived. In Figure 12.14 an offer curve with a constant supply of labour is shown on the left. Good b is the country's export good and good a its import good. Point A is the initial position. The slope of the line OA shows the terms of trade P_b/P_a. When P_a falls a new point B is reached which means that the country imports greater quantities.

The diagram to the right of Figure 12.14 shows what can happen to the offer curve when the supply of production factors is no longer constant. The lowest part of the offer curve corresponds to the lowest part of the supply curve for labour in Figure 12.13. The upper part of the offer curve corresponds to that part of the supply curve for labour when higher real earnings reduces the supply of labour.

Figure 12.14: Offer curves for respectively constant and variable supplies of labour

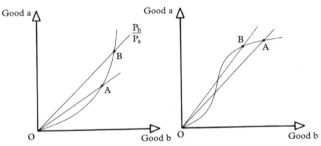

On the upper part of the offer curve a fall in the price of good a will mean a move from point A to point B. A fall in the price of good a means that imports of this good fall.

There are again two conflicting influences. With a constant labour supply a fall in price for good a will increase the country's demand and reduce the country's production of good a. This means that imports will increase. On the other hand, a reduction in the supply of labour, as a result of the increasing real earnings, particularly hits the production of the labour intensive good b. The overall result can therefore be that production of good b falls and production of good a increases.

If the domestic production of good a increases more than demand, imports of good a will fall, even though the price of good a falls. This is the case illustrated on the right in Figure 12.14.

12.8 A model with three sectors

A three sector model can give different results

In international economics it is traditional to work with a model with two goods, an export good and an import-competing good. This is a simplification, but it has the advantage that the model is relatively easy to work with and it is possible to represent it graphically.

It is more realistic to have a model with three sectors: an export sector, an import-competing sector and a domestic market sector, in which goods and services are not traded internationally.

The terms 'tradables' and 'non-tradables' are often used. Tradables are goods which can be traded internationally and which are traded if the trade barriers are not too great. The trade barriers can be political, in the form of tariffs, or natural, in the form of high transport costs. Non-tradables are typically services which are provided locally and which do not form a part of international trade.

In the model there are three goods X, M and H which are, respectively, export, import and home market goods. The three goods are produced using two production factors K and L. The three goods can be ranked according to their capital intensity. It is assumed that X is more capital intensive than M which in turn is more capital intensive than good H. This means that $K_X/L_X > K_M/L_M > K_H/L_H$.

It is assumed that, just as in the traditional two sector model, there are perfect markets for capital and labour. This means that capital and labour flow to where the returns are highest, without any problems of adjustment. When the relative factor prices r/w are given, the relative finished goods prices P_X/P_M and P_H/P_M are also given.

In the three sector model it is more difficult to draw general conclusions. To illustrate this it is assumed that the price of the import good M falls because of conditions on the world market.

In a two sector model, where there is a constant supply of factors, a falling price of an import good will lead to increased imports. The relationship is simple. A falling import price increase demand and reduces production, both of which mean that imports rise.

The relationship is not so simple in a three sector model with constant supply of factors. In a three sector model a falling price of the import good M can mean that the quantity of imports falls. It is the same result as is reached when the total supply of labour is no longer constant, as shown in the preceding section.

When the price of the import good M falls, the price of labour will fall in relation to the price for capital if the production of the import good is labour intensive. With a falling price P_M, in the initial situation there will be a fall in the production of good M, which releases more labour than capital. Therefore the price of labour falls.

This means that P_X/P_M will rise and that P_H/P_M will fall, because the home market good is more labour intensive than the import good. Production in the home market sector is reduced. Thereby production factors are released, especially labour, which can be used in the production of the export good X and the import good M.

The result of this example will be that the falling import price will increase the demand for the import good. On the production side there are contrary forces in play. In the initial situation the falling price for the import goods will reduce production. Consequently the production of the home market good will be reduced. This releases production factors which will be used in the import and export sectors. The end result can be that production in the import competing sector is increased. If the increase in production is greater than the increase in demand, there can be a reduction of imports.

It is important to emphasise that such a situation can arise in a three sector model, but that the traditional situation, where falling import prices leads to increased import quantities, can also result.

A three sector model with externally determined international prices

In this model there is a small country which has three sectors. The export sector produces X_X and the price of the export good is P_X, the import competing sector produces X_M at the price P_M, and in the home market sector the production and the price are X_H and P_H respectively.

Since it is a small country its terms of trade are externally determined. This means that the two goods which compete abroad can be considered as one good, where the production of the composite good X_Q can be described as:

$$X_Q = X_X + \frac{P_M}{P_X} \cdot X_M$$

This means that one unit of the export good is always equivalent to P_X/P_M units of the import competing good.

The model can be illustrated using an ordinary diagram where the composite product X_Q constitutes one axis and production of the domestic product is the other axis.

In Figure 12.15 TT is the transformation curve and C_1 is the indifference curve which touches the transformation curve at R_1. The point of equilibrium for both consumption and production will always be on TT. This fits with the fact that production and consumption of the home market good shall always be identical, because the home market good is not traded internationally. The slope at the tangent P_1 indicates the price relationship between P_Q and P_H.

If consumer preference moves to the advantage of the home market product, there will be a new indifference curve, the dotted line C^*. This will touch the transformation curve at R_2, where consumption of the home market good increases, and there will be a corresponding fall in production and consumption in the other two sectors that compete abroad.

Figure 12.15: A three sector model where the terms of trade are externally determined

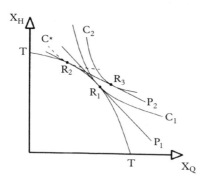

At R_2 there will still be a point of equilibrium because R_2 is a common tangent point for TT and C^*. At any common tangent point it applies that:

$$X_Q = C_Q$$

which means that:

$$X_X + \frac{P_M}{P_X} X_M = C_X + \frac{P_M}{P_X} C_M \quad \rightarrow$$

$$\tag{12.12}$$

$$X_X - C_X = \frac{P_M}{P_X} (C_M - X_M)$$

which is the same as saying that there is equilibrium in the balance of payments. P_M and P_X are determined by the world market, and they are determined in foreign currency. When Equation (12.13) applies, the country has a nominal rate of exchange ExR_N, which means that the foreign prices are converted to domestic prices so there is a domestic price structure that ensures that Equation (12.13) is fulfilled.

We will now turn to a different situation in which the initial position is at R_1. Preference is unchanged at C_1. There is now inflationary pressure in the country since the production factors wish to increase their earnings by, e.g. 10 per cent. This means that all producers within the three sectors wish to raise the prices of the goods by 10 per cent. This can be done without any problems for the home market good, but not in the two sectors which compete abroad. These prices are calculated in foreign currency and they remain unaltered because there is no inflation abroad. When the nominal exchange rate is unchanged P_X and P_M will remain constant, calculated in domestic currency, but P_H will rise by 10 per cent.

This means that the price relation P_Q/P_H falls by 10 per cent. The new pricing conditions are given by P_2 which touches the transformation curve at R_2 and the indifference curve C_2 at R_3. This is not an equilibrium situation since the demand for the products that are traded internationally is greater than the production. There will therefore be a deficit in the balance of payments.

The real exchange rate can be defined as follows:

$$ExR_R = ExR_N \cdot \frac{P_Q}{P_H}$$

where ExR_R is the real exchange rate and ExR_N is the nominal exchange rate, and where P_Q is the price of the goods which are traded internationally, calculated in foreign currency.

What happens in the above example is that inflation in the country leads to P_H rising while P_Q and ExR_N are unchanged. This means that the real rate of exchange falls which is the same as a real revaluation of the currency. The real revaluation means that production X_Q in the sectors competing internationally falls, because the relative factor remuneration falls in these sectors while the demand for these goods goes up because they have become relatively cheaper.

The model shows how inflation in a country can contribute to the distortion of the industrial structure. The model can also illustrate the problems caused by an expansion of the public sector (which is a significant part of the domestic market sector) if there is unwillingness to pay for it.

Staying with the case of inflation in Figure 12.15 it can be said that the solution to the problem is simple. The country's currency can be devalued so that that real rate of exchange is unchanged. In this case the slope of P_1 will still be the relative prices for final goods (P_Q/P_H) and situation will still be at the point of equilibrium R_1.

If there is full utilisation of all resources, and if the public sector is increased without consumers changing their preferences, there are two possibilities. Either the purchasing power of consumers is limited so that R_2 becomes the new point of consumption, or the country will experience a deficit in its balance of payments. This is illustrated in Figure 12.16.

Figure 12.16: Expansion of the home market sector with and without limitation of purchasing power

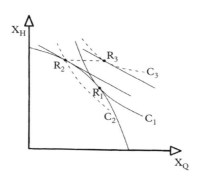

The initial situation is the point of equilibrium R_1. If public expenditure is increased at the same time as taxes are augmented R_2 will be the new point of production and consumption. The indifference curve C_2 which passes through R_2 lies lower than C_1. Welfare falls while there is equilibrium in the balance of payments. If purchasing power is not limited by taxation and public expenditures are increased, the position R_3 can be arrived at, where demand for the public goods corresponds to their production, while demand for goods in the sectors which compete abroad is greater than the production of these goods. The result will be a deficit in the balance of payments equal to R_2R_3. This leads to foreign indebtedness which is not sustainable.

The expansion of the public sector at the same time as maintaining the balance of payments will lead to a de-industrialisation of society because production will fall in the sectors which compete abroad.

12.9 The Dutch disease

As shown above, if there is a strong expansion of the public sector, which is a significant part of the domestic market sector, this can result in de-industrialisation.

De-industrialisation can also take place in connection with what is called the 'Dutch disease'. The phrase Dutch disease originates from the circumstances in which the development of natural gas production diminished the competitiveness of Dutch industry. Other countries, such as Great Britain and Norway, have seen the same effect in connection with the substantial development of oil and gas production. The phenomenon has also been seen with the mining of minerals, e.g. in Australia. In Denmark oil and gas production pays for the deficit in the balance of payments which would otherwise have occurred without this production.

The development of production based on natural resources reduces production in traditional industries which are export or import competing. This means that a country which is subject to de-industrialisation has a significant deficit in the balance of payments when exports based on production form natural resources, which finance the deficit, are disregarded. The problem is that when the natural resources are exhausted, a country may have an insufficiently developed industrial structure.

The Dutch disease can be analysed in a three sector model where there is a export sector, an import sector and a home market sector. In the initial situation the export sector is traditional in the sense that it is based on the use of capital and labour. There is then the discovery of natural resources, for example oil. The production to which this discovery gives rise is exported. The export sector is thus divided between two sub-sectors, 'traditional' export production and production based on natural resources.

In the traditional export sector, the import sector and the home market sector, production takes place using sector-specific capital stocks which are constant. In the sector with natural resource exporting production, production involves the natural resources, capital and labour. The labour is mobile between the all sectors which means that the earnings of labour are the same throughout. However, the sector-specific capital cannot be moved, and capital earnings are therefore different in the different sectors.

If the country is small it is natural to assume that the prices of import goods and the prices of export goods, regardless of whether they are traditional exports or exports based on natural resources, are fixed exogenously. This means that, just as above, it is possible to treat all the goods which compete abroad as one composite product. The export goods and import goods are considered as one composite good Q and the other good is the home market good H.

Figure 12.17: De-industrialisation as a result of Dutch disease

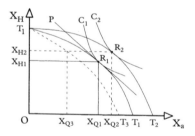

The quantities of the two goods is set out along the axes in Figure 12.17. $T_1 T_1$ is the transformation curve before the discovery of the natural resources which are the basis for new production in the export sector. The point of equilibrium R_1 is the point where the indifference curve C_1 touches the transformation curve. There is X_{Q1} production of the traditional export good and import good. There is X_{H1} production of the home market product, and the relative prices P_Q/P_H are given by the slope at the tangent P.

Now production of the new natural resource based product, for example oil, is started. This means that the aggregated transformation curve, including oil, is T_1T_2. The transformation curve excluding oil will be the dotted line T_1T_3. The new point of equilibrium is R_2 where the indifference curve C_2 touches the new transformation curve.

At the point R_2 production and consumption of the home market product is OX_{H2}. Production of the composite product Q is OX_{Q2}. OX_{Q3} represents the traditional export good and the import good together. $X_{Q3} X_{Q2}$ is the production of oil, which is exported and which finances the increased import and falling export of the traditional export good.

The above analysis can be supplemented with an analysis that concentrates on the labour market. As previously mentioned, the capital in the three sectors is sector-specific. This means that in each sector there is a fixed capital stock. There is full mobility in the labour market, so the earnings of the work force are the same in every sector. It is assumed that the labour in each sector is rewarded in accordance with the marginal productivity of labour. When w is the nominal wage, which is the same everywhere, and when P_M, P_X and P_H are the prices of the goods in the import, export and home market sectors, the following applies:

$$w = \frac{\partial X_M}{\partial L_M} P_M \quad \text{or} \quad \frac{w}{P_M} = \frac{\partial X_M}{\partial L_M}$$

$$w = \frac{\partial X_X}{\partial L_X} P_X \quad \text{or} \quad \frac{w}{P_w} = \frac{\partial X_M}{\partial L_M} \cdot \frac{P_X}{P_M}$$

$$w = \frac{\partial X_H}{\partial L_H} P_H \quad \text{or} \quad \frac{w}{P_M} = \frac{\partial X_H}{\partial L_H} \cdot \frac{P_H}{P_M}$$

$\partial X/\partial L$ is the marginal productivity of labour which, in each of the three sectors, falls with an increased employment of labour. L_M, L_X and L_H are the amount of labour used in the three sectors.

In Figure 12.18 the length of the horizontal axis shows the total size of the labour force. This labour force is divided between the three sectors. w/P_M is shown on the vertical axis.

In the initial situation O_H measures the demand for labour in the home market sector. In the initial situation O_Q measures the demand for labour in the import competing sector L_M, and if, on the horizontal axis, one adds to this the demand for labour in the export sector, one gets the total demand for labour L_Q in the two sectors which trade internationally.

In the initial situation the real earnings are w_0, and the demand for labour in the sectors H, M and X are $O_H h_1$, $O_Q m_1$ and $m_1 h_1$ respectively.

What now happens is that production based on natural resources begins in the export sector, e.g. because of the discovery of oil. This means that the demand for labour goes up in the sector. Therefore L_Q moves to the right to $L^\star_Q$. Prices P_X and P_M are unchanged because these are determined externally. With an unchanged price for the home market good P_H, the new point of intersection will mean that the real wages increase to w_1. However, this is not a new point of equilibrium. The price of the home market good H will go up, unless the domestic market good is an inferior good. Society will be richer because of the discovery of oil, so P_H/P_M will rise, since P_H rises and P_M is an externally determined constant. Therefore L_H moves to the right to $L^\star_H$. At the new point of intersection C the real wages will be w_2.

With the higher wages w_2 employment in the import competing sector will fall to $O_Q m_2$ and in the traditional export sector employment will fall to $m_2 h_2$. As the capital stock in the two sectors are unchanged production in the two sectors will also fall.

Figure 12.18: The distribution of labour between sectors

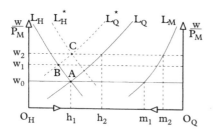

Therefore, all things being equal, the discovery of natural resources will mean that production in the traditional export sector and in the import competing sector will fall. As the domestic demand for the goods supplied by the two sectors will rise, imports will go up and exports of traditional products will go down. Exclusive of the production based on natural resources, the society will have a deficit on the balance of payments which will be financed by the export of the good, for example oil, which is extracted. The long term problem is that when the day arrives that the natural resources are exhausted, the society lacks a production capacity so it becomes difficult to achieve equilibrium in the balance of payments.

12.10 Summary

Economic growth is the result of an increase of the quantity of production factors together with an improvement in the quality of the production factors.

In this chapter the increase in factor endowment is considered as being exogenously determined. It is the results of economic growth that are the subject of analysis. Economic growth affects the volume of trade and it can also change the mix of goods traded. Economic growth affects international terms of trade, factor prices and income distribution.

The analysis is made on the basis of a neo-classical general equilibrium model of the same type as is used in factor proportion theory. It is a 2 country/ 2 goods/ 2 factors model, using comparative statics. It enables the comparison of the equilibrium situation before and after economic growth.

The effects of economic growth depend on whether it is the stock of capital or the size of the population which is increased, or whether it is technological progress that is the source of the growth. The effects of technological progress in their turn depend on whether it is neutral, labour saving or capital saving technological progress.

The effects of economic growth also depend on the country in which it takes place, and in which sector and whether, in the initial situation, it is an export or import sector.

Normally economic growth is associated with a rise in per capita national income and thus a rise in the standard of living. If economic growth is defined as an increase in production potential shown by the transformation curve moving to the right in the co-ordinate system, it is not a given fact that per capita national income increases. There can be a fall in welfare if it is the population that increases, or if the growth leads to a strong deterioration of the country's terms of trade because of very small elasticities in consumption and production.

The results given by the model depend on the assumptions fed into it. If the supply of labour is no longer constant but is endogenously determined by real earnings, there will be different results as to how economic growth affects the extent of trade.

If one moves from the assumption that there are only two sectors, the import and export sectors, and operates instead with a three sector model, which also includes a home market sector, there will be different results. In a three sector model it is possible to analyse the significance of inflation for those sectors that are subject to competition abroad. It is also possible to analyse the effects of an increase of production in the public sector, and explain the effects of the phenomenon known as 'Dutch disease' on the economy of a society.

The whole chapter looks at the changes which exogenously determined growth gives rise to in connection with trade. It is important to be aware that there is also a connection the other way round, from trade to growth. How do different trade policies affect growth? This core relationship is dealt with in 'International Trade Policy', Copenhagen 2001, by the present author.

Literature

Bhagwati, J., 'Immiserizing Growth: A geometrical Note', *Review of Economic Studies*, 25, 1958.

Corden, W.M. and J. P. Neary, 'Booming Sector and De-industrialization in a Small Open Economy', *Economic Journal*, 92, 1982.

Findlay, R., 'Growth and Development in Trade Models' in Jones, R. W. and P.B. Kenen (eds), *Handbook of International Economics*, Volume 1, 1984.

Findlay, R. and H. Grubert, 'Factor Intensities, Technological Progress and the Terms of Trade', *Oxford Economic Papers*, 11, 1959.

Johnson, H.G., 'Economic Expansion and International Trade' *Manchester School of Economics and Social Studies*, 23, 1955.

Johnson, H.G., 'Economic Development and International Trade', *Nationaløkonomisk Tidsskrift*, 97, 1958.

Rybczynski, T.M., 'Factor Endowments and Relative Commodity Prices', *Economica*, 22, 1955.

Singer, H. W., 'The Distribution of Gains between Investing and Borrowing Countries' in Caves, R. E. and H. G. Johnson (eds), *Readings in International Economics*, George Allen and Unwin, 1968.

United Nations, *The Economic Development of Latin America and its Principal Problems*, New York, 1950 (Prebisch-report).

13. International factor movements

In factor proportion theory it is assumed that only trade takes place between countries, but there are no factor movements. There is no transfer of capital or migrations of labour. The relative prices for final goods are established so that there is equilibrium in the balance of payments on the current account. This means that the savings in a society are equal to the investments.

If it is recognised that there can be international loans and borrowings between countries, a country can either be a net borrower or a net lender. This means that there is no longer equilibrium in the balance of payments on the current account. In a country that is a net borrower there will be a net import corresponding to the amount by which investments exceed domestic savings. Conversely, a country which is a net lender will have domestic savings which are larger than its investments.

13.1 International lending and borrowing

Hitherto the analyses have been of a single period. With lending and borrowing it is necessary to look at conditions in two consecutive periods. What happens in the first period influences the conditions for the second period. The two periods need not be limited to one year. They can well cover a longer period, for example 10 or 30 years.

In Figure 13.1 consumption in the two periods is drawn on the axes. In a closed economy the situation is at point A, which makes it possible for consumption to be at A_1 in the first period and A_2 in the second.

The indifference curve U_1 passes through point A, and at point A it has the slope $1 + t$, where t is the time preference. It is the case that:

$$- \frac{\Delta C_2}{\Delta C_1} = 1 + t$$

which means that there is indifference if during period 1 consumption ΔC_1 is sacrificed in order to gain $\Delta C_2 = (1 + t) \Delta C_1$ in periode 2. The time preference t varies with the slope of the tangent to the indifference curve. The smaller t is, the higher will be the prospect of future consumption compared with current consumption.

Figure 13.1: Consumption in two periods

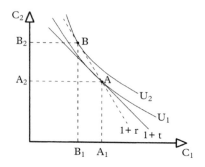

The international interest rate is r, which is assumed to be greater than t. The dotted line with the slope 1 + r is drawn through A in Figure 13.1. It touches a new indifference curve U_2 at point B.

There is now a possibility of international lending and borrowing. When the international interest rate is greater than the time preference, the country can consume at point B which is where the straight line with the slope 1 + r touches the indifference curve U_2.

Point B means that consumption in period 1 will be B_1 and consumption in period 2 will be B_2. This point can be achieved if the country makes a loan to the outside world which corresponds to the value of consumption A_1B_1 in period 1 on the basis that the loan will be repaid with interest to the value of A_2B_2 in period 2.

In period 1 the country will be a net exporter of goods to the extent of A_1B_1. The country being looked at is a creditor and the outside world will be a debtor. The country can change its pattern of consumption through international lending because the time preference is less than the international interest.

The reason why the time preference is relatively small can, for example, be due to the demographic structure of the country. If the age distribution is such that a larger group of people will be pensioners in period 2, it can be sensible to build up net assets in period I which can be used for consumption in period 2.

If the international interest rate is lower than the time preference, the country will be able to increase its welfare, i.e. be situated on the higher indifference curve by taking up a loan which will be repaid later. Consumption in the first period is increased through imports, while it is reduced in the second period by exports.

In the example in Figure 13.1 there is only one combination of consumption, as long as there is no international capital market. This combination of consumption is point A.

This is a simplified assumption since, without the existence of an international capital market, a country can move its consumption possibilities between time periods through savings and investments. The good which the country produces can either be used for consumption or investment. The more that a country saves in the first period, the lower the consumption and the larger the investments. Larger investments in the first period enable larger consumption in the following period.

In Figure 13.2 the curve TT is a kind of transformation curve which shows the combinations of consumption in the two periods which it will be possible to achieve.

For example, point A in Figure 13.2 corresponds to point A in Figure 13.1. By saving in the first period the country can increase its scope for consumption in the second period. If in the first period the country saves A_1B_1 it reduces its consumption in the first period, but in return it increases it by A_2B_2 in the following period.

Figure 13.2: An international capital market in a situation where the country's production conditions are changed

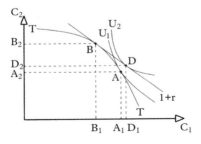

If there is no international capital market the optimal point will be A because the indifference curve U_1 touches TT at point A.

The slope of the tangent at point A is $1 + t$, where t equals the time preference. Point B is not the optimal combination since B is on a lower indifference curve (which is not drawn).

When a country can save and invest, and an international capital market is introduced, it can be optimal to produce at point B. This will be so if the international rate of interest is of such a size that the line with the slope $1 + r$ touches TT at point B and touches the indifference curve U_2 at point D, where welfare is greater than at point A.

The international capital market makes it reasonable for the country to give up consumption combination A. It is reasonable to save and invest A_1B_1 in the first period. This enables a production increase of A_2B_2 in period 2. Without a capital market the consumption point would be B. With an international capital market the country can borrow B_1D_1 in the first period to finance the import of goods in the same period. In the following period the country must export goods to the value of B_2D_2 to service and repay the debt.

The borrowing in the first period makes it possible, through increased savings, for a country to develop its capital stock without reducing its consumption. This larger capital stock ensures that in the following period the debt can be serviced and repaid while in the current period consumption is greater than in the initial situation A.

This is a problem which is known to developing countries. Imports in the first period financed by loans enable development to be made of the basis for production in the following period.

In this example the time preference is greater than the interest. The fact that the time preference is large can be explained by the fact that the country is poor. It attaches relatively more importance to the present than to the future.

The marginal return on investment can be measures by the slope of the tangent to the transformation curve TT. The investment is shown as the drop in the production of consumer goods in the first period. The return on investment is the increased production which is thereby obtained in period 2. At A the return on investment is more than the international rate of interest. Therefore it can pay to borrow.

13.2 *Capital movements and trade*

A country's balance of payments is the balance sheet of the country's economic transactions with the rest of the world. Different transaction are divided into two types. First, there are current items, which includes trade in goods and services, as well as current transfers, and second there are movements on the capital account. These capital items are in turn split between direct investments and portfolio investments.

There is a close correlation between the current account and the capital account. If a country has an excess of imports on the current account, this must be financed through a capital import. If, on the other hand, a country has a capital import, this is first realised in the economy when the capital import is shown as a corresponding net import.

What is the difference between foreign direct investment and portfolio investments? There is a foreign direct investment when a person or a company in one country acquires an enterprise in another country over which that person or company has direct control. With foreign direct investment an asset is acquired which gives proprietary rights, in contrast to portfolio investments which concern the acquisition of financial claims.

Portfolio investments can either be long-term or short-term. They can either be used to finance increased consumption or increased investment. In principle a portfolio investment can merely mean that part of the existing capital stock is now financed by foreign investors. In other words this does not refer to an increase in the capital stock. In what follows in this chapter only portfolio investments are dealt with. The question of foreign direct investment is dealt with in the next chapter.

The preceding paragraph refers to portfolio investments. In the first example, illustrated in Figure 13.1, the production conditions are unchanged. There was a shifting of consumption between two periods. In the second example, illustrated in Figure 13.2, the portfolio investments affected the capital formation and thereby the production conditions in the country.

In this section it is assumed that the portfolio investments, i.e. the financial lending, causes a corresponding expansion of the capital stock. The purpose of the analysis is to show how capital movements which give a corresponding expansion of the capital stock, affect the structure of production, trade and welfare in society.

Trade or capital movements

There are two countries A and B in which the labour force is the same and where country A has a smaller capital stock than country B. Both countries produce two goods a and b, where a is a labour intensive product and b is capital intensive. It is assumed that all the standard conditions of factor proportion theory are met. The transformation curves are drawn in Figure 13.3.

Figure 13.3: Transformation curves with and without capital movements

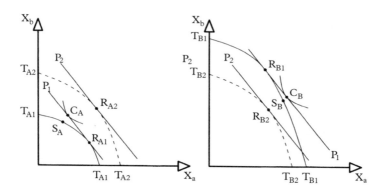

In the initial situation the transformation curves for country A and country B are $T_{A1}T_{A1}$ and $T_{B1}T_{B2}$ respectively. Without trade and without factor movements the countries produce and consume at points S_A and S_B respectively.

The introduction of trade

There is now trade, but without the possibility of factor movements. International terms of trade are established P_a/P_b, which are equal to the slope of the tangent P_1.

Following the introduction of trade the two countries A and B will produce at the points R_{A1} and R_{B1} respectively. Consumption will be at the points C_A and C_B. When the conditions of factor proportion theory are met, the factor return in the two countries will be the same when the countries trade with each other.

If the possibility of international capital movements is now introduced, there is no basis for such to take place. It is assumed that it is different returns on capital which cause capital movements. When there is trade the return on capital is the same, therefore there is no incentive for capital to move from one country to the other.

When international trade is entirely free there is no economic basis for international capital movements, even though they are possible.

There are capital movements

As an alternative it is now assumed that in the initial situation there is no trade. This is because, for example, country A imposes a tariff on good b so that the country is at point S_A. Correspondingly country B puts a tariff on good a, so that country B produces at point S_B. There is a situation of self-sufficiency, where there are no imports.

When both countries protect their potential import-competing goods this means that the return on capital in country A is greater than the return on capital in country B. Capital will now move from country B to country A. When all the conditions of factor proportion theory are met it can easily be shown that capital movements from country B to country A will establish a factor remuneration in the two countries which will be the same as the factor return that would result if there were trade.

In Fig. 13.3 the dotted transformation curves $T_{A2} T_{A2}$ and $T_{B2} T_{B2}$ are the new transformation curves after the capital movements have taken place. The new transformation curves are identical because the size of the labour force in the initial situation is the same, and because capital will move from country B to country A until the capital stocks of the two countries are the same.

When the factor remuneration is the same the price of the finished goods will also be the same. The new relative prices given by the slope of the tangent P_2 are the same as the relative prices, given by the slope of P_1, which obtain in the trade situation. Country A will now produce at point R_{A2} and country B will produce at point R_{B2}.

The foreign capital in country A gives a return which it is assumed is paid without deductions to the owners of the capital in country B. The line P_1 indicates the consumption possibilities in country A after the remuneration of foreign capital. Measured in the quantity of good b, the vertical distance between P_2 and P_1 is the remuneration paid on the foreign capital. The vertical distance between P_1 and P_2 is the same for both countries, which is due to the fact that country A pays the same for foreign capital as country B receives.

The remuneration paid on the domestic production factors is exactly the same as the remuneration obtained in a free trade situation without factor movements.

This means that for the citizens of country A the consumption point, after the payment of remuneration on foreign capital, is C_A. The same consumption point is obtained under free trade. The remuneration of the foreign capital occurs through a combination of exports of the two goods a and b so that there is movement from the production point R_{A2} to the consumption point C_A.

The opposite occurs in country B. After the capital has been reduced in country B, production will be at R_{B2}. Remuneration is received on the capital which has been lent to country A. This income is received in the form of imports of the two goods. This means that the consumption point will be C_B, which again is the same consumption point which would have been achieved if there had been trade without capital movements.

If one compares the situation where there is trade, but no capital movement, with the situation where there is no trade initially, but where there is capital movement, it is possible to draw some interesting conclusions.

Firstly, one can conclude that where there is free trade there will be an equalisation of factor prices so there will not be capital movements even though these may take place.

If there is no trade in the initial situation, capital movements will mean that the factor endowment will be the same in the two countries. This means that there is no scope for any trade other than that resulting from the capital exporting country taking its return on its capital invested in the other country through combined imports of goods a and b.

Secondly it can be seen that the welfare in the two countries will be the same, regardless of whether there is trade without factor movements or there are capital movements that involve the transfer of income equal to the return on the capital loans. The domestic consumption of the two goods will be identical in the two situations in each of the countries.

Compared with a situation of self-sufficiency, trade will create greater welfare. Trade enables advantage to be taken of the fact that the marginal productivity of capital is higher in country A than country B in the initial situation.

It is reasonable to assume that the difference in return is the reason why capital movements take place. The gain which is achieved by this, compared to a situation of self-sufficiency, is illustrated in Figure 13.4 which is a one product model.

Figure 13.4: The effects of capital movements

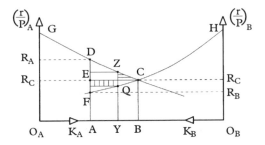

The vertical axis measures the real return on capital in the number of product units r/P, where r is the nominal return on capital and P is the price of the good produced.

The length of the horizontal axis is the sum of the capital stock in the two countries. The marginal product of capital in country A is drawn with the starting point O_A, and the marginal product of capital in country B is drawn with the starting point O_B.

The two curves are identical. This is due to the fact that the functions of production are assumed to be the same, and the quantity of labour is assumed to be the same in the two countries. In the initial situation country A and country B have capital stocks that are $O_A A$ and $O_B A$ respectively. The national product calculated in product units is $O_A ADG$ in country A and $O_B AFH$ in country B.

In this situation the real retrurn on capital in country A is equal to $O_A R_A$ and in country B it is $O_B R_B$. This difference in real interest will lead to capital movements from country B to country A. This will continue until the marginal product of capital is the same in both countries. In country A the capital stock will be larger, $O_A B$, while in country B it will be smaller, $O_B B$.

The national product in country A will now be $O_A BCG$, and in country B it will be $O_B BCH$. In country A the national income, which takes account of the international transfers, will be equal to the national product minus the area of ABCE. The area ABCE is the amount of foreign capital in country A times the return on capital $O_A R_C$. In country B the national income will be the national product plus this area.

When comparing the situation in the two countries before and after the capital movements, it will be seen that the global income has increased by the area CDF. This additional income will be divided between the two countries. Country A will receive the area CDE and country B the area CEF.

For the sake of completeness it should be mentioned that the distribution of income between the owners of capital and the wage earners will be affected by capital movements.

In the initial situation the national income in country A equals the area O_AADG. Of this the area O_AADR$_A$ will be paid to capital, and the area GR$_A$D will be paid to wage earners. Following the movement of capital AB has increased the capital stock in country A, the domestic owners of capital will have an income equal to O_AAER$_C$. The wage earners will receive increased income since they will now receive income corresponding to the area GR$_c$C.

The increase in wage earners' incomes is greater than the fall in income of the domestic owners of capital.

By looking at Figure 13.4 it seems obvious that in country B, which provides the capital, the incomes of the owners of capital will rise while the incomes of wage earners will fall.

What happens when the capital is taxed?

In the above it has been assumed that the foreign capital is not taxed in the host country. In practice capital will be taxed in both countries. It is now assumed that foreign and domestic capital are taxed equally.

Without taxation the curves GC and HC illustrate the economic returns for society which are the same as the private economic returns. If there is taxation of the capital then the private economic returns will be lower than the social economic returns. If the taxation of capital is the same in country A and country B, then the private economic return on capital will lower the curves GC and HC in Figure 13.4 similarly. This means that the new point of intersection C will still be on the same vertical axis above B. The existence of the same level of taxation in the two countries will therefore not affect the extent of capital movements.

If the taxation of capital in country A is higher than in country B, the point of intersection C will be moved to the left. This means that the capital movements will be reduced. On the other hand, the heavier taxation of capital in country A means that country A gets a share of the social economic returns to which the foreign investments give rise and which would otherwise go to country B. The heavier taxation of capital will also hit domestic capital, unless there is a differential between the taxation of domestic and foreign capital.

Perhaps country A wants to impose a special tax on country B's investments in order to obtain an advantage. The special tax ZQ is imposed on country B's investments in country A, see Figure 13.4. This naturally restricts country B's capital movement to country A, which are now AY. With this tax country A now gets the vertically hatched area which, without tax, would go to country B. On the other hand country A loses the horizontally hatched area which it would otherwise get if it had not imposed a special tax on foreign investments.

If the vertically hatched area is bigger than the horizontally hatched area, then country A makes a gain. This gain is at the cost of country B.

In this analysis it is assumed that the foreign capital in country A gets the same private economic return as the domestic capital in country A. This is a natural assumption in the case of portfolio investments. If the foreign owned investment is subject to costs which are not applied to the domestically owned, this will naturally reduce the movement of capital. This is dealt with in connection with foreign direct investment in Chapter 14.

13.3 Trade will not always equalise differences in factor remuneration

The foregoing analysis covers two countries in which it is assumed that the conditions for factor proportion theory apply. This means that it is the relative factor endowment in the two countries which determines the remuneration of capital and labour which will be different in the two countries.

If there is free trade but without the possibility of capital movements, the trade will create uniform prices for final goods, and thereby equal factor remuneration. Even if capital movements are subsequently made possible there will be no economic basis for them since the return on capital will be the same in both countries.

If free trade is not possible in the initial situation but there is the possibility of capital movements, these will create equal factor remuneration, which will make trade superfluous when the demand structure is the same and when the utility function is homothetic. However there will be an export of goods from the capital importing country to the capital exporting country which will be equal to the return on capital which is provided by the capital exporting country.

Finally there is the possibility that both free trade and capital movements are allowed simultaneously. In this situation there can both be trade and capital movements. It is not immediately possible to state the extent to which it is trade or factor movements that create equal prices and equal factor remuneration. It is necessary to look into the process of adjustment in more detail. Which becomes established more quickly, trade or capital movements?

In general it can be concluded that as long as the conditions of factor proportion theory apply, trade and capital movements are interchangeable methods for establishing a new equilibrium. If trade is allowed to flourish there is no basis for capital movements. If there is freedom of movement of capital, there is no basis for trade.

However, this conclusion cannot be sustained if the conditions of factor proportion theory do not apply. Even if there is free trade there will not be equal factor remuneration between the two countries. This can then give rise to capital movements where this is possible.

There can be a number of reasons why there may not be equalisation of factor prices. This will be the case if:

a. At least one country specialises in the production of one good.
b. There are barriers to trade, either in the form of tariffs or transport costs.
c. There are domestic taxes or subsidies, or the market is imperfect.
d. There are economies of scale of an external nature.
e. There are differences in production technology so that the functions of production are not the same in both countries.

To illustrate these problems it can be helpful to look at a couple of examples. In one case it is the transport costs of international trade, and in the other case it is technological differences which mean that the remuneration of the production factors are different between countries.

Transport costs

In this example the transport costs mean that there is a difference between the cost of goods in the two countries A and B. Producer and consumer prices are identical in each of the two countries.

$P^A = P_a^A/P_b^A$ are the relative prices between good a and good b in country A, and $P^B = P_a^B/P_b^B$ the relative prices in country B.

When good a is country A's export good and b is its import good, the following applies:

$$P_a^A (1 + t_a) = P_a^B$$
$$P_b^A = P_b^B (1 + t_b)$$

where t_a and t_b are the transport costs for the two goods. This means that P^A is less than P^B.

This is illustrated in Figure 13.5, from which it appears that each of the countries has less specialisation, compared with a situation in which there is free trade without transport costs.

If good a is a capital intensive good, the capital return in country A will be lower than in country B. It is the case that $(r/w)_A < (r/w)_B$. Therefore there will be capital movements from country A to country B, if this is possible. If the international capital market is perfect there will be capital movements until the remuneration on capital is the same in both countries. If it is assumed that labour is not internationally mobile then capital movements will continue until the relative factor endowments in the two countries are the same.

Figure 13.5: Transport costs and trade

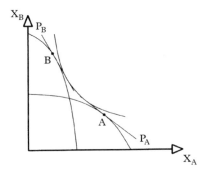

Gradually, as the relative factor endowment in the two countries gets closer, there will also be a reduction in trade. In the new equilibrium situation, where the relative factor endowment is the same, there will not be a basis for trade.

Here we have a situation in which the conditions of factor proportion theory do not apply, because there are transport costs. Trade cannot bring about price equalisation. However, this can be brought about by capital movements, which also have the effect of eliminating the trade which took place before the freeing of capital movements. Just as in the case where there were no transport costs, capital movements can function as a substitute for trade.

If the barriers to trade are not transport costs, but political measures in the form of tariffs or other trade barriers, the result will be just the same.

Differences in production technology

If there are differences in production technology between two countries, trade will not bring about an equalisation of factor prices. This means that there will be a basis for capital movements.

In the initial situation there are two countries which are identical. In Figure 13.6 $T_A T_A$ is the transformation curve for the two countries. They both produce at Q, and there is no trade.

There is now technological progress in the sector that produces the capital intensive good a in country B. Technological development can be of different kinds. For example the production function can be of a Cobb-Douglas type:

$$X_a = A \cdot K^\alpha \, L^{1-\alpha} \qquad\qquad (13.1)$$

If A increases without a change to α, it will be a case of neutral technological progress. If A increases at the same time that α increases, it will be a case of a capital intense innovation. If A increases while α falls, it will be a case of a labour intensive innovation. The simplest case is that with neutral technological progress. It is now assumed that there is neutral technological progress in sector a in country B. As a result of this, there will now be transformation curves $T_A T_A$ and $T_B T_B$ for the countries A and B respectively.

The relative good prices P_a/P_b are given by the slope of the tangent P. Country A produces at Q_A and consumes at C_A. Country A exports

the labour intensive good b, and country B exports the capital intensive good a, in which the country possesses better technology.

The situation in Figure 13.6 is in equilibrium with regard to trade.
However there is now different capital remuneration in the two countries. This is discussed in Section 12.5. In Figure 12.11 Z_1Z_1 is the
curve for country B, where there is neutral technological progress.
When there are relative good prices in international trade which correspond to the slope of P in Figure 13.6, there will be differing capital
remuneration in the two countries. With the help of Figure 12.11 it is
possible to see that if the relative international goods prices are B,
then the capital remuneration will be higher in country B than in
country A.

Figure 13.6: Different production functions in the two countries

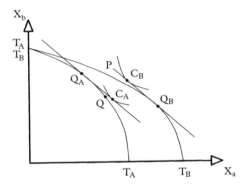

It is also possible to illustrate the conditions as shown in Figure 13.7.

Figure 13.7: Capital remuneration when production functions differ

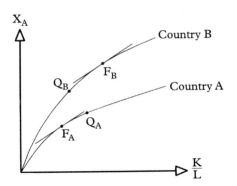

The production function, Equation (13.2), can be written as follows

$$X_a = A \left(\frac{K}{L} \right)^\alpha \cdot L \tag{13.2}$$

This production function for the two countries A and B is drawn in Figure 13.7. The lower curve, where the constant A in Equation (13.2) is relatively small, describes the situation in country A. In country B there is technological progress which means that A in Equation (13.2) increases. Therefore country B's curve is positioned higher than country A's. The slope of the tangent at a given point indicates the size of the marginal product of capital in sector a.

In a state of equilibrium the marginal product of capital is equal to the real return on capital (r/P_a). When there is international trade, as shown in Figure 13.6, the capital remuneration is greater in country B than country A. For example, country B is at Q_B and country A at Q_A, see Figure 13.7.

If there is the possibility of capital movement, there will be capital movements from country A to country B, until the return on capital is the same in both countries. In Figure 13.7 the properties at points F_A and F_B mean that the slope of the tangents at the two points are the same. This means that the marginal product of capital and thus the capital remuneration are the same in both countries.

What the model shows is that technological progress which occurs in one country but not in another will contribute to the factor endowments, and thus the economic activity in the two countries, becoming more unequal, because of the capital movements. To start with the conditions in the two countries are the same. Through technological progress country B obtains a comparative advantage in the production of good a. When the technological progress in country B further contributes to capital movements from country A to country B, these comparative advantages will be further developed. Factor movements therefore create the basis for increased trade.

This model shows that if there is technological progress in one country in one sector but not in another country, there will be a basis for trade. This trade will not bring about factor price equalisation. There will be the basis for capital movements which will strengthen the country's comparative advantages, which will in turn lead to increased trade. In this example capital movements and trade will both take place in a transition period. Once capital movements have taken place and there is trade there will no longer be capital movements while the return on capital is the same.

13.4 Advantages and disadvantages of capital movements

If factor proportion theory applies countries can obtain advantages through trade. The same advantages can be obtained without trade if there are capital movements. The immediate thought is that capital movements could be preferable to trade. One achieves the same result without the costs of international transport, while reducing external disadvantages in the form of the environmental problems associated with transport.

This is based on the premisses of factor proportion theory. However, a growing share of trade between industrial countries is intra-industry trade, where the motives for the trade are the advantages of firm specialisation, the advantages derived from being in an industrial environment (external economies of scale), as well as the consumer benefits linked to a greater variety of goods on offer. These advantages can only be obtained through trade and not through capital movements. Instead of considering trade and capital movements as alternatives, which is far from always being the case, it is more reasonable to look at the consequences of capital movements themselves.

The background to capital movement is that the return on capital is different in different countries. Even if there is trade, the return on capital is not necessarily the same, as shown in the preceding section. Figure 13.4 shows that *as long as the marginal return on capital is different* in two countries, there will be gains to be made by moving capital from the country with a smaller marginal return to the country with a larger marginal return. Both countries will gain by this.

It has also been shown that a borrowing country can obtain a gain by *taxing foreign capital*, even though the incentive to invest in the country is reduced. The gain of the borrowing country is balanced by a corresponding loss for the lending country. Total welfare for the two countries together will decrease compared with the situation where foreign capital is not taxed separately.

Capital movements can also lead to a change in the *terms of trade*. For one reason or another the return on capital is greater in country B than in country A, even though there is trade. If the relative good prices are constant, production of the capital intensive good a will increase in country B, and production of the labour intensive good b will fall, cf. the Rybczynski theorem. In country A the opposite will occur, so production of the capital intensive good a will fall and production of good b will increase. Taking the two countries together, the production of the capital intensive good a will increase more because the production technology for this product is better in country B, to which capital now moves.

There will be an increase of income in both countries, cf. Figure 13.4, since it is assumed that the capital return on country A's capital in country B will be transferred back to country A. If the demand conditions in both countries are such that the demand for good b increases more than the demand for good a, the relative good prices will change to the disadvantage of good a.

If good a is country B's export good this means that country B's terms of trade will deteriorate. The country with the higher capital return, which receives the loan capital, has worsened its terms of trade. However, if country B imports good a, country B improves its terms of trade.

In other words, capital movements can influence the terms of trade either to the advantage or disadvantage of the borrower. When looking at the advantages or disadvantages to an individual country, possible changes to the terms of trade must be included in the analysis.

When looking at the changes in the terms of trade from an overall point of view, the gain of one country will equal the loss of the other country. Terms of trade affect income distribution. If capital movement means that the poorer countries will suffer from a deterioration of their terms of trade, this can of course be a problem in itself.

This problem of terms of trade also turns up in connection with capital transfers in connection with aid or war reparations. Capital transfers can be compared with capital movements, but with capital transfers there is no interest payable as the capital is provided as a 'gift', without obligations.

Capital movements can also be the consequence of a country introducing *trade barriers*, for example tariffs. If country B introduces a tariff on good a which is capital intensive, it may be because the country has relatively little capital and wants to support the sector. As a relatively scarce factor, capital will get a better return when the capital intensive sector a is protected.

When capital in country B gets a better return there will be capital movements to country B. This means that sector a will be developed. This contributes to the increase in the production of good a in which country B has a comparative disadvantage. Imports of good a will fall, and the same applies correspondingly to exports of good b. Through free capital movements there is a development of the country's industrial structure which is not in compliance with the theory of comparative advantage.

Apart from this disadvantage, capital movements also have the disadvantage that they reduce a country's revenues from customs duties. When capital movements have eliminated imports of good a, the customs revenue of country B will also disappear.

Four different effects of capital movements have been identified here, related to different marginal returns, taxation, terms of trade and tariffs. The total effect depends on the circumstances of the case. If the country analysed is so small that it has no influence on its own terms of trade, the advantages or disadvantages of changes to its terms of trade are not relevant.

Many readers will perhaps be surprised that there is no reference to the increased employment which can be the consequence of the increased activity brought about by capital movements. This is because the analysis is made within the context of a neo-classical model in which there is, by definition, full employment. If one departs from this model and uses instead a Keynesian model, taking account of unemployment, then the question of employment is included.

Of the four circumstances listed above it is the difference in return on capital which is used as an argument in support of free movement of capital. As shown above, this argument is not valid as long as the differences in capital returns are caused by trade barriers. The argument only applies if the difference in capital return is caused by economic effectiveness. Even in such a case one should be aware that free capital movements can cause problems in the form of greater differences of activity in the two countries. Free movement of capital can lead to greater industrial concentration.

It is also appropriate to make clear that when references are made to differences in capital returns, these refer to the differences in the real economic returns. This real economic return can well be the same in different countries even if the interest paid on financial claims is different because the countries conduct different economic policies.

13.5 Trade, capital movements and economic inequality

The existing economic inequality between industrial and developing countries is usually measured by per capita GNP. As previously mentioned in Chapter 11, it is problematic to divide the world into to categories of countries. There are considerable differences within each group of countries. This is especially the case with developing countries.

Factor proportion theory is a neo-classical theory with which a number of assumptions concerning production, demand and market conditions are associated. According to factor proportion theory international trade should benefit both industrial and developing countries compared with a situation of self-sufficiency. The result of trade is that the factor prices are equalised. Equalisation of factor prices does not mean equalisation of per capita GNP. The country which has the bigger capital endowment has a bigger per capita income than the country with a smaller capital endowment.

In practice it can be seen that trade does not lead to equalisation of factor prices. The question is, therefore, whether the differences in return on capital when there are differences in factor endowment, should lead to significant capital movements from industrial countries to developing countries.

The production function for country A is drawn in Figure 13.7. If the production function is identical for industrial and developing countries, the production function for country A describes the production conditions for both of the groups of countries. K/L is greater in industrial countries which means that production is greater in industrial countries. This means that the marginal product of capital is lower in industrial countries than in developing countries, and when there is free movement of capital this should mean that that capital will flow from industrial countries to developing countries.

There is not the movement of capital from industrial countries to developing countries that might be expected. This is because the assumptions of factor proportion theory about uniform technology do not apply. Figure 13.7 shows that, if technology is more advanced in industrial countries (country B) than in developing countries (country A), then it is possible for the marginal return on capital to be the same in the two groups of countries. For example, this would be the case if the developing countries were at point F_A and the industrial countries were at point F_B.

When the capital return in industrial countries can be at the same level as in developing countries, despite the relatively plentiful capital, this is due to the better technology in individual firms, combined with the existence of an industrial environment in the industrial countries (external advantages). For individual firms it is in itself a great advantage to produce in an industrial environment, with the availability of inputs such as semi-manufactured goods and know-how from other firms. In addition there are advantages of infrastructure and institutional conditions. A high return on capital is based on the existence of an effective transport and communication system. Capital returns are also dependant on institutional conditions which ensure efficient markets, including financial markets and, for example, efficient services from public authorities.

Can free movement of capital create greater economic equality? According to factor proportion theory free trade should, in itself, create equal factor remuneration in industrial and developing countries, when they have the same production technology. When industrial countries have higher technology it is possible that the capital return will be higher in industrial countries than developing countries. This means that the capital return can be higher in those countries which already have relatively plentiful capital. The consequence is that the free movement of capital leads to an even more intensified capital accumulation in the industrial countries and weaker capital accumulation in developing countries. A new equilibrium is reached when capital movements have brought about an equal return on capital.

If there is continually greater technological progress in industrial countries than in developing countries there will be a tendency for capital returns to be greater in the richer countries. This again means that there will be a tendency for capital to move from poorer to richer countries. These factor movements will smooth out differences in capital returns, but if there is further technological progress in the industrial countries, new differences in capital remuneration will arise, giving further capital movements from developing to industrial countries.

If there is different technological progress in two regions, this can lead, via capital movements, towards a situation where the activities in the two regions become more unequal. There will be a potential for increased factor remuneration in the industrial countries without any corresponding development in the developing countries.

It is therefore important, if the economic situation in developing countries is to be improved, that there should be a transfer of such technology to these countries as they have the capacity to exploit. Consideration should be given to the large labour forces which developing countries can take advantage of, as long as there is the transfer of relatively simple technology which is non capital intensive. The transfer of high technology is problematic. On the one hand a well educated labour force is needed to make use of the high technology, and on the other hand there is a need for on-the-spot skills for maintaining and repairing advanced capital equipment.

13.6 Migration of labour

In factor proportion theory it is assumed that there is full mobility of production factors within the borders of a country, but no transnational mobility. This does not apply to capital movements in today's world. Nor does it apply fully to the movement of labour, though the assumptions of factor proportion theory apply to a greater extent to the labour force. There is a greater mobility for highly educated employees than for the labour force in general. In general the well educated workers move to where there is already a large pool of well educated workers. This is described as a 'brain drain' which is what occurs when employees who have received a high level of education either leave their country or do not return to their country because it is more attractive to get a job in a centre of high technology in another country. The fact that it is the best educated and most enterprising workers that emigrate can contribute to increased inequality between industrial and developing countries.

Historically there have been periods of significant migration of labour, for example from Europe to North America in the nineteenth century. Europe has also experienced immigration from Africa and Asia, even though this has been relatively small. There has also been relatively small migration of labour between EU countries, even though the legal barriers have been removed. It is to be expected that the mobility of the labour force within Europe will also be limited in the future.

If there are international migrations of labour, these can be included in the models in the same way as the movements of capital looked at above. Since the labour force has low mobility and since migration of labour can be analysed in the same way as movements of capital, the point of interest here is why international labour mobility is so low.

Migration of labour are dependant on three factors: the conditions in the country of origin, the conditions in the destination country, and the barriers to migration. The conditions for employment, wage levels and the cost of living in the country of origin and in the destination country are decisive for how great the potential is for labour migration between countries. The conditions in the country of origin are 'push' factors, and the conditions in the destination country are 'pull' factors.

The extent to which potential labour migration occurs depends on the extent of the barriers. The greater the barriers the less mobility there will be on the international labour market. Mobility is also dependent on the physical distance and the costs associated with it. These transaction costs are related to the fact that a migrant has to 'liberate' himself from his old place and establish himself in a new place. These costs can be significant. Apart from this, mobility can be limited by the fact that workers have families and friends where they are. For a worker to tear himself out of his home environment becomes more complicated when he moves to another country with another language and another culture. The perception of the surmountability of these linguistic and cultural barriers depends on the educational level of the labour force. Everything else being equal, people with a high educational level will judge these barriers to be lower than people with a lower educational level.

Figure 13.8 illustrates the conditions that affect the extent of labour migration. The vertical axis shows the extent of international migration. One of the horizontal axes shows the difference between the standard of living in the country of origin and the country of destination. This difference is assumed, everything else being equal, to show the potential labour migration between two countries. The greater the rise in living standard to be obtained by moving abroad, the greater the incentive.

The other horizontal axis shows the living standard in the country of origin. The international mobility of the work force is assumed to be associated with the living standard in the country of origin.

Figure 13.8 illustrates three cases. There are countries of potential emigration with a low, a middle and a high living standard. In all three cases the actual level of emigration will be almost non-existent up to a certain level of difference between the living standards in the country of origin and the living standards in the potential country of desti-

nation. Up to a given level of living standards, potential migration will
not become actual because of the barriers to migration. At the point
where living standards cross a threshold value the barriers will no
longer be a complete bar to migration.

Figure 13.8: Living standards and labour migration

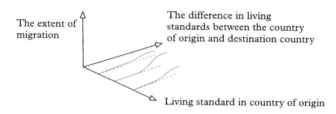

As appears in the figure, once the difference in living standards crosses
the threshold value, the extent of migration depends on the conditions
in the country of origin. If the potential country of origin has a low or
a high average income, migration will be low even if there are large
differences of income between the country of origin and the destination country.

In poor societies the barriers are great because of ignorance and low
educational levels. In rich societies these barriers do not exist. However, if the migration levels are still low this is because even large
differences of income are not such an incentive to migration, because
of the sharp decline in the marginal utility of income.

In a society which lies between the rich and the poor, the barriers
to migration are lower and the benefits of a higher income are greater.
Therefore migration will be relatively larger when a substantial rise in
income can be obtained by taking work in another country.

13.7 Summary

The existence of an international capital market makes it possible for
a country to shift its consumption from one period to another. An
international capital market also means that a country is not limited
to a level of investment determined by its domestic savings. This
means that in the following period there must be a surplus of savings,

i.e. I (investments) must be lower than S (savings) in order to service and repay debts.

If it is assumed that factor proportion theory applies, capital movements will not have advantages which cannot be obtained through trade. Capital movements and trade are interchangeable on the basis that free trade makes capital movements superfluous and capital movements make trade superfluous.

If the conditions of factor proportion theory do not apply, there will be capital movements even though there is trade, when the return on capital is different in two countries. If there are transport costs or political trade barriers, e.g. in the form of tariffs, capital movements will replace trade. If the differences in return on capital are caused by different production technologies in the two countries, there will be capital movements at the same time as trade. At the new point of equilibrium there will be increased trade and capital movements will stop, because an equalisation of factor prices will have been reached.

Several advantages and disadvantages of capital movements can be identified. The advantage which can be used as an argument in favour of free movement of capital is the difference in the real return on capital. There is a more effective use of a given amount of capital at a given moment if it is invested where there is the highest return on capital. However the problem is that capital movements can lead to a greater inequality of economic activity between countries. It can lead to a concentration of industries in the wealthier region.

International migration of labour are less significant, especially when highly educated labour is excluded. With highly educated labour the 'brain drain' can cause problems. Since the effects of labour migration can be analysed in the same way as capital movements, it is worth looking at the factors which explain why labour migration is not more widespread. There are a number of barriers to migration which can explain why the international mobility of labour is limited.

Literature

Bhagwati, J.N., 'International Factor Movements and National Advantage', *Indian Economic Review*, October, 1979.

Bhagwati, J.N., and R. Brecher, 'National Welfare in an Open Economy in the Presence of Foreign-owned Factors of Production', *Journal of International Economics*, 10, 1980.

Jones, R.W. and R.J. Ruffin, 'Production Pattern with Capital Mobility' in R.W. Jones, *International Trade: Essays in Theory*, Amsterdam, 1979.

Mac Dougall, G.D.A., 'The Benefits and Costs of Private Investments from Abroad: A Theoretical Approach', *Economic Record*, 36, 1960.

Markusen, J.R., 'Factor Movements and Commodity Trade as Complements', *Journal of International Economics*, 13, 1983.

Purvis, D.D., 'Technology, Trade and Factor Mobility', *Economic Journal*, 82, 1968.

14. Direct investment

14.1 Different kinds of direct investment

As stated in Section 13.2, the decisive distinction between portfolio investment and direct investment is the question of control. Portfolio investments consist of financial loans or the purchase of shares with a view to obtaining a good financial return, but without the intention of acquiring the right to direct the management of the firm. With direct investment the aim is to take on the management of a firm, either by setting up a new unit or by the purchase of an existing unit.

A distinction is made between a firm and a firm unit. A firm is an economic entity which often consists of several technical units. Direct investments abroad can either be in sales subsidiaries or manufacturing subsidiaries which, together with the parent company, constitute the whole company or the whole firm.

Foreign direct investment can be of different kinds, depending on the nature of the integration in question. There can be vertical investments, horizontal investments or investment in the production of goods which the company has not previously produced.

Vertical investments can either be 'backward' investments of 'forward' investments. Backward investments take place when a company invests in the production of raw materials which are processed in further steps within the company. These investments are often made by parent companies in industrial countries which invest in developing countries. Investments in sales subsidiaries are forward investments, and they are mostly undertaken by companies in industrial countries investing in other industrial countries.

When there is the establishment of units producing the same goods as the parent company this is called *horizontal investment*. This type of investment primarily occurs between industrial countries and it has increased particularly in the post war period.

Direct investments which lead to an *increase in the product range of the company* are rare. The parent company usually produces a range of products that are related either in production or marketing, though this is not necessarily the case. If the company extends its range of products this most frequently occurs by the parent company extending its range. The establishment of investment abroad with a view to starting production of a new product usually occurs after production has been established in the country of the parent company.

When reference is made to foreign direct investment this usually refers to the multinational companies which have arisen through the setting up of production units in several countries with the management of the business situated in one country. However, also in smaller countries where even the bigger companies are small or medium sized by international standards, even smaller companies which cannot be described as multinationals are making foreign direct investments in the form of sales or production subsidiaries.

In the following, a number of theories on direct investment will be examined. The theories apply both to multinational companies and to other companies which invest abroad. However, certain elements of the theories can have different significance depending on whether the investment is made by a multinational company or another company.

14.2 Why make direct investment?

The previous chapter analysed capital movements in the form of portfolio investments. It is assumed that there is a perfect capital market in each of the countries. The interest generated in the capital market is assumed to be equal to the marginal productivity of the capital. It is assumed that investors will continue to increase the capital stock until the point is reached where the marginal return on capital is equal to the interest rate.

In Figure 14.1.a it is assumed that the production function is the same in the two countries A and B. This means that the marginal productivity of capital r is described by the curve RR. The capital markets of the two countries are separated. In country A the interest rate is i_A which results in a capital stock of OA, and in country B, where the interest rate is i_B, the capital assets will be OB. There is now the possibility of capital movements, and if there is an integration of the capital markets in the two countries the interest rate will be i_i. This means that loans move from country B to country A, which leads to the capital stock being lower in country B and correspondingly higher in country A.

Figure 14.1: The marginal return on capital and interest rates

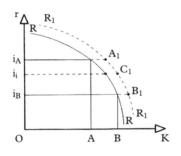 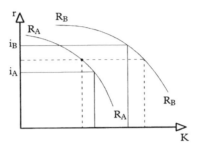

a. Identical production functions   b. Different production functions

In Figure 14.1.b it is assumed that the production functions in the two countries are different. Country B has better technology than country A. When international lending is introduced, country B borrows in country A. The capital stock in country A is diminished, and the capital stock in country B is increased.

In both cases there will be a national reallocation of the initial capital stocks in the two countries. In practice it is the growth in the capital stock which is shifted through loans. There may be technological progress which leads to an increase in the marginal return on capital. This means that the RR curve in figure 14.1a moves upwards to R_1R_1. If there is not an integrated capital market, but only national capital markets with interest rates of i_A and i_B respectively, in country A there will be investments of AA_1, and in country B there will be investments of BB_1. If there is an international capital market with an interest rate of i_i, the greater part of country B's savings will be lent to country A, which will see an increase in its capital stock from A to C_1, and country B will not increase its capital stock from B to B, but only from B to C_1.

The central point is that an international capital market will allocate savings where they will give the best return on investment. It is a precondition that there are a number of national capital markets which operate perfectly. In addition it is a pre-condition that these capital markets are integrated internationally so that overall there is a perfect international capital market.

If some of these conditions are not sustained, the marginal return on capital can vary from country to country, even though there may be international portfolio investments. This means that there is also a basis for foreign direct investment.

As long as there is perfect competition in an integrated international credit market it is reasonable to assume that international differences in the profitability of businesses will be smoothed out through the capital markets rather than through foreign direct investment.

This is linked to the fact that while portfolio investments are 'cost free', in the sense that the transaction costs of moving capital are close to zero, additional costs are to be expected when making foreign direct investments. It is to be expected that a given investment made by a domestic investor will give a higher domestic return than will be the case with foreign direct investment. Subsidiary companies abroad usually have higher costs than national companies.

This is linked to a number of factors. There are transport costs for managers and employees who have to co-ordinate the activities between the parent and subsidiary companies. There are costs of communication. Especially prior to the technological developments within the transport and communication sectors these were considerable additional costs. Cultural and linguistic difficulties can cause problems which involve extra costs. A foreign owned subsidiary often has poor knowledge of the national laws and regulations, as well as an inadequate understanding of the customs and unwritten rules in the host country, including an understanding of the practices of the labour market. It may be necessary to post management and employees from the home country in the host country, which often involves considerably higher salary costs to make the international transfer attractive. Finally, there can be risks involved in being subject to the jurisdiction of a foreign country. There can be a risk, for example, of nationalisation or other encroachment on the rights of ownership. There can also be a risk from changes to the exchange rate, though this risk should not be given undue weight since the foreign direct investment itself includes the possibility of covering this risk through borrowing in the host country.

In the real world both portfolio investments and direct investments are made across national borders. Normally portfolio investments go only one way, from an area with low returns to an area with high returns. In contrast to this, direct investments flow both in and out of individual countries.

As has been mentioned already, if the international capital market is not perfect this can mean that both portfolio and direct investments take place simultaneously.

Even if the international capital market is perfect, there can be circumstances which mean that there is scope for foreign direct investment. There are a number of circumstances which can help to explain why there are foreign direct investments. These circumstances are as follows:

a. It is not the same agents that decide the financial capital dispositions and the direct investments, and their aims will often be different. Thus there can be portfolio investments and direct investments simultaneously.

b. Direct investments made by foreigners need not have a lower domestic return than corresponding investments made by a country's own citizens. The parent company abroad may have some special know-how which can best be exploited through direct investments.

c. Direct investments can be competitive because there are advantages of specialisation, economies of scale, and advantages of co-ordination.

d. Direct investments can be the consequence of imperfections in the markets for the goods in question in the form of an oligopoly.

e. Trade barriers and exchange rate problems can have an influence on the establishment of foreign subsidiaries.

When analysing direct investments it is reasonable to start by considering the theory of the product life cycle, cf. Chapter 8.5. This is the only trade theory which also allows for the possibility of direct investment. The core of the theory of the product life cycle is that a good will be produced in different countries, depending where it is in its cycle. Innovations occur in the wealthiest countries. Later, production moves to other industrial countries, and later still it moves to developing countries.

However, the product life cycle theory does not say anything about who shall produce the product in the other countries when production moves. There are three possibilities. First, a producer in another country can start production, for example upon the expiry of a patent. Secondly, the company which made the innovation can directly establish production in other countries. Thirdly, the innovating company can sell its know-how to local producers in other countries, who then start production.

The five circumstances set out above, and which are dealt with below, can explain the foreign direct investments undertaken.

14.3 Different objectives

There are differences between those who make direct investments and those who make portfolio investments. These differences are apparent in their different objectives and different behaviour.

Direct investments are almost exclusively made by companies. By contrast, for all practical purposes, individuals only make portfolio investments. Companies also play a role in credit markets, but in this role the aims and activities of companies are similar to those of individuals.

When individuals buy securities they aim to maximise their returns. The decisive elements of an investment decision therefore are, on the one hand the expected returns, and on the other hand an assessment of the risks of the investment.

When a company is setting up a subsidiary it takes account not only of the expected returns and the various risks; apart from maximising gain the company will also often be aiming for growth. If a company is assured of profit, above a certain minimum level, the company can be more interested in long term growth.

There are thus different objectives behind the decision making process for individuals who make portfolio investments and companies which make direct investments.

Even if both individuals and companies include expected profits and risks in their investment decisions, these two elements have a very different significance for the two categories of investors.

For the individual investor the *expected return* means the interest on a loan made abroad or the dividend on shares bought. For a company the expected return means the profit to be gained by establishing a unit abroad, either by taking over an existing firm or with a start-up. The profit that a company can make through its investment can be very different from the return obtained on a portfolio investment, including passive ownership of shares. The investment horizon for a private investor with a portfolio investment is much shorter than the investment horizon of a company. A company does not set up in a foreign country for short terms gains, but for long term profit.

The *risks* which an individual investor is interested in are linked to fluctuations in the values of the shares or securities. These fluctuations depend not only on the profits of the companies connected with the securities, but also on the effectiveness of the functioning of the foreign capital market. In contrast to this the establishment of a subsidiary abroad will always be considered in the light of the company's total 'global strategy'.

A company will be willing to take greater risks on a single investment to avoid the threat of a competitor establishing itself instead. The economic risks associated with an individual investment can seem great, in the context of that investment alone, but seen in relation to the whole company these risks will naturally appear much smaller, by avoiding the loss caused by a competitor gaining a foothold.

The different objectives in relation to investments made by private persons and by companies can explain foreign direct investment, even if portfolio investment is more profitable in the short term.

14.4 A comprehensive theory for foreign direct investment

A foreign subsidiary company can very well have an internal profit which is the same as or higher than the internal profit of locally owned companies. This can be the case when the parent company has some special knowledge which locally owned firms do not have.

Under such circumstances it will be best for a company which has some special knowledge or know-how to exploit it abroad through direct investment.

The theory of firm-specific advantages

How can a foreign subsidiary company compete with the local producers? There is an initial assumption that a foreign subsidiary company is in a weak competitive position against national companies. This is so as long as there is perfect competition in the national market for the goods concerned and as long as the production techniques are the same in the two countries. In such a case the foreign subsidiary company will have higher costs than the local competitor. This is due to a) the costs of communication between the subsidiary and the parent company, b) the lack of knowledge about the institutional conditions in the local market, and c) complications in adjusting to existing local customs, for example in the labour market.

These disadvantages arise because the subsidiary and parent company are geographically separated and the subsidiary company has to work in a foreign environment. When subsidiary and parent company are separated there are organisational problems which the national competitor does not have. Large concerns which have a widespread network of subsidiary companies cannot avoid these problems which naturally increase with the number of subsidiaries. Among other things the foreign working environment means that the subsidiary does not know the rules and regulations as well as domestic companies and does not understand the habits and attitudes of the employees.

When direct investment is made it is often because the market for the goods is not perfect and because the production conditions for the foreign subsidiary are different to those of the domestic firms. In spite of the cost disadvantages of the subsidiary compared with national competitors, it will be able to compete, for example because it has know-how which the national firms do not have. This know-how is transferred from the parent company.

A firm which considers investing abroad can have special skills in the form of technical, managerial and marketing know-how.

The technical know-how may consist in being able to produce a product which is not available on the market. In this case there is a monopoly. Even if there is not a monopoly, but there is a market with monopolistic competition, each producer's product can have particular characteristics which gives the producer a special position.

The technical know-how can also be linked to the production process. The company can have knowledge about a special production process which is the basis for the final product being either different or cheaper. There can also be special machines or workers which other businesses do not have.

The specific advantages of the company are not necessarily related to technology. The company can also possess managerial or marketing knowledge which gives it a competitive advantage.

However, the parent company's greater or more advanced knowledge compared with that of a foreign country is not sufficient to explain having direct investments abroad. The special know-how of a company can generate foreign earnings by a) export of goods produced with the help of the know-how in question, b) sale of the relevant know-how to foreign producers and c) establishing a production unit abroad.

An explanation of why production units are set up abroad must therefore include an explanation of why the parent company does not choose to export the goods or sell its know-how instead of making direct investments.

The theory of location

There are two countries A and B. The company in country A must choose between exporting and establishing a production unit abroad. Which factors are decisive in making the choice? First, there are the different production conditions in the two countries, for example because of different factor prices. Next, there are the barrier costs of exporting and of setting up an establishment abroad. These barriers can be 'natural' in the form of technical or cultural barriers or 'artificial' in the form of political barriers. These conditions can be described using Figure 14.2.

Figure 14.2: Barriers to trade and direct investments

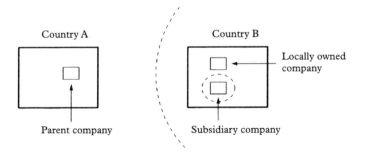

The dotted line around the subsidiary indicates the natural barriers (lack of knowledge about institutional conditions and complications in adjusting to existing local customs) which the subsidiary meets in country B.

The dotted line around country B indicates the barriers to country

A's transactions with country B. These barriers can be linked both to exports and to direct investments.

With exports the parent company meets natural obstacles in the form of increased production, transport and sales costs. The product must be adapted to the market, which leads to extra production costs compared with the costs of producing for the home market. The physical distances in foreign trade give increased transport, financing and warehousing costs. Finally sales and marketing in export markets are more complicated and therefore more costly. In addition to this, exports can meet a number of artificial obstacles in the form of customs tariffs, import restrictions and exchange restrictions, and invisible trade barriers such as technical and health related provisions, as well as exchange rate risks.

There are natural obstacles for subsidiary companies with problems of organisation and co-ordination. Apart from this there can be political obstacles between countries in the form of currency restrictions which limit the movement of capital between the parent company and the subsidiary. Also the subsidiary can be subject to a different legal system. The subsidiary can be at risk from nationalisation. Finally, there is the exchange rate risk. However, in a world of fluctuating exchange rates this need not be a disadvantage, but rather an advantage to have units abroad, because it gives greater possibilities of covering the exchange rate risk.

It is now possible to identify the extent to which it is possible for a company in country A to export to country B. It is also possible to determine whether there is a good basis for establishing a unit in country B. In this assessment a number of elements will be included: P, B_e, B_d and V.

P is: The difference in the production costs between country A and country B with the technology which is used by country B's own producers. The differences in cost are based on the different production conditions in the two countries, for example the different factor prices.

B_e is: The barrier costs for exports from country A to country B.

B_d is: The barrier costs of production related to direct investments by country A in country B.

V is: The economic advantage associated with the possession of the specific know-how of the parent company which can be transferred to subsidiaries.

Whether the company in country A is able to export profitably to country B depends on whether the economic advantage linked to the specific knowledge of the company is greater than the country B's production advantages plus the barrier costs of exporting. Expressed by the symbols defined above, it is the following relationship which is of interest:

$$V \gtreqless P + B_e \qquad (14.1)$$

where P is reckoned as positive if the production costs of the technology used in B are lower in country B than in country A.

If the left hand side of the equation is greater, country A will be able to export, since the advantage of country A's know-how exceeds the sum of country B's advantage in production costs together with the export barrier costs of country A. If the right hand side of the equation is greater there is no basis for export from country A.

Whether the company in country A will choose a direct investment abroad rather than exporting depends on the expression of Equation (14.2):

$$P + B_e \gtreqless B_d \qquad (14.2)$$

By establishing a subsidiary rather than exporting, the company obtains a gain of $P + B_e$. There are costs savings by producing in country B, and the extra costs of exporting are avoided. On the other hand, the subsidiary is subject to additional costs by comparison with local producers, and these are expressed as B_d. If the left hand side of Equation (14.2) is greater than the right hand side, then a direct foreign investment is preferable.

From the expressions of Equations (14.1) and (14.2) it appears that establishing a subsidiary can be considered even though it may not be more profitable than exporting. This will be the case as long as $P + B_e > V > B_d$. However, in practice, it is rare for there not to be exports prior to the establishment of a subsidiary.

The different elements dealt with here are measured as capital values. The element P is thus the present discounted value of the differences of production costs between the two countries with country B's technology. As always with investment calculations, there are problems in estimating the values of the elements relevant to the calculations. In making such estimates it is necessary to consider that the value of some elements will change over time, even over the shorter period which may correspond to the investment horizon of the enterprise.

This applies, for example, to the barrier costs. When starting to export the costs of adjusting to the export market and some of the additional sales and marketing costs must be paid. These are one-off payments. The greater the exports the better understanding of the market and the fewer the costs incurred in obtaining knowledge about the market. Something similar applies to the barrier costs with production by a subsidiary. Once production starts, knowledge of the institutional conditions and the scope for adjusting to the country's customs and tastes is significantly increased.

Also, the economic advantage associated with know-how can change with time. The know-how will be disseminated to a greater or lesser extent. The company thus loses its monopoly of this knowledge. In order to maintain an advantage over competitors the company must continually develop new knowledge.

Finally, there are differences in production costs. These change relatively slowly. In the short term, cost developments can vary from country to country due to differing inflation rates. However, these differences are not based on the real economic conditions and will mostly be corrected through changes to the exchange rate. In the longer term production conditions will be influenced by trade and by the subsidiary companies established.

If $P + B_e$ is bigger than B_d, cf. Equation (14.2), then setting up a subsidiary will be preferable to exporting. If B_d is bigger than $P + B_e$ then exporting will be preferable. This is a theory which can identify whether it is preferable to locate production domestically or abroad.

However, there is nothing in this theory to explain why a company does not choose to sell its know-how to a foreign manufacturer rather than manufacture abroad itself.

The theory of internalisation

Even though foreign direct investment is subject to a number of costs which local competitors do not have, such investments are made because subsidiary companies are able to make use of know-how which local competitors do not have. The value of this know-how (V) is greater than the barrier costs (Bd) of the subsidiary. In other words the subsidiary has greater benefits than local competitors. The value of this benefit is $V - B_d$.

The question now is whether the parent company could not have obtained even greater benefit by selling its know-how to a competitor abroad rather than setting up a subsidiary.

By not setting up a foreign subsidiary the average profit (G) obtained by the local competitors is lost, as well as the extra profit $V - B_d$. By selling the know-how there is a gain of the profit V, as well as releasing the capital which would otherwise have been bound up in the foreign investment.

If this freed capital can generate a return that corresponds to the profit level of the foreign producers, G, then the parent company will make a bigger gain by selling its know-how than by foreign direct investment. However, this assumes that the parent company in fact wants to maximise its gains and that the company can sell its know-how at the value which it has for the parent company itself, and that the parent company does not ascribe value to the control of its own specific knowledge.

Firstly, the aim of a company can be to obtain maximum growth or the maintenance of a given market share. This can mean that setting up a subsidiary will be preferable to the sale of know-how, even though the gain of the latter would be greater.

Secondly, the price the parent company can obtain for its know-how is usually lower than the value of such know-how when exploited by the parent company itself. In other words the market for the sale of know-how is imperfect. This is linked to a number of factors. It is difficult to draft a know-how contract. It is complicated to formulate exactly what knowledge is being sold. This applies perhaps less to manufacturing know-how, but maybe more to knowledge of marketing, organisation and management. Finally it is usually difficult to put a price on such know-how even when its content is clearly specified. The purchaser will often be unwilling to pay the full value of the know-how because of uncertainty about its exploitation. The purchaser cannot assess what is a reasonable price. This is because the potential purchaser does not have the same information about the value of the know-how as the potential seller. There are limits to the amount of information a potential seller will give away. If specific information is given away the potential buyer obtains knowledge so that there is no further interest in buying the know-how. In addition to this, the know-how is of greater value to the parent company because it is cumulative to its other stock of know-how and because it is often part of a continual production of new know-how. Therefore the know-how in question is worth more when it is exploited by a subsidiary than when it is sold to an independent company, unless the potential buyer of the know-how can enter into a more long term co-operation with the owner of the know-how. For the potential buyer this can mean an undesirable state of dependence. Because of the uncertainties referred to, the potential buyer will not pay a price which is acceptable to the potential seller. The potential seller of know-how will prefer direct investment, and the potential buyer of know-how will prefer to sell its firm to the foreign company.

Imperfections in the market for know-how and objectives other than maximising profits can thus each explain why direct investment is preferred to entering into contracts for the sale of know-how to independent companies.

A third factor is that by selling its know-how a company loses control over the use of the specific know-how. With direct investment there is an internal sale of know-how from the parent to the subsidiary. The company thus retains control of what constitutes its competitive strength. The internalisation of this within the enterprise is preferred to using the market for the sale of know-how.

With vertical investments there is also an internalisation, rather than a use of the market. There are numerous examples of processing firms buying up suppliers of particularly important inputs, for example vital raw materials, so that future supplies can be secured. If the producer of raw materials has a strong market position, or if the producer can obtain a strong position by establishing a cartel, there is a risk that prices of the raw materials will go up. If the manufacturer of final goods buys up the producer of the raw materials, this risk is eliminated.

It is possible that the producer of raw materials also supplies some of the competitors of the manufacturer of final goods. In such a case then, following the acquisition of the producer of raw materials, the manufacturer of final goods will be able to put up the price of raw materials to its competitors. This naturally weakens the other manufacturers' competitiveness.

A manufacturer of final goods which invests in a sales subsidiary also makes an internalisation, rather than using the market. The manufacturer obtains greater control over its sales and marketing and gets closer contact with the foreign market. A certain amount of information is internalised which would otherwise have to be bought in the market.

A comprehensive theory of direct investment based on sub-theories

A comprehensive theory on foreign direct investment must explain a number of things. Firstly it must explain how it is at all possible for foreign subsidiaries to compete with local producers. It is the theory of company-specific advantages linked to the possession of specific assets in the form special know-how. Secondly, it must explain why direct investment may be preferable to exports. This is done using the theory of location, taking account of comparative advantages and barrier costs. Thirdly, it must explain why direct investment is preferable to the sale of know-how. This is done by using the theory of internalisation. Table 14.1 shows which circumstances the individual sub-theories can explain. The theory of the specific know-how which a given company has can explain why it can be best to set up a foreign subsidiary. But this theory also allows for the possibility that the company could exploit its knowledge through exports or through the sale of know-how.

When it comes to the theory of location, it is possible to show that it can be reasonable for a company to exploit its know-how through direct investment rather than through export. As against this, the theory cannot explain that direct investment is preferable to the sale of know-how.

The internalisation theory can explain why direct investment may take place in preference to entering into an agreement for the sale of know-how.

Taken together the three sub-theories make it possible to explain why decisions are taken to make direct investments and why these are preferred to export or sale of know-how.

Table 14.1: What possibilities do the sub-theories open up?

The theory opens up for:	Company-specific advantages	Location	Internalisation
Exports	Yes	No	No
Know-how contracts	Yes	Yes	No
Direct investments	Yes	Yes	Yes

14.5 *Which kinds of companies prefer direct investment?*

The theory of direct investment explains why direct investment may be preferred to exports or sale of know-how. The theory can be supplemented with a theory on the particular characteristics of different companies which determine which choice is best for each type of company.

A company which acquires some special knowledge, either by developing a new product or a new production process, will go through several stages of development. To start with, after the appearance of the new product, the business will supply foreign markets through exports. When a foreign market reaches a certain size the local producers will be interested in producing under licence. Because of the lower production costs abroad local producers will be able to pay the innovating company for the relevant know-how. For the innovating company it is more advantageous to give up the exports and to sell the know-how instead. The establishment of a production unit in the export market will not be an alternative to export for the innovating company. The company's turnover in the export market in question will be too small for this.

However, if the company's exports to the foreign market grow to a substantial level, this will make it more profitable to set up a unit within the market, rather than sell the know-how. This will apply when the potential buyer of know-how is unwilling to pay a price corresponding to the actual value of the know-how for the potential seller.

Whether a company chooses to make foreign direct investment or to sell its know-how to a foreign manufacturer depends on two closely related things: the company's share of the foreign market and the size of the company.

If the company has only a small share of the market there is no basis for making a direct investment which requires a certain level of turnover before the capacity of the investment can be exploited. On the other hand other manufacturers will have a large share of the market, so there should be a good possibility for a company which has the specific knowledge selling its know-how to one of these manufacturers.

If, on the other hand, the company has a large share of the market, there is a basis for direct investment. The investment must be of a certain size in order to be profitable, and there will now be a sufficient basis of sales for this to be achieved. In addition to this, the better the company can serve the market, the less likely it is that other manufacturers will penetrate the market once the subsidiary has become established. Through the establishment of a subsidiary, the company will have far better control over how its know-how is used.

From the above it can be deduced that small enterprises prefer to sell their know-how, while big enterprises prefer to set up subsidiaries. Apart from the differences in market share, there can be other reasons for this. Big companies find it easier to raise the capital necessary for the investment. As a rule big companies have a continual production of new know-how which can be used by its subsidiaries. The know-how created by small companies is often a one-off event. When the innovation becomes obsolete the small enterprise is left standing with a foreign subsidiary which has difficulty in competing because it no longer has any special knowledge.

14.6 The advantages of specialisation, economies of scale and co-ordination in cases of direct investment

It has been shown above that a company which has acquired specific know-how can advantageously undertake direct investment under given circumstances. There are other conditions, apart from the possession of know-how, which can make it advantageous to set up foreign subsidiaries. There can be advantages of market specialisation, economies of scale and improved co-ordination.

Even if the company does not possess any specific know-how, these other advantages can in themselves mean that it can be worthwhile setting up foreign subsidiaries. If the company has special know-how as well as the advantages referred to, both sets of factors will contribute to making foreign subsidiaries profitable. It is clear that a given know-how becomes more valuable when it is combined with other advantages.

With vertical investments the parent company invests in the production of the raw materials and semi-finished goods used in its manufactures. Thus the company ensures its supplies of raw materials and semi-finished goods. If there is imperfection in the markets for raw materials and semi-finished goods it is also possible to save costs by taking over a former supplier's firm or by a start up. There can also be cost savings through better co-ordination of the production of raw materials and final goods when these units are part of the same company.

With horizontal investment it is possible to obtain advantages of economies of scale and of specialisation. By having several units gathered together in one company it is possible to achieve the traditional advantages of economies of scale which are associated with sales, finance and research, cf. Chapter 8.3. The fixed costs can be spread over a larger production and it is possible to employ more specialist labour in the areas concerned. The advantages of economies of scale referred to here give subsidiaries a competitive advantage over local producers.

If a company produces several products then horizontal investment creates the possibility of product specialisation within the individual units belonging to the company. For example the business can produce a variety of manufactured goods which are included in an assortment, or it can produce a number of components in different units which are included in the production of a final product. If the parent company has a number of subsidiaries, there is the possibility of co-ordinating the manufacture of the different final products or its components so that production can take place in the country with the best manufacturing conditions. The gathering of all the units in one company makes it possible to co-ordinate the manufacture of the final products with its necessary components. At the same time it is possible to co-ordinate the investment programmes of the different units. Instead of allowing independent companies to undertake the production of single components, which are then bought, there can be an exact planning of production in all details. The market mechanism is replaced by the planning mechanism.

Even if a horizontally integrated concern does not have specialised production in its individual units, it is possible, within the company, to smooth out the effects of the fluctuations caused by different economic conditions in different markets. It is possible to re-direct manufactures from a unit in a market with low growth to a market with high growth. Of course, in the above instance, horizontal investment will only be an advantage if the market mechanism cannot solve such problems satisfactorily.

14.7 *Oligopolies and direct investment*

Foreign direct investment is especially prevalent in sectors character-ised by oligopoly. There can be two reasons for this.

The first is that it is possible that the specific know-how which is the incentive for foreign direct investment can most advantageously be developed in companies in oligopolistic markets. It is also possible that the exploitation of the benefits of economies of scale coincides with the existence of oligopolies. In this case it is the possession of specific know-how and the exploitation of economies of scale more than the existence of an oligopoly that are the motives behind the foreign direct investment.

Secondly, the existence of an oligopolistic market can itself influ-ence the making of foreign direct investment. This can be because big companies in oligopolistic markets are more inclined to go for growth rather than profit maximisation.

In an oligopolistic market each company will have a substantial market share. Companies behave conjecturally, which means that when deciding its business policy each company takes into account the expected reactions of its competitors. This means that competition is often neutralised. The individual company's desire to expand cannot be satisfied unless the company takes on other products or invests abroad. If an individual company tries to enlarge its share of the domestic market it risks that the neutralisation of competition will break down to the disadvantage of all in the oligopoly. Nor is growth by acquisition of competing firms in the same sector a possibility if competition law restricts mergers and acquisitions, for example.

The existence of an oligopoly and competition law together can thus mean that companies must either extend their product range or invest abroad, or both. Direct investments made as a result of this can be called *active* investments since they represent an attempt to achieve the goal of maximum growth.

In the above it has been assumed that the individual company in an oligopoly strives for the greatest possible growth. As said, this can lead to an active interest in foreign investments. It is also conceivable that the aim is not the greatest possible growth, but growth which is as big as its competitors' so that market shares are not upset.

If a big company has sales interests in the form of exports to a market, the desire to secure the position in that market can lead to direct investment. There is a desire to protect against competition from local manufacturers and from other foreign companies making direct investments. Local competition can be avoided by buying a local manufacturer. The fact of being first in the market can also give advantages against other foreign interests on the market. The reaction in an oligopolistic market will often be that other companies will follow suit to prevent the company which is first to establish itself on the market obtaining a dominant position in the market.

The driving force behind direct investment in such cases is the desire not to lose a market to other competitors, whether they are companies which can become big and thus dangerous competitors, or other big companies in the oligopolistic market. In this market all are alert to whether a competitor grows and thus gains market share. Foreign direct investment is a measure taken to counteract this risk. In this case the setting up of a foreign subsidiary to achieve this can be seen as a *defensive (passive)* measure.

There is an example of this in the oil industry. In connection with oil extraction from new oilfields consortiums are established, with agreements on the conditions under which the oil extraction shall take place. All the big oil companies are interested in joining in setting up these consortiums. Even if an individual company reckons that the chances of profit are not particularly good it will be interested in joining in. If it does not join, its market share might fall and competitive conditions might change to the advantage of those who do join. This will happen in those cases where the company may have underestimated the chances of profit.

Today in China there are considerable foreign investments, many of which are loss-making. For example, there is an oligopoly in the motor car industry. When passenger car makers enter the Chinese market at an early stage it is on the strategic consideration that early establishment will prevent others entering the market and taking an early foothold, whether they be Chinese manufacturers or other foreign car manufacturers.

14.8 Trade barriers and the rate of exchange

Trade barriers

In connection with Section 14.4, which discusses a comprehensive theory of direct investment, trade barriers, for example in the form of customs tariffs, are built into the theory. It is necessary to look at the significance of trade barriers in more detail.

Does the establishment of a customs union help or hinder the setting up of foreign subsidiaries? There are three countries A, B and C. In the initial situation there are customs barriers between each of the countries. A and B enter into a customs union, which removes the internal barriers to trade and builds up a common customs barrier against country C.

If, before the establishment of the customs union, the companies in country A have invested in country B in order to avoid tariffs, internal free trade will mean that the assumptions which were the basis for the direct investment no longer apply. Under free trade it is better to export from country A. If the core reason behind the direct investment is to save tariffs costs, this incentive will be removed by establishing the customs union.

The converse of this is that the removal of tariffs between A and B will lead to more companies making direct investments in future. In the initial position the customs tariffs have hindered exports from country A to country B. As shown in Section 14.5 the typical development pattern for companies will be that they first export to another country before they consider making direct investment. With the removal of country B's tariffs more companies now have the opportunity to export in greater amounts. This brings nearer the time when it is reasonable to replace exports with direct investment.

What the net effect will be for country A's investments in country B will depend on which goods country A produces. A distinction is made between cost sensitive goods and goods for which the conditions of demand are most important. For costs sensitive goods the reduction of tariffs will have a restraining effect on direct investment. The opposite applies to goods for which the conditions of demand are most decisive. A tariff reduction will increase exports and thus direct investment in the longer term.

What is the effect on country C which is outside the union, of the setting up of the customs union between countries A and B? Before setting up the customs union companies in country C exported to both A and B. After the customs union takes effect C's exports will be exposed to stronger competitive pressures. This can lead businesses in country C into replacing exports by setting up subsidiaries in either country A or B. Before setting up the customs union direct investment in country A or B could not be considered because, for example, the market was too small. Now it becomes possible to supply both markets from a production unit in one of the countries. The trade discrimination against C's exports together with the bigger sales potential from a production unit within the customs union can mean that country C will now make direct investments.

The rate of exchange

In equilibrium models for international trade it is assumed that import costs are equal to export earnings. There is equilibrium on the current account of the balance of payments. This in turn means that there is equilibrium in the rate of exchange.

In the real world the rate of exchange is not always in equilibrium. If country A has an export surplus and country B has a corresponding import surplus, the rate of exchange is not in equilibrium. In fact in country A the rate of exchange will be undervalued compared to the rate which would give equilibrium. Country A must revalue its currency in order for there to be equilibrium in the balance of payments.

When country A's currency is undervalued, country A has a general production advantage compared to country B. A company in country A which has some specific know-how will therefore exploit this through exports. As a result of the higher production costs in country B, measured in country A's currency, and the barrier costs related to subsidiaries, the value of the specific know-how in question must be high before it can pay to set up a subsidiary in country B. On the other hand, it is an incentive for companies in country B to make direct investments in country A if their currency is overvalued.

The conclusion is that if the rate of exchange does not smooth out the general differences in the level of production costs in the two countries then, all things being equal, there will be an incentive to set up subsidiaries in the country whose currency is undervalued. The experience of the post-war period show that a currency can be overvalued or undervalued for several years.

14.9 The pattern of foreign direct investment

The theory of foreign direct investment considered above consists of a number of separate elements. The starting point is that certain companies possess specific know-how.

Whether this specific know-how is exploited through exports, sale of the know-how or through setting up foreign subsidiaries depends on a number of factors. What are the costs of exporting from the home country? What are the advantages and disadvantages of selling the knowledge? What are the costs of production abroad? Is it possible to exclude competitors by direct investment? As shown in Section 14.4, it is an overall evaluation of all of these factors which determines whether foreign direct investment is made.

The fact that special know-how included in the theory is business-specific can explain why in a country like Britain there are both British investments abroad and foreign investments in Britain. Some companies in Britain have a special know-how which leads them to invest abroad. In other sectors foreign companies have special know-how which leads them to invest in Britain.

It is therefore to be expected that in a country like Britain, and in other industrial countries, there will be both *outward flowing* and *inward flowing* direct investments. If the net effect is calculated, in other words if the inward flowing investments are deducted from the outward flowing investment, it cannot be assumed that the net flow is nil. Even though statistical data on foreign direct investment is defective, there is no doubt that in the case of Britain there has been a tendency for the outward flowing investments to be larger than the inward flowing investments. If one looks at the net flows between Britain and the various world regions, for example North Europe, North America, Central and Eastern Europe, and developing countries, the net flows differ. In relation to North America the inward investments have been largest. In relation to Central and Eastern Europe and developing countries, British outward investments have been larger than its inward investments.

The net flows of foreign investments between two areas will depend on the economic levels of the two areas. It is reasonable to start with the ranking of countries shown in Figure 11.1 in Chapter 11, where the different world regions are ranked according to their per capita GNP.

In the nineteenth century and at the beginning of the twentieth century there were considerable investments by industrial countries in developing countries. There were investments in gathering natural resources in the form of raw materials such as tropical crops, minerals (copper, tin etc.) and oil which industrial countries could exploit by exporting them to other industrial countries. The developing countries did not themselves have companies which could exploit these resources.

Today industrial countries' investments in developing countries are not as large, relatively, as previously. These days, instead of investing in developing countries, industrial countries invest in other industrial countries. The investments of industrial countries in Sub-Saharan Africa and South Asia are small. Such investment as does take place in developing countries takes place in the richer developing countries in Southeast Asia and Latin America. These areas have reached a stage of development where simpler manufactures, which previously took place in industrial countries, can now be undertaken advantageously from a cost point of view. This is often in connection with vertical specialisation which involves contracting out the production of individual components or semi-finished products to these areas. Sometimes goods are supplied under contract by local producers, sometimes through joint ventures and sometimes by setting up direct subsidiaries under the control of parent companies in industrial countries.

Most investments by industrial countries are made in other industrial countries. It is usual for industrial countries with the same high level of per capita GNP to invest in each other.

The investments made between developing countries are not as large. Usually any such direct investment is made by the richer developing countries, for example the newly industrialised countries, (South Korea, Taiwan, Hong Kong, Singapore) in the less wealthy developing countries, where there are lower manufacturing costs.

A pattern therefore develops. Industrial countries are responsible for much the greatest part of direct investments. Among the industrial countries it is those that have the largest GNP that make the most investments. Only a small amount of direct investment is made by developing countries. Again, it is the richer developing countries which make these investments. The higher the GNP, the greater the amount of outward investment.

With regard to inward investments, it also applies that the industrial countries with the higher GNPs receive the most foreign direct investments. These are investments by companies in other industrial countries which also have a high GNP. Industrial countries with a lower per capita GNP and developing countries with a higher GNP receive direct investments primarily from industrial countries with a higher per capita GNP.

If the pattern were presented schematically one could say that the extent of the outward investments is proportionate to the per capita GNP of the country in question. The extent of the inward investments is also dependent on the country's per capita GNP. The inward investment of a country corresponds to the outward investment of another country which either has a higher per capita GNP than the receiving country, or a per capita GNP of a similar level. It is unusual to see outward investment from a country with a low per capita GNP to a country with a high GNP.

What kind of manufactures are typically contracted out for production abroad? Here, a distinction must be made between goods in which some specific know-how is critical and goods in which the specific know-how of the company is less important.

If the goods in question are research-based products in which there is innovation either of new products or new production processes, the specific know-how will be of central importance. These are products which are less cost sensitive and which can only be produced in a developed industrial environment. If advanced products are produced by setting up foreign subsidiaries, these subsidiaries are typically set up in an industrial country with high per capita GNP, which itself makes investments in other industrial countries with a per capita GNP at around the same level.

If, on the other hand, the products concerned are more traditional, both as regards the products themselves and their manufacturing processes, then specific know-how is less important, and the products will be more cost sensitive. Such manufacturing will often be contracted out by countries with a high per capita GNP to be produced in countries with a lower per capita GNP where costs are lower. The more traditional the goods and the more standardised the manufacturing process, the more significant are the production costs.

14.10 The effects of foreign direct investment

Establishing a baseline reference

It is important to emphasise that portfolio investments and foreign direct investments are two entirely different things. With portfolio investments, as discussed in Chapter 13, the lending country has a smaller capital stock than it would otherwise have had. Correspondingly the borrowing country gets a greater capital stock than it would otherwise have had. The capital movement is the key element.

With foreign direct investments, subsidiaries are set up abroad, because they have some specific know-how in relation to production technology, management skills and/or marketing. There can be advantages of co-ordination in having a company consisting of a number of units. The decisive factor with direct investment is the transfer of know-how. With direct investments this specific know-how is kept within the company. It can, of course, also be transferred through the sale of know-how, but this means that the company loses control of its know-how.

When there are direct investments this does not necessarily mean that there will be simultaneous capital movements. This will only be the case if the company finances its foreign investments through domestic borrowings. If, on the other hand, a company finances its setting up of a foreign subsidiary through borrowings in the host country, there will be no capital movement.

Foreign direct investment does not necessarily mean that the host country gets a bigger capital stock. It there is a sale of a company in the host country to a foreign company, the host country's capital stock will not be increased. However, if the company makes new investments in the host country obviously this should mean that there will be a growth in the capital stock. However, this will sometimes only be the case if the direct investment is financed from outside the host country. If there is borrowing in the host country this can often be at the cost of other domestic investments which are then not made because there are insufficient resources for them.

Market conditions can also be affected differently. Foreign direct investment does not take place exclusively in oligopolistic markets, but this type of market is often associated with foreign direct investment. If there is investment in the form of setting up a new business unit, the number of competitors will increase. If the investment takes the form of acquisition of an existing firm, the initial number of competitors is unchanged. If the firm set up as a result of foreign direct investment is strongly competitive, some of the domestic companies can be competed out of the market. In the longer term this can lead to a stronger oligopoly.

These different possibilities with foreign direct investment make it difficult to generalise about the economic effects of direct investment in the host country.

As with all economic analyses, the effect of one measure can only be evaluated when there is a clear baseline for reference to indicate what would otherwise have happened. When analysing the effects of direct investment, the baseline can be the situation in which the potential host country buys the specific know-how from abroad. It would be possible to create the conditions for increased investments through borrowing, and to obtain the necessary know-how through know-how contracts or through a joint venture.

A discussion of the effects of foreign direct investment is very much linked to the question of the significance of multinational companies for their host countries and their home countries. In the following some of the core questions concerning multinational companies will be discussed.

The internal planning mechanism

A central feature of multinational companies is that a central planning mechanism replaces the market mechanism. This need not be a problem since there can be imperfections in the market mechanism that can be eliminated by rational planning. Conversely, it cannot be assumed that a private planning mechanism is better than the market mechanism when it functions effectively and if the companies try to maximise their profits. If the internal planning mechanism does not ensure that ineffective production is eliminated, as would happen if the multinational company's units were independent, there will be inefficiencies in the private planning mechanism. In other words there can be cross-subsidies from a profitable unit to a less profitable or even loss-making unit. The risk of such a situation will be greater if the multinational company prioritises growth, combined with a desire for an overall 'reasonable' or 'acceptable' profit for the company as a whole.

The individual units of a multinational company supply goods and services to each other. Typically the parent company provides specific know-how to the units abroad and it will also provide capital goods for the establishment and development of the subsidiaries. There will be internal flows of raw materials, semi-finished goods and final products between the parent company and subsidiaries and between subsidiaries themselves. These internal flows are made at internally fixed prices which do not necessarily reflect the market prices for equivalent supplies. In an internal accounting system, where each unit is a profit centre, the internal prices ought naturally to reflect market prices, if the management of the company is to obtain an accurate picture of the effectiveness of the various units. With the preparation of the accounts which form the basis for the taxation of the units in different countries, there can naturally be an incentive to ensure, through internal price-fixing, that the greatest profit is made in the country with the lowest company taxation. If there are significant customs duties on imports, then the internal pricing can operate to reduce the costs of customs duties.

Internal pricing with a view to minimising the tax liability obviously creates problems for host countries which have high rates of company tax. It is also clear that the company taxation rules in the parent company's own country are important. In the USA before 1962 a subsidiary company's earnings abroad were not taxed in the USA before the profits were repatriated. Since 1962 the rule has been that foreign earnings shall be taxed in the USA when they arise, regardless of when the earnings are repatriated. This has meant that the incentive to invest abroad rather than in the USA was reduced. It is also clear that international double-taxation agreements to avoid double taxation are significant for total tax payments.

Internal pricing which is totally out of step with market conditions will not be accepted by national tax authorities. Even if there is no empirical basis for quantifying the extent of the problem, it can be assumed that internal pricing makes tax gains possible.

The effect on trade and the balance of payments

As has been made clear above, foreign direct investment will give rise to internal business decisions which affect trade.

If foreign direct investment means that domestic production in the host country replaces former exports from the parent company's country or deliveries from another country, then the host country's imports of the goods will be reduced. On the other hand, there can be new trade because the parent company supplies capital equipment for setting up the foreign subsidiary. Similarly there may be imports of raw materials and semi-finished goods to the subsidiary's host country. Likewise there can be exports resulting from the direct investment in the host country, either to the parent company's country or to other countries including partner countries of the host country if the host country is part of a customs union or free trade area.

The statistical material about direct investments and internal trade between units is inadequate. But such figures as do exist show that foreign direct investment grew strongly in the post-war period, even more strongly than international trade. The share of foreign owned capital, as percentage of the total capital stock, rose in industrial countries. The picture for developing countries is less clear, but it shows the same trend.

Through their international manufacturing, multinational countries can influence the pattern of trade; international trade between units in the same company is a large share of the exports of several countries. In the USA, Great Britain, Japan, Sweden and Belgium, international trade between units in the same company consists of approximately 30 per cent or more of the total exports of the company. For the figures on this see Cantwell (1994).

It is thus obvious that the changes to the pattern of trade and the extent of trade which goes with multinational companies affect the balance of trade in goods and service between countries. This is so both for the parent company's country and the countries where subsidiaries are situated. Other items on the balance of payments account are also affected. Capital movements are affected. If direct investments are financed by the parent company's country the host country will experience inward capital movements. This will not be the case if financing is arranged through the host country. At the same time there will be income transfers from the host country if the parent company repatriates the profit of the subsidiary. If the profit is not repatriated but re-invested in the host country, the host country will get a greater benefit from the foreign investment, and there is no burden on the balance of payments.

It is impossible to generalise about the overall effect on the balance of payments. The bigger the share of financing that comes from outside, the more the subsidiary uses domestic suppliers in the host country, the greater the share of profit reinvested in the host country then, everything else being equal, the greater will be the benefit to the host country from the foreign investment.

The external effects of direct investments

The core element of direct investments is technology transfer, whether this means manufacturing technology, management skills or marketing skills. It is constantly claimed that this gives a number of external benefits to the host country. The employees of the subsidiary receive training in the workplace which they would not otherwise get. There is dissemination of know-how from the subsidiary to the rest of society through subcontracts with suppliers in the host country. There can be a development of new know-how through contacts between the subsidiary and the national institutions for research and development. The chances of theses positive effects are greatest when it is an industrial country which is host to the direct investment.

Even in this case, the advantages can be limited. It is claimed that many multinational companies prefer internal company supplies from abroad, rather than contracting with suppliers in the host country. There is also a risk that subsidiaries will attract the specially trained employees, including managers and researchers, from the host country. Instead of national companies which develop management and research and development on the basis of their own strategies, the country will get a number of foreign subsidiary companies where skilful managers and researchers are moved abroad as a part of a company's global strategy. As for research and development, these are typically carried out in larger units located in the country of the parent company. Therefore there is a risk that there will be an 'export' of managers and researchers from the host country. This is the phenomenon often referred to as the 'brain drain'.

With investments in developing countries the problem is often even more severe. There are often investments which are like enclaves in the national economy without any substantial links with the domestic economic sector. These are referred to as 'dual economies' where on the one hand there is a sector which has relatively high technology and is capital intensive, while on the other hand there is a local sector with low technology and labour intensive production. These two sectors exist separately without contacts between them. The highly developed capital intensive sectors are more closely related to the economies of the industrial countries than to the economies of their host countries.

Many developing countries have chosen the strategy of setting up development zones to attract foreign investments with advantages in the form of tax exemptions and duty-free imports of raw materials and semi-manufactures products. The advantage of this can be an increase in foreign currency earnings. This advantage should not be underestimated, but it is clear that the development effect which could result from a close integration with the local economy is often very limited.

Other developing countries, for example India, have in the past chosen a different policy, under which a number of conditions are laid down before foreign direct investment is accepted. Joint ventures are preferred in which local companies are involved together with foreign companies with a view to setting up common enterprises with shared ownership. The joint venture agreement can include provisions to the effect that a given percentage of the senior personnel shall be Indians and that there shall be help with training to enable more Indians to become managers. There can be requirements that a certain percentage of the semi-manufactured products used shall be made in India. There can also be requirements that a given proportion of the production shall be exported and a share of the profit shall be re-invested in the country. These pre-conditions for foreign investments, on domestic supply of semi-manufactured products and the export of a part of the production, are called TRIMs (Trade Related Investment Measures).

Conflicts between multinational companies and national interests

Multinational companies possess specific know-how. They try to exploit this through foreign direct investments, in which they retain control over their know-how. Host countries can have an interest in receiving these foreign investments, by which they can benefit from the specific know-how. The direct investments can create jobs which would perhaps not otherwise have been created. There can be a series of external advantages which have positive effects on the host country. But there can also be problems from the point of view of the host country. Multinational companies have control over the subsidiaries. Often the partners in the host country will feel they do not get a fair share of the profits. In developing countries the situation may amount to what some will consider 'exploitation'.

When multinational companies have control over subsidiaries, the future of a subsidiary is determined by the goals of the parent company. For example, a parent company may see an advantage in closing a subsidiary in one country in order to expand production in another country or to set up a subsidiary in a new country. Obviously this creates problems of adjustment in the host country where production is closed down and where there may already be high unemployment. The multinational company can threaten closure if there is not some easing of the national rules which the subsidiary is required to abide by. For example, there can be a demand for an easing of taxation.

The concept of 'exploitation' requires a more precise definition. Power relations are inherent to the form of the market. Where there is a developing country and few companies and a labour force which either may not or has not been able to form trade unions, the employer has a situation akin to a monopoly without resistance. If trade unions and employers organisations are formed, there is a bilateral monopoly. If in developing countries farmers on the one hand have inputs supplied by large companies, and on the other hand there is a sole purchaser of agricultural products, in other words a monopsony, they will be in a much weaker market position than if they could themselves supply inputs and sell agricultural produce through co-operatives.

It is obvious that some power relations are built into the market. It is equally clear that the power relations are affected by the alternatives available to those involved. If an employee has a poor education, or only a few opportunities for employment because there are few companies or because there is high unemployment, the employee is in a weak position.

By comparison, the subsidiaries of a multinational business are in a strong position. This also applies in relation to the national authorities which want the foreign currency earnings and employment that goes with subsidiaries.

When there is a general desire to host foreign subsidiaries, there can easily be competition between countries which takes the form of giving economic advantages for setting up subsidiaries such as cheap locations, easing customs restrictions on the import of semi- manufactured goods, relaxation of tax regulations as well as easing foreign exchange restrictions on the repatriation of profits.

Competition between countries to attract foreign direct investment can make it more difficult to attract investment if conditions are imposed for the setting up of subsidiaries. However justified they may appear to be from the point of view of the host country, national requirements of governments, e.g. in the form of TRIMs provisions, can lead to multinational companies avoiding such countries.

The idea of an international set of rules for conditions for foreign direct investment is of special interest to developing countries, and it is included in the WTO co-operation.

One of the strengths of multinational companies is that they can make available a ready made package of capital, management and technology. Obviously their strength is reduced if there are realistic possibilities of a less comprehensive package in the form of a joint venture where the host country provides part of the capital and management. Also, if a country does not depend on the delivery of a total package solution, but can raise capital in the financial markets, as well as buy the necessary know-how through management contracts and know-how contracts, the host country will be in a stronger position.

14.11 Summary

Foreign direct investments are different from capital movements in the form of portfolio investments. Portfolio investments are discussed in Chapter 13, and it is assumed that there is a change in the capital stock of a country which corresponds to the portfolio investments.

With foreign direct investments there is a parent company which acquires the right to control a subsidiary abroad. The financing of this investment can be through the country of the parent company, the host country, or some other country. It is not necessarily the case that foreign direct investment involves an increase in the capital stock of the country because the foreign investment might take the form of the acquisition of an already existing firm.

The significant basis for direct investment is that the parent company possesses some business-specific know-how. The parent company can use this know-how either through exports, through setting up foreign subsidiaries, or through sales of know-how to another manufacturer.

It is a combination of three part theories that, together, can explain whether direct investment is chosen. These three part theories are: the theory of business-specific know-how, the theory of location, and the theory on internalisation.

There are also other circumstances that can lie behind direct investment decisions. There can be goals other than the maximisation of profit. The aim may be growth or a large market share. Corresponding to the advantage of possessing specific know-how, a multinational company can have an advantage in having several units under the same control. It is possible to exploit the advantages of specialisation, economies of scale and co-ordination. If the market is oligopolistic this can also have an influence, because in such markets there may be strategic considerations that can persuade a company that direct investment is the best solution. A company can thus actively seek to achieve its goals (active investment) or it can aim to prevent others getting too large a market share (passive investment). Finally customs tariffs and rates of exchange can influence the choice in favour of direct investment, rather than one of the alternatives.

A large proportion of direct investment is made by multinational companies. Therefore a discussion of the effects of direct investment must take account of the advantages and disadvantages of multinational companies. Any worthwhile discussion must have a baseline as a basis for comparison with alternative scenarios. There are a number of possibilities to choose between. In general it can be concluded that there can be disadvantages as well as advantages, because there can be significant conflicts between the interests of multinational companies and national interests.

Literature

Balasubramanyam, V.N., 'Foreign Direct Investment and the International Transfer of Technology' i D. Greenaway (ed), *Current Issues in International Trade*, Macmillan, 1985.

Cantwell, J., 'The Relationship between International Trade and International Production' in D. Greenaway and L.A. Winters (eds), *Surveys in International Trade*, Blackwell, 1994.

Dunning, J.H., 'The Eclectic Paradigm of International Production: An Update and Some possible Extensions', *Journal of International Business Studies*, 19, 1988.

Hymer, S.H., *The International Operations of National Firms: A Study of Direct Foreign Investment*, Cambridge, 1976.

Markusen, J.R., 'Multinationals, Multi-plant Economies and the Gains from Trade', *Journal of International Economics*, 16, 1984.

Vernon, R., *Sovereignty at Bay: The Multinational Spread of U.S. Enterprises*, London, 1971.

Vernon, R., *Storm over Multinationals: The Real Issues*, Cambridge M.A., 1977.

15. Cumulative processes

15.1 Trade and factor movements are treated separately

In traditional theory it is customary to treat trade and factor movements separately. Chapter 6 deals with factor proportion theory. This theory assumes that production factors are internationally immobile. Equalisation of factor prices is brought about through trade, so there is no scope for factor movement, even if it were made possible.

In Chapter 13 capital movement is analysed. If in the initial situation there is no trade, for example because of high tariffs, then factor movements will bring about an equalisation of prices, so that the relative prices of the goods will be the same. This means that if, thereafter, the tariff protection is removed, there will be no incentive to trade, because the factor prices are the same.

This theory for explaining trade and capital movements gives the result that both countries have advantages from both trade and capital movements. There is a new point of equilibrium in which the welfare potential is greater in both societies.

Trade and factor movements can be, but need not necessarily be, substituted for each other, as long as the pre-conditions of factor proportion theory are disregarded. In Section 13.3 it is demonstrated that if there are different manufacturing technologies in the two countries, trade will not bring about an equalisation of prices. Therefore trade will be supplemented by e.g. capital movements which can contribute to the enlargement of the relative difference in factor endowment of the countries. A new point of equilibrium is reached at which there is trade but there are no factor movements. Sections 13.4 and 13.5 show how a combination of trade and capital movements can create greater inequality of economic activity between the two countries. Section 13.5 also shows that if, in one of the countries, there is continuous technological development but there is not technological development in the other country, then greater inequalities will develop between the economic activity of the two societies.

It is this problem which is considered in greater depth in this chapter. The use of the traditional factor proportion model with its traditional assumptions has been criticised as it has been pointed out that it does not allow for the possibility that trade or factor movements can give rise to a number of self-reinforcing processes, which can in turn lead to greater inequalities in the location of production and greater inequality in welfare between different areas.

The theory of international trade and investment includes a theory of the location of the country in which production will take place. However the international location theory differs from the location theory used in regional economics. Regional economics is the discipline which looks at the interaction between the various regions within a country. Of course, there are many similarities between the issues of regional economics and international economics. Regional economics is concerned with the theory of location in the regions within a country. International economics is concerned with the theory of location between countries.

However, the models that are used in the two disciplines are very different. First, the geographic element plays a central role in regional economics. Regions have a geographical extent, so that distance is a core issue. In international economics individual countries are considered as points, without geographical extent. Normally there is assumed to be no barrier of distance in the economic transactions, apart from barriers introduced by the trade policy of individual countries. Since each individual country is a single point, there are no regional differences within a country, which are therefore considered to be homogenous in all respects, and without geographical extent.

Secondly, the model assumptions are normally different. In international economics it is traditional to distinguish between trade and factor movement. By contrast, in regional economics, internal trade and internal factor movements take place together.

In studying international trade and investment there are many reasons for looking at the issues dealt with in regional economics. Firstly, the geographical extents of different countries vary widely. The USA is bigger than the present EU. Yet, economic relations within the USA are of a regional economic character, while economic relations between EU countries traditionally come within the sphere of international economics.

Secondly, economic relations between EU countries and between countries in other similar kinds of co-operation are changing towards the kind of internal relations that exists between states within the USA, because there is both full freedom of trade and of factor movements. In international economics it is generally the case that the removal of trade barriers together with the free movement of capital means that international economic relations increasingly take on the characteristics of regional economic relations.

Thirdly, one can say that international economic relations are a further development of the internal regional economic relations that take place within an individual country.

There are therefore good reasons for believing that international economics can benefit from looking more closely at the problems and the models used in regional economics.

15.2 Characteristics of regional development

In a review of the regional conditions in a country, it is usual to find substantial differences. There will be some regions with large populations, high production levels and high incomes. Other regions will be thinly populated, have low levels of production and have lower incomes. There will be a number of centres with a positive economic situation, and a number of less developed regions where the situation is less satisfactory. Governments try to equalise the economic conditions of different regions through policies of taxation and expenditure.

Firstly, it must be recognised that there are significant regional differences within individual countries. Secondly, these inequalities can increase with economic growth. Thirdly, when once concentrations of population and production have arisen, the resulting inequalities have a tendency to continue over very long periods. Fourthly, it is possible for new centres of growth to arise.

There are many examples to illustrate this. In the USA the Atlantic states were first populated by European immigrants. The arrival of industrialisation was concentrated in the Northeast states, from New York to Chicago. There was a considerable concentration of economic activity. This has been maintained, even though in reduced strength and even though new centres such as California have appeared. In Great Britain business activity is concentrated in the Midlands and around London, while the fringe areas of Scotland, Wales and Cornwall etc. have become less developed regions. In Germany, industrialisation was centred in the Ruhr district. In Italy, economic development has been concentrated in Northern Italy.

In Europe today there is reference to the so-called 'banana', which stretches from the South (Barcelona, Lyons, Marseilles, Milan) through the middle (Zurich, Stuttgart, Munich) and on through Northern Europe (Frankfurt, Rhine-Ruhr district, the large Dutch towns and the Paris area) to end in Great Britain (London and the Midlands). There is a considerable concentration of European economic activity in this area.

If one looks at developing countries today one of the greatest problems concerns the urban concentrations that have accumulated in recent decades. In China it will be seen that most economic growth has been regionally concentrated in the East.

The question is, what factors can explain the almost universal phenomenon of the regional concentration of economic development? To start with it is necessary to divide economic activities into primary, secondary and tertiary sectors. In terms of location there are large difference between the three sectors. Agriculture, fisheries and mining are all primary industries whose production is based on natural resources. In the case of agriculture this production is geographically spread over the area where there is land which can be used for production.

When industrialisation started in the past, industries were more dependent on energy and raw materials. Also energy and raw materials were less mobile as there was no energy distribution network and the transport costs for heavy raw materials were too great. Developments have tended to make the location of industrial production less dependent on proximity to energy and raw materials. These inputs can now be supplied everywhere at reasonable cost. With this development old industries have become more 'footloose', as there is a much wider freedom of location for production. In addition to this there are many new industries which are free to locate wherever there is an established industrial environment.

Finally there is the tertiary sector, which includes the provision of services. The location of this production will take place where there is a demand for the services. Service industries will therefore be concentrated in larger centres of population.

15.3 A regional economic model

In what follows a model is used which is based on some assumptions about the key factors which influence the choice of location of a company. The three key factors are assumed to be transport costs, the extent of economies of scale and the extent of demand. Many of the individual elements included in the model have been recognised and used previously. The gathering together of the individual elements was made by Krugman (1991), whose model is discussed here.

There is here one country which can be divided into two equally large regions, the northern region (N) and the southern region (S). There are two business activities, agriculture and industry. The total share of employment in agriculture in the whole country is j, and the remainder 1 – j is the employment in industry. Employment in agriculture is evenly divided between regions N and S, since agriculture is based on natural resources which are evenly divided between the regions. However, the labour needs of industry are not the same in the two regions. The share of industrial employment for region N and S is designated S_i^N and S_i^S respectively. Employment in industry in the two regions depends on the extent of industrial production in each region. There is assumed to be a direct proportion between industrial employment and industrial production.

The regions' share of the population depends on industrial employment

Using the symbols which are used above, it is possible to compile Table 15.1 which shows the individual sectors' and the individual regions' share of total employment. When the two sectors' employment is added together, the result is the individual region's share of the total employment, referred to as S^N and S^S, which together are equal to 1.

Table 15.1: The distribution of employment

The share of employment by sector:	The share of employment by region:		
	Region N	Region S	All country
Agriculture	$j/2$	$j/2$	j
Industry	$(1 - j)S_i^N$	$(1 - j)S_i^S$	$1 - j$
All businesses	S^N	S^S	

It is assumed that the figures for the distribution of employment are equal to the figures for the distribution of the population since the average ratio of people in employment to people not employment is constant. It appears from Table 15.1 that the total proportion of the population in region N is

$$S^N = \frac{j}{2} + (1 - j) \, S_i^N \qquad\qquad (15.1)$$

which means that region N's share of the population increases together with its share of industrial employment.

Factors influencing the location of industrial companies

In the market for goods it is assumed that each inhabitant demands k units of goods. This is naturally a simplification for the sake of the model. Even if in practice the demand is dependent on price, this does not fundamentally change the model. The total population B therefore determines the size of the market which is $k \cdot B$.

It is also assumed that if a company sells it goods in the region where it is located there will be no transport costs. However, if the company sells it goods outside the region where it is located, there are transport costs of t per unit. Again, this is a simplification, since in general there is a more or less continuous correlation between increased distance and increased transport costs. However, neither does this simplification significantly affect the key issue of the model.

If a company wishes to supply the whole market from one manufacturing unit, it will have to take on the transport costs of selling to that part of the population which does not live in the region where manufacturing is located. The company can avoid this by manufacturing in two units, one in each of the regions.

The company therefore has the following transport costs:

	Transport costs
1 manufacturing unit in N	$S^S \cdot B \cdot k \cdot t$
1 manufacturing unit in S	$S^N \cdot B \cdot k \cdot t$
2 manufacturing units, one in each region	0

Finally, it is assumed that there are economies of scale in the production. These can either be 'internal' or 'external' economies of scale, cf. Sections 8.1 to 8.3.

Figure 15.1: Internal and external economies of scale

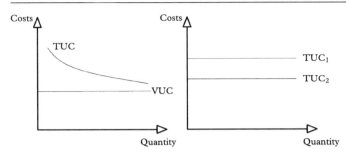

In Figure 15.1 the production costs are shown. In the left hand side of the figure the variable unit costs (VUC) are assumed to be independent of the quantity of production. The economies of scale are associated with the fixed costs, F, which are reduced per unit as the quantity of production increases. The right hand side of the figure illustrates the external advantages, which are the advantages of producing in an industrial environment. Where there is an industrial environment it is possible to buy a number of inputs at a lower price. This means that the total unit costs will be TUC_2, which is lower than TUC_1, which represents the costs when production is not located in such an environment. For the time being the external advantages will be ignored.

When a company decides whether to locate a unit in region N or region S, or to locate a unit in both regions, there are three factors that are decisive. The first is the extent of the economies of scale measured by F. The second is the cost of transport on sales to the other region, measured by t. And the third factor is sales volume to the two regions. It is here that the regional distribution of the population comes into the picture, measured by S^N and S^S.

By establishing one manufacturing unit there will be extra transport costs which would not be incurred by setting up a manufacturing unit in each region. On the other hand there will be the installation costs of a manufacturing unit equal to F.

The following expression will therefore be decisive:

$$S^S \cdot B \cdot k \cdot t \gtrless F$$

$$S^N \cdot B \cdot k \cdot t \gtrless F$$

(15.2)

where the left hand side is the cost of transport to which the company becomes liable by locating in region N or region S. The right hand side is the costs of setting up a manufacturing unit, which are saved by building only one manufacturing unit.

The expression in Equation (15.2) can be recast as:

$$S^S \gtrless F/Bkt = Z$$

$$\tag{15.3}$$

$$S^N \gtrless F/Bkt = Z$$

where the sum of S^N and S^S is equal to 1.

If Z is greater than 1, the economies of scale will be so advantageous compared with the cost of transport that it will be decided to produce in one manufacturing unit. Region N will be chosen if $S^N > \frac{1}{2}$, since the cost of transport will be less than if region S were chosen.

If Z lies between $\frac{1}{2}$ and 1 it will not be possible for both S^S and S^N to be bigger than Z. Therefore production will be placed there where the share of the population is larger.

If, however, Z is less than $\frac{1}{2}$ then there are three possibilities:

$$S^N < Z \text{ and } (1 - S^N) > Z \tag{15.4.1}$$
$$S^N > Z \text{ and } (1 - S^N) > Z \tag{15.4.2}$$
$$S^N > Z \text{ and } (1 - S^N) < Z \tag{15.4.3}$$

In the first case it will be best to locate manufacturing in region S. If the conditions shown here apply to all manufacturing then all manufacturing will be located in region S.

In the third case it will still only be worthwhile establishing one manufacturing unit. This time it should be in region N which will attract all manufacturing.

In the second case (15.4.2)

$$S^N > Z \text{ and } S^S > Z$$

which means that, regardless of whether production is located in region N or S, sales to the region where manufacturing is not located will be subject to such high transport costs that it will be best to establish two manufacturing units, one in each region. This means that the share of industrial employment in, for example, region N will be directly proportional to the region's share of the total population.

It can be concluded from this that the question of how many manufacturing units will be set up depends on three factors: the extent of the economies of scale, the level of transport costs, and the regional distribution of the population. The greater the economies of scale the fewer will be the manufacturing units. The greater the costs of transport, the greater the number of manufacturing locations. The more even the distribution of the population between the regions, the more manufacturing units there will be.

The analysis also shows that if it is only worthwhile manufacturing in one location, it will be in the region with the bigger population.

The relationship between the size of population and employment in industry

In an individual region the size of the population depends on the employment in agriculture and industry. This is apparent in Equation (15.1). The share of employment in agriculture is assumed to be exogenously determined at j/2. The greater the employment in industry in region N, the greater will be the total population. Equation (15.1) is drawn in Figure 15.2.a. The greater the share of the population employed in agriculture, the larger will be the line segment OA.

Conversely, the share of employment in industry in region N depends on the share of the total population in region N. Whether there is industrial employment in regions N and S depends on the equations in (15.2). If the left hand side in the two equations in (15.2) are greater than the right hand side, then there will be industry in both regions. If these conditions are not met, there will only be industry in the region where the population is larger. If the economies of scale are big, compared with the transport costs, there will only be industrial employment in this one region.

Figure 15.2: Relationship between population and industrial employment in region N

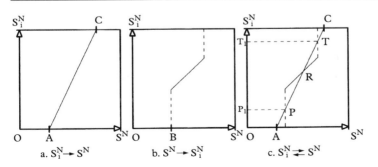

Equation (15.3) is directly derived from (15.2), and it means that there is only a possibility of industrial employment in both regions as long as Z is less than ½. When Z < ½ there will be three possibilities, cf. Equations (15.4). Z is drawn on the S^N axis as OB in Figure 15.2.b. If Equation (15.4.1) applies, $S_i^{\ N} = 0$. If Equation (15.4.2) applies, $S_i^N = S_N$. If Equation (15.4.3) applies, $S_i^N = 1$.

In Figure 15.2.c, the Figures a and b are superimposed. It shows that there are three points of intersection, P, R and T. It can easily be shown that R is the only stable point of equilibrium of the three.

The starting point is Equations (15.1) and (15.2). The first equation determines the total share of the population as a function of the share of industrial employment. The second equation shows how the share of population in region N determines the changes in the share of industrial employment over time in the region.

There are the following:

$$S_i^{\ N} \rightarrow S^N$$
$$S^N \rightarrow dS_i^{\ N}/dt$$

If, in the initial situation, $S_i^{\ N}$ is greater than P_1 and less than T_1, then there will be movement towards the point of equilibrium R, which means that the two regions N and S each have half the population and half the industrial employment. If, in the initial situation, $S_i^{\ N}$ is less than P_1 there will, in the longer term, be no industry in region N. There will be movement towards point A. If in the initial situation $S_i^{\ N}$ is greater than T_1, region N will move towards point C, which means that all industry will be located in region N.

The result of the analysis, with the assumptions made, is that points A, R and C are points of equilibrium. The analysis can be used to illustrate a number of key conditions that can be observed in the real world.

What does the analysis show?

The first thing the analysis shows is that once a point of equilibrium has been established, whether it is A, R or C, there is considerable inertia which means that the situation will stay that way. The advantages and disadvantages which have been established historically in the region will be self-reinforcing. A region which has historically had large industrial employment will have a large population which, in itself, makes it attractive to locate future industrial activity in the region. This also applies to the provision of services in the tertiary sector. If a region has not had a share of industrialisation it will be difficult for it to attract new industry. This is not least because the underlying population, which is based on primary production, is too small.

The second thing the analysis shows that, when there is industrialisation, the regional distribution of industry depends on the extent of economies of scale and the transport costs and the other impediments to trade. Barriers to trade in the form of customs tariffs, import restrictions etc. can be considered as equivalent to transport costs.

In comparing the USA with Europe it is interesting to see that the geographical concentration of manufacturing is considerably higher in the USA than in Europe. In Europe, agriculture has played a central role for centuries, which means that the population has been relatively evenly spread throughout the regions. In the USA agriculture developed from the middle of the 1800's in conjunction with building the railways, which meant that immigrants went West.

Agriculture has created the basis for manual work and light industry everywhere. The development of industry in Europe took place at a time when the costs related to distance were high. This was due not only to the transport technology of the time, but also to trade barriers in the form of customs and import restrictions. In other words, most countries in Europe were already industrially active when there was a breakthrough in new transport technology and economies of scale.

The conditions in the USA were different. Industrialisation arrived later in the USA and the costs of trade were lower because there were not the same trade barriers as in Europe. In addition to this the population in the USA was concentrated in the north-eastern states.

In a historical description of the pattern of settlement it is important to note that the locations of industries were previously more regionally restricted than today. For example the existence of iron and usable energy, e.g. coal, was decisive when choosing a location.

This is not included in the model discussed above, where only the population base is decisive in selecting a location. This is truer today than previously, but even today there are other influences than the population. For example this applies to the existence of external economies of scale which are dealt with later.

It is obvious that economies of scale can vary in extent in different industries. Therefore the degree of concentration also varies in different industries. It is also obvious that transport costs, as a share of the price of the goods, vary from industry to industry.

The third thing that the model shows is that there can be changes to the regional distribution of employment in the long term. If a region has strong population growth, the population increase can create the basis for starting regional industrial production. An increase in the population can come from migration to the region, for example as the result of the discovery of oil or minerals in the region. Such a growth of the population, accompanied by a rise in purchasing power, can form the basis for a relative shift in the location of manufacturing. The industrialisation of California is a good example of this. If, for example, technological development increases the economies of scale in relation to the costs of transport, this will also strengthen the tendency towards concentration. This applies to both the internal and external economies of scale. Production becomes more and more dependent upon specific know-how. This means that it can be more important to be located in a region or a centre where there is close contact with the know-how that is developed in the industry.

The central importance of the model is that it shows how cumulative processes can arise which cause economic activities and business structures to vary from region to region. Some regions will be centres of growth and some regions will become less developed.

Even within a region there will not, of course, be an equal distribution of population and economic activity. In growth areas there will be one or more big conurbations which will be the engines of development. Primary industries, including agriculture, will be dependent on supplies made to the towns. In less developed regions the primary industries will be relatively more important. Towns in these areas are smaller. Their role is to service the population that is linked to the primary industries which will be a large share of the population.

The model illustrates how the centres and the peripheral areas develop, and how the centres grow while the periphery stagnates.

The model is simple and while it oversimplifies the conditions, it does say something important about the forces which cause increased concentration. As an example one can look at the self-reinforcing forces which link the development of regional transport system to regional concentration.

Figure 15.3 shows a region in which there are 4 towns which, in relation to their distance from each other, are symmetrical. The four towns have the same population, so they have the same demands. If the transport system between the four towns is the same, then the transport costs from one town to the other three towns should be the same, regardless of where a business is located. It is therefore unimportant where a new business is located.

Figure 15.3: The relationship between transport systems and regional concentration

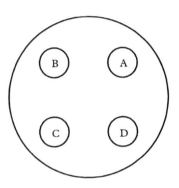

If the transport system is developed between A and B, so that it is better than the rest of the transport system, then other things being equal, it will be beneficial to be located in either A or B. A and B can thus have a population advantage which leads to industrial activity being concentrated in A and B. This means that the trade between these two towns is developed, so the transport costs per unit are reduced. This will stimulate industrial concentration in A and B, which in turn makes it more economical for society to invest in further improvements to the transport system between A and B. An improved transport system between A and B leads to industrial concentration in A and B, which leads to falling transport costs, which in turn increases industrial concentration. In other words there is a virtuous spiral which reinforces the link between industrial concentration and falling transport costs, when the transport sector is characterised by high fixed costs.

15.4 External economies of scale

In the above a model has been used to illustrate how divisions develop between growth regions and less developed regions. Part of the explanation lies in economies of scale. These can be internal or external economies of scale. In his book The Principles of Economics (1920), the English economist Alfred Marshall was the first to distinguish clearly between the two types, and he pointed out the significance of the latter. The fact that there are economies of scale in moving from a smaller size to larger size in manufacturing is well known. At a certain level of production the internal economies of scale are assumed to stop. The fact that it is nevertheless not unusual to see several manufacturing units in the same industry in the same place is linked to the existence of external economies of scale which are considered in more detail below.

The concentration of several manufacturing units in the same place is due to the advantage of having a more concentrated labour market rather than a labour market spread throughout the region. The external advantage of a concentrated location can be the greater possibility of obtaining the necessary inputs. Finally there is an advantage in there being a central location, as technological developments can be promoted through closer contacts.

The advantages of a concentrated location of the labour force

It is assumed that there are two regions where production can be located and two companies which produce goods. They can either each locate their activities in their own region, or they can both decide to locate their production in the same region. Each of the two companies demands specialised labour. This labour force is 400. Under normal conditions each company has a demand for 200 employees.

For each of the two companies there is uncertainty about their sales potential. Each of the companies only employs 150 workers in bad times, but in good times they can employ 250.

It is assumed that there is a negative correlation between the sales potential of the two companies. The success of one company is at the expense of the other. For example, this could be a case of two textile manufacturers where one has better luck with its design and obtains better sales at the expense of the other.

Through an agreement between the labour market organisations wages are fixed at a level where there is no unemployment when each company employs 200 workers. Under these conditions it will be an advantage if both companies are located in one area, and if the labour force lives in the same area.

If each company is located in its own area, each with its share of the labour force, then in one region production will only be carried out with a labour force of 150. In the other region, where there may be a demand for 250 workers, it is still only possible to employ 200 workers, because of the size of the available labour force.

From the point of view of the companies and of the employees it would be better if production were concentrated in one region. Behind this conclusion there is an assumption that there are internal economies of scale for each of the companies. If there are no internal economies of scale, each company could set up two manufacturing units, one in each region. In this situation the advantage discussed above will be obtainable in each region through the establishment of two manufacturing units in each place.

It is accepted that the sales of the companies are seldom totally correlated as shown above. However, the argument is still valid to the extent that there is some significant negative correlation.

The example shows that companies and employees who have special skills can both have an interest in being located in a centre where there are already several companies and employees in the same industry.

There is an opposite argument for companies to disperse their locations, and that is the desire to exploit a monopsony. It is possible to imagine that a company would want to locate in a place where there is no pre-existing manufacturer in the same industry. It will thereby establish itself in a monopsony position in the labour market. The company would be the sole purchaser of the specialised skills which should enable it to put downward pressure on wages. If there is a large supply of the specialised labour, this makes it difficult for trade unions to intervene. Even without the intervention of trade unions the possibility of exploiting a monopsony position is limited. Employees will not live in such an area but move to the centres where they will have more opportunities for employment and avoid being dependent on one employer.

Supplies of inputs

In the model which is discussed in Section 15.3, the manufacturer of final goods will locate where there is a large market, i.e. where there is a concentration of population.

The manufacturer of final goods needs a number inputs. If the transport costs for these inputs is high in relation to the transport costs of the final goods, which will often be the case in the early phase of industrialisation, then the manufacturer of final goods will locate close to the inputs. Historically industrialisation was concentrated close to coal and iron.

The example considered here is of a case in which neither the transport costs of the final goods nor the inputs are decisive. In other words there are no naturally determined links between either the production of final goods or the production of raw materials, semi-manufactured goods or services.

The manufacturer of final goods will therefore locate in population centres where the transport costs are low and where there are significant internal and external economies of scale. One of the external economies of scale is that producers of inputs will locate where the manufacturers who are their customers are located. The model in Section 15.3 can also be used in relation to producers of inputs, where the demand for final goods is merely replaced by the demand for input factors.

Where there is already a concentration of manufacturers of final goods there will also be suppliers of semi-manufactured goods, capital goods and services. In such a centre there will be a number of sub-contractors supplying semi-manufactured goods and producers of special machinery. It will therefore be sensible for a new manufacturer of final goods to locate in such a centre where these special products can be found. Sub-contractors locate in the same centre, where the transport costs are low and where there are economies of scale for their products.

It is usual to talk of linkage between the different parts of the industrial complex. There is income linkage, forward linkage and backward linkage. For producers of final goods consumer income is decisive. The producer will locate in a centre of population with large purchasing power, giving large income linkage. The manufacturers of final goods in a growth centre also creates backward linkages in the sense that they have a demand for a number of necessary inputs in the form of raw materials, semi-manufactured goods, machines, special skills and services. Input producers which locate themselves in a growth centre give rise to forward linkage to the manufacturers of final goods which buy their production. Besides this, the producers of inputs have a number of backward linkages, since they have demands on their input suppliers.

Transfer of knowledge through contacts between suppliers and purchasers

When a company is located close to a significant market it is in close contact with the developing trends in the market for final goods.

This close contact with suppliers, manufacturers of machinery, technological institutes, research centres, universities etc. can make it easier to find solutions to new problems. There is a body of special know-how which is more easily exploited through contact between those who have the know-how and those who seek the solutions.

It is difficult to judge how much this factor is worth. The cost of communication has fallen sharply, so that distance is no longer such an inhibiting factor to the spread of know-how. On the other hand close contact will still be important for obtaining special know-how and knowing where such know-how can be found.

Proximity is probably important for obtaining an overview of existing solutions. Proximity and contact with the 'right people', of which there will be more in an industrial centre, make it easier to find new solutions in the form of developing new products and new technologies.

How does a centre for a given industry become established?

The model in Section 15.3 shows that once a centre has been established there will be a tendency for more and more companies connected with the industry in question being established in that centre. Not least the external economies of scale, which are discussed above, will contribute to this.

What causes such a centre to be started in the first place? It is not easy to give a universally applicable reason. Through the course of history expertise of various kinds can be built up in a centre. Certain cumulative processes come into play. What the original reason is for the development of a centre can be more or less accidental. A single entrepreneur with special skills can be the explanation.

Today, when advanced technology products are based on special know-how on different topics, companies are often located in university centres with associated research parks. In California Silicone Valley, with its links to Stanford University, is a centre for advanced technology in the are of electronics. A similar centre has grown up around the universities in the Boston area.

15.5 Regional economic analysis applied to countries

In individual countries there can be industrial centres or centres for service industries. Thus in an individual country there can be one or more industrial concentration as well as a number of less developed regions. In the case of Western European countries each individual country cannot be considered as a 'closed' region. Some industrial centres cross national boundaries. This is the case with the industrial concentration of the Ruhr district, north-eastern France and southern Belgium.

National concentrations have been developed with the movement of capital and labour to these centres from other regions within national borders. For most of the twentieth century there has been low mobility of capital and labour between countries. Over the past couple of decades there has been freedom of movement of capital in Europe, while labour is still relatively immobile because of the linguistic and cultural barriers. In the USA, throughout the whole period of industrialisation there has been a situation where there have been no hindrances in the form of trade barriers and there has been internal mobility of both capital and labour. This is the background to the much greater concentration of business activities in the USA.

With the establishment of the internal market in the EU it is possible to foresee much greater business concentration. However, it is unlikely to be as great as in the USA because Western European countries already have a multiplicity of centres established due to former internal trade barriers, and the lack of mobility of European capital and labour.

There can be a problem for regions with production based on primary products in securing business development, because the underlying population has been reduced. It is possible that there may be greater intra-sectoral specialisation in the EU so that more knowledge based manufactures may be concentrated in certain centres in the North, with lighter consumer goods industries more concentrated in the South. This raises problems in connection with Central and Eastern European association with the EU.

It is questionable whether, in the foreseeable future, the internal market of the EU will come to function like the internal market in the USA. This is due to the differences in regional economic and international economic problems. The differences between international economics and regional economics is often linked to the differences in four conditions:

a. the mobility of production factors
b. national currencies
c. national economic policies
d. the special characteristics of markets

As has been mentioned already, in the USA there is full internal mobility of capital and labour. In the EU there is close to full mobility of capital, but national labour markets are not integrated with each other.

Unless an economic and monetary union is established with a common currency for all countries, it will still be possible for countries outside the monetary union to adjust their exchange rates. Exchange rate adjustments can contribute to keeping the national 'balance' in relation to maintaining employment.

In the USA there is a common economic policy, and there are no political trade barriers in the form of customs, import restrictions etc. In the EU the internal market means that trade policy barriers are excluded. In economic policy there is still room for national ma- noeuvre unless a centralised economic and monetary union becomes a reality.

Finally, tastes and preferences differ in different European coun- tries, as a result of historical developments. These differences do not exist to the same extent in the USA.

Even if the relations between European countries become more like relations between states in the USA, there are still significant differ- ences which mean that the regional concentrations will not be as big as in the USA.

It cannot be concluded that integration will harm smaller countries and benefit bigger countries if there are industrial concentrations in both types of country.

In Figure 15.4 there is a large country with an industrial concentra- tion at A, and a small country with an industrial concentration at B. The national border is the line with small dashes. When trade barriers are removed the small county's sphere of interest can be expanded so that its economic border becomes the dotted line.

A problem arises if the smaller country does not have an industrial concentration of sufficient strength because the primary sector is too dominant. An example of this is the position between Canada and the USA in the nineteenth century. When industrialisation started in the USA, Canada was an agricultural society which was thinly populated. Following industrialisation in the USA, Canadian labour migrated to the USA. In order to create the basis for industrialisation in Canada high protective tariffs were introduced against imports form the USA, while heavy subsidies were introduced for transport between East and West Canada, in order to bind the country together. This created the basis for building up a viable Canadian industry which could employ a growing population. Today Canada's industry is so competitive that Canada has been able to enter into the North American Free Trade Agreement (NAFTA) with the USA and Mexico.

Figure 15.4: Integration between a large country and a small country

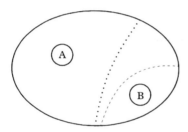

If Canada had not protected its industry it is reasonable to believe that Canada would have developed into being a peripheral area with the north-eastern part of the USA as its centre. Without protection, industry located in Canada would have been located in the USA.

It is therefore possible to hypothesise that there is a correlation between the level of transport costs and living standards when two regions are compared. In Figure 15.5 there are two countries C and P. In the initial situation the transport costs are OB. In each of the two countries agriculture is the main activity, combined with craft manufactures and small scale industry. When the transport costs fall to OA the living standards will rise in both countries because there will be an increase in trade. When the transport costs are OA there will be a concentration of industrial production in country C, as a result of economies of scale.

Figure 15.5: The development of transport costs and the standard of living in a two country model

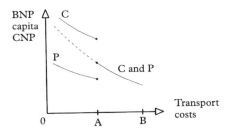

The income in country C will rise and the income in country P will fall because there is no longer the basis for industry in country P. Gradually, as the transport costs fall further, the per capita GNP will rise in both C and P, though at different levels, because country C has developed as a centre for industry and service, while country P has become peripheral and has no basis for larger industrial activity. If country P had imposed customs duties when the transport costs were OA, then both countries could have developed industrial production, which could have meant that the per capita GNP would have followed the dotted line.

15.6 Polarising forces

Once economic inequalities have arisen between countries there are a number of economic mechanisms which operate to make the inequalities greater. To illustrate this one can look at conditions in richer industrial countries compared with poorer developing countries.

In industrial countries there is a large and growing demand for goods. This creates the basis for large investments, and it is possible to exploit internal and external economies of scale, as well as take advantage of technological developments. In this way companies can make productivity gains which can bring about a rise in the standard of living without rising prices. This in turn creates an increase in purchasing power, so that companies want to invest further. The demand for capital is big, and this demand is met through the supply of capital through savings. In a richer society it is normally easier to achieve a higher savings ratio.

In a rich country there is a demand for well educated labour and for new technology. A richer country can also allocate resources for education and research.

The conditions in the poorer developing countries are the opposite of this. The opportunities for capital formation in the form of physical assets and human resources are much more limited. The result is that there are in-built mechanisms that mean that industrial concentrations are established in industrial countries while developing countries become peripheral, mainly supplying primary products.

Trade, capital movements and migration can contribute to the reinforcement of these cumulative processes, so that there is a polarisation of industrial activities.

Trade

If transport costs are low and the advantages of being in an industrial centre are high, then trade can contribute to a further concentration of business activity. Competition from industrial countries means that it is difficult to sustain manufacturing in developing countries. Even if the wages are low, the costs can still be high because of the relatively low productivity in the developing countries.

Problems of balance of payments can make it difficult for developing countries to import the capital goods necessary for industrial development. The problems will be increased if industrial countries put trade restrictions in the way of, for example, agricultural and textile industries where these countries usually have a comparative advantage.

Capital movements

Capital movements between the two areas can also increase the inequality. The return on capital will often be higher in a growth area than in a stagnating area. For an industry there are a number of advantages connected with being located in a developed area with growth. A lack of capital in a less developed area will not manifest itself as a demand for capital because of the relatively poor private economic return.

There are a number of explanations for this. There is a lack of public infrastructure in less developed areas. This concerns the means of communication, sources of energy, educational institutions, effective public administration, etc. Nor are there service providers in the private sector, as there are in industrial countries, in the form of a well developed banking system, or organisations providing trade and technical assistance.

There is also a lack of well educated or well trained labour and technicians. Finally, there will often be an absence of the laws and regulations and institutions that are necessary for directing capital towards productive investments.

Labour migration

With a labour force of a given size expansion will be restricted in industrial countries. This restriction can naturally be overcome by the immigration of workers. The labour which migrates to the growth areas can form the basis of further growth in the areas of immigration. Without this immigration growth will be limited by the lack of labour. In the areas from which the labour has migrated growth can also be limited. This is connected with the fact that it is especially younger men that migrate. Thus the proportion of the actively employed part of the population falls in relation to the total population. Further, it is often the part of the male population with greater initiative that emigrates. In other words, the emigrants will predominantly come from those sectors of the population which are most needed to bring about growth in society.

In developing countries there is a particular lack of educated labour. Despite this it is often the higher educated people from developing countries that obtain jobs in industrial countries because the employment prospects are better.

15.7 Disseminating forces

While there are a number of polarising forces between different regions in individual countries and between countries at different economic levels, there are also a number of disseminating forces.

These apply between regions within a country. In a growth centre there can be a number of disadvantages of scale when a centre of concentration becomes too big. There can be a lack of labour. There can be environmental and transport problems. The cost level can be too high. This can prompt an exodus of activities and can be an incentive for new businesses to locate away from the centre. For example, improved communications systems and information technology can mean that it becomes less important to be in the centre.

Correspondingly there can be factors between countries which can contribute to the dissemination of activities. Trade and capital movements can contribute to this. Increased activity in industrial countries means that there are possibilities for developing countries to increase their exports. Because of lower costs it can be possible to be competitive on more simple product types where wage costs are an important element.

It can also be possible to set up direct investments in developing countries to exploit the special cost advantages in these countries. In this way there can be an accumulation of capital, training of the local labour force and a dissemination of technology through the production methods used.

The extent to which the polarising or the disseminating forces will dominate depends on the product categories in question and the developing country in question.

In the case of goods with high wage costs there is a greater probability that the disseminating forces will dominate, compared with more advanced products where technology, design and other qualities are important.

The question of which developing country is involved is also decisive. If it is a richer developing country in which manufacturing centres have already been established and where there are external economies of scale, there is a better chance for further development than in a less developed country. Today, in Southeast Asia, manufacturing centres have been established with considerable purchasing power and with infrastructures which make competitive production possible. In Africa such conditions do not exist. Even though there is a potential lack of capital, the private economic return on investment is not up to expectations. This is due to the additional costs and the great complications associated with the inadequate institutional conditions in these countries.

15.8 Summary

In the traditional theory trade and factor movements are considered as two separate phenomena, and attempts are made to explain each of them in isolation. In the traditional neo-classical factor proportion theory it is usual to disregard the problems of distance, economies of scale, whether internal or external, and concentrations of population. These elements are included in analyses of regional economics. In these models trade, capital movements and labour migration are included. The use of such models can help to explain how industrial centres, associated with growth, arise at a regional level, and how less developed regions with weaker economic development will appear.

Regional economics has to do with the national location of economic activity. International trade and investment theory has to do with the international location of business activity. In many ways the problems are thus very similar.

One of the central features of the regional economic models is that there are a number of cumulative processes which contribute in many ways to greater inequality. Institutional development, including the establishment of industrial environments, environments of high technology, know-how and differentiated services, are essential in this connection.

It can be helpful to use such models in relation to issues of international economics. At the international level simultaneous trade and factor movements can lead to a polarisation between countries, so that economic activity is concentrated in certain areas while other areas fall further behind. However, there are also a number of factors which can contribute to activities being disseminated between countries. The existence of an institutional structure, including an industrial environment where there are external benefits in setting up firms, is decisive in determining whether the polarising or disseminating forces will prevail.

Literature

Bairoch, P., *Cities and Economic Development,* Chicago, 1988.

Isard, W., *Location and Space Economy,* Cambridge M.A., 1956.

Kaldor, N., 'The Irrelevance of Equilibrium Economics', *Economic Journal,* 82, 1972.

Krugman, P., 'History and Industry Location: The Case of the US Manufacturing Belt', *American Economic Review,* No. 2, 1991.

Myrdal, G., *Economic Theory and Underdeveloped Countries,* London 1957.

Porter, M., *The Competitive Advantage of Nations*, New York, 1990.

Young, A., 'Increasing Returns and Economic Progress, *Economic Journal*, 38, 1928.

Index